INSPIRING FELLINI

Literary Collaborations behind the Scenes

Federico Fellini (1923–1993) is considered one of the greatest auteurs in the history of film, and the very symbol of the golden age of Italian cinema. What is not well known, however, is that many of his films are the result of collaboration with some of the greatest scriptwriters of twentieth-century Italy. *Inspiring Fellini* re-examines the filmmaker's oeuvre, taking into consideration how it was influenced by his prominent writers and intellectuals, including Pier Paolo Pasolini, Ennio Flaiano, Tullio Pinelli, and Andrea Zanzotto. Federico Pacchioni presents a complex portrait of Fellini that goes beyond that of the stereotypical solitary genius, as he has often been portrayed by critics.

Pacchioni explores the dynamics of Fellini's cinematic collaborations through analyses of his contemporaries' other creative projects, their contributions to the conceptualization of Fellini's films, and their conversations with Fellini himself. Drawing extensively on public and private archival sources, this book offers new appreciation of Fellini's work and insight into his artistic development.

(Toronto Italian Studies)

FEDERICO PACCHIONI is the Sebastian Paul and Marybelle Musco Endowed Professor in Italian Studies in the Department of World Languages and Cultures at Chapman University.

FEDERICO PACCHIONI

Inspiring Fellini

Literary Collaborations behind the Scenes

UNIVERSITY OF TORONTO PRESS
Toronto Buffalo London

© University of Toronto Press 2014
Toronto Buffalo London
www.utppublishing.com
Printed in Canada

ISBN 978-1-4426-4499-1 (cloth)
ISBN 978-1-4426-1292-1 (paper)

Printed on acid-free, 100% post-consumer recycled paper with
vegetable-based inks.

Library and Archives Canada Cataloguing in Publication

Pacchioni, Federico, 1978–, author
Inspiring Fellini : literary collaborations behind the
scenes / Federico Pacchioni.

(Toronto Italian studies)
Includes bibliographical references and index.
ISBN 978-1-4426-4499-1 (bound).   ISBN 978-1-4426-1292-1 (pbk.)

1. Fellini, Federico – Criticism and interpretation.   2. Fellini,
Federico – Friends and associates.   I. Title.   II. Series: Toronto Italian
studies

PN1998.3.F45 P33 2014   791.4302'33092   C2013-906474-5

University of Toronto Press acknowledges the financial assistance to its
publishing program of the Canada Council for the Arts and the Ontario
Arts Council.

University of Toronto Press acknowledges the financial support of the
Government of Canada through the Canada Book Fund for its publishing
activities.

For Julie, a collaborator of a lifetime

Contents

Acknowledgments

One of the greatest rewards and pleasures of writing a book such as this lies in the exchanges with the many brilliant and generous people who inspire the discovery of ideas and who collaborate on the retrieval of sources and the compilation of the text. The roots of this book are deep, reaching back to the years when, in the company of a few good friends, I voraciously watched all of Federico Fellini's films and heatedly debated them. Without all the friends and colleagues who shared and cherished the experience of relating to and understanding an artistic creation, this book would have never come to be.

I am most grateful to Peter Bondanella, who introduced me to the Fellini-Pinelli archive in the Lilly Library of Rare Books at Indiana University Bloomington by inviting me to assist him in editing and translating a few unpublished scripts in the summer of 2006. His continued support has been invaluable to the life of this project.

I want to acknowledge the late Tonino Guerra and Tullio Pinelli, whose hospitality, intellectual generosity, and kindness, even during my insistent questioning at the early stages of this research, largely fuelled my motivation.

I am enormously grateful to those who read all or parts of the manuscript, especially Antonio Vitti, Colleen Ryan, Marco Arnaudo, Andrea Ciccarelli, and John Welle. Even though they might not be aware of it, this book owes a great deal to the people with whom I talked about key issues in these past few years; among them are Millicent Marcus, Gian Piero Brunetta, Vito Zagarrio, Claudio Bondì, Enrico Bernard, Manuela Gieri, Fabrizio Natalini, Massimo Scalabrini, and Ernesto Livorni.

I am indebted to my colleagues at Chapman University who provided guidance and supported my research at very critical moments, in particular John Boitano, Polly Hodge, Wendy Salmond, and Patrick Fuery, and to the helpful staff of the Wilkinson College of Humanities and Social Sciences and of the Leatherby Libraries. I am grateful to the staff of numerous archives and libraries for assistance, including the Lilly Library and the Herman B. Welles Library of Indiana University Bloomington, the Fondazione Federico Fellini, the Cineteca of Bologna, the Mediamuseum of Pescara, the Biblioteca Malatestiana of Cesena, and the Homer D. Babbidge Library at the University of Connecticut. I was fortunate to work with editors at the University of Toronto Press such as Anne Laughlin and the late Ron Schoeffel, who, with their patience and kindness, allowed for the conditions that my project needed to evolve naturally and fruitfully; moreover, the careful eye of Angela Wingfield helped much in refining my style.

I wish to acknowledge my supportive family: my wife, Julie, who was most instrumental during many midnight brainstorming sessions and who patiently read through many rough drafts; my in-laws Christa and Martin Jenner who have believed in me and supported me throughout my career; my mother, Carla, for her constant enthusiasm and help in tracking down and shipping books and magazines from Italy; and my brother Francesco, who assisted in designing the cover of this book.

Finally, my sincere gratefulness goes to Sebastian Paul Musco, Frank De Santis, and their families, who provided significant financial support for the realization of *Inspiring Fellini*.

Illustrations

All illustrations are from Federico Fellini's *The Book of Dreams* (Milan: RCS Libri Spa, 2008), on the pages noted, and are reprinted courtesy of Fondazione Federico Fellini in Rimini, Italy.

INSPIRING FELLINI

Literary Collaborations behind the Scenes

Introduction

As foreshadowed nearly a decade ago by Millicent Marcus's volume *After Fellini: National Cinema in the Postmodern Age*, study of Federico Fellini (1920–93), who had become the very symbol of the golden age of Italian cinema, was increasingly moved to the margin of scholarship in order to make space for an emphasis on contemporary and popular cinema. In the wake of a forceful shift away from auteurism, even Peter Bondanella, the author of one of the most successful auteurist monographs on Fellini, has attempted to curb the prominence of the great auteur's weight in a new edition of his history of Italian cinema.[1] Indeed, auteurism, along with realism, has been at the centre of a number of convincing attacks by recent scholars in an effort to free Italian film studies from institutional narratives of criticism.[2] This turn away from auteurist studies, and the marginalization of Fellini, has understandable and justifiable reasons. The fact that "Italian auteur cinema is not so much a distinct entity in itself, as [it is] the intellectual and/or better funded end of national genre production," as film historian Mary Wood clearly puts it, has deflated the prestige of auteur cinema by bringing it to the same level of other commercial genres, and has consequentially raised doubts about the objectivity of auteurist monographs that appeared to be chiefly legitimized by their fandom for the auteurs.[3]

Without question, this dynamic has been especially marked in Fellini criticism, built on producers' authorial propaganda that eventually included the director's name in the films' titles. It was not for the sake of vanity that Fellini began releasing, as early as 1954, public statements minimizing the roles played by his screenwriters.[4] What appeared to be Fellini's disloyalty towards his collaborators, with whom he had spent many months researching, imagining, and writing the scripts before arriving on the set, was actually a more or less conscious alignment with the marketability of auteur cinema, which required the signature of a clearly identifiable artist.

Fellini became a brand, the adjective *felliniesque*, and his image was transfigured both in Italy and abroad by comics, films, murals, novels, and urban legends into the myth of the sublime art-director: a being made of pure inspiration, a sorcerer heroically facing the unknown, summoning rows of voluptuous women and fanciful atmospheres. Auteurist scholarship around the world capitalized on and enlarged this very myth, even while examining the philosophic and stylistic traits central to his films. This book hopes to not only foster a less stereotypical image than that of Fellini as a solitary genius but also advance the ongoing effort to deepen the understanding of the classics of Italian cinema by exploring them through new routes that extend to film studies and cultural studies at large. In Fellini's case, recent books like Thomas Van Order's *Listening to Fellini: Music and Meaning in Black and White* (2009), Andrea Minuz's *Viaggio al termine dell'Italia: Fellini politico* (2012), and Hava Aldouby's *Federico Fellini: Painting in Film, Painting on Film* (2013) indicate how much the study of auteur cinema still has to offer when examined beyond the traditional auteurist approach.

Inspiring Fellini argues for the instrumentality of the screenwriting collaborations of Federico Fellini in supporting and shaping a cinema endowed, in both content and form, with an extraordinary penchant for expressing the fluidic relationship between the real and the fantastic, bearing phenomenological instability, and exposing the consequences of nihilism and self-delusion alike – a body of work that continues to be a point of reference for a still-growing number of directors around the globe.[5] During his life Fellini worked with some of the most talented Italian screenwriters of the last century, including Tullio Pinelli (1908–2009), Ennio Flaiano (1910–72), Brunello Rondi (1924–89), Pier Paolo Pasolini (1922–75), Bernardino Zapponi (1927–2000), and Tonino Guerra (1920–2012). Through the vantage point of a systematic study of Fellini's screenwriting partnerships – considered in relation to their philosophic and stylistic common denominators and elements of friction – the chapters of this book disclose new artistic and cultural associations regarding Fellini's cinema. Even though much of the scholarship on Italian cinema has largely shifted away from the study of the Italian film canon, this book is part of a minor but growing trend to keep alive the exploration of auteur cinema through fresh perspectives that are suited to revealing new contextual information and textual interpretations. In re-examining the cinema of Federico Fellini within a cultural map drawn on his screenwriters' artistic and intellectual identities and his creative exchanges with them, this study aims to further contextualize the discussion on central issues of Fellinian authorial poetics, with a special focus on the role played by the screenwriters in inspiring and challenging the well-known and ever-ambiguous spiritual quality of this director's work.

A Not So Solitary Genius: Traversing Authorial Politics and Methodological Anxieties

The study of collaboration in art cinema has always been controversial, often disapproved of by scholars and directors alike, a fact that suggests its methodological, theoretical, and political complexity. It seems therefore necessary to elucidate at the onset the issues that generally discourage or are thought to hinder the study of screenwriting collaborations in art cinema. The solutions proposed below present a multi-authorial perspective directed at identifying the fields of creative forces and describing their artistic and cultural significance wherever they are traceable in the conceptualization, production, or aftermath of a film.

Lino Miccichés essay "Un cinema senza sceneggiatori?" ("A Cinema without Screenwriters?"), published in the inaugural issue of the official journal of the Fondazione Federico Fellini in 2001, provides a significant example of the theoretical impasse of single-authorship that entailed seeing collaboration and authorship as mutually exclusive.[6] Here, the late critic attempts to resolve the challenge of celebrating Fellini's vision while at the same time acknowledging the uncomfortable presence of other authors, namely the screenwriters. Miccichés solution exemplifies the basic elements of traditional auteurist principles. He begins by celebrating the poetic value of art film where the script is seen as secondary to visual improvisation, and follows by confirming Fellini's centrality in the creative process, concluding that "there would be nothing more erroneous than to explain Fellini's cinema according to the order of his screenwriting collaborations."[7] Indeed, statements such as these manifest the disciplinary politics that have traditionally delegitimized a comprehensive study of the functions of Fellini's screenwriters. While the realities of authorship and of collaboration are not seen as incompatible in the present study, Fellini's relationship to the script is assessed in all its conflicting dimensions. His well-known struggle with the narrative nature of cinema is examined here within the varying collaborative contexts across Fellini's career, revealing the ways in which this director tried to achieve his ideal of non-narrative cinema through specific choices of screenwriters and approaches to the script.

When the film critic Robert Carringer shared with Orson Welles his study about the contributions of collaborators on *Citizen Kane* (1941), such as the cinematographer Gregg Toland, the screenwriter Herman Mankiewicz, and the art director Perry Ferguson, the director, after an outburst of irritation, proceeded to clarify that "collaborators make contributions, but only a director can make a film."[8] Actually, Carringer's work did not contradict Welles on this point but rather fostered an understanding of the fact that "the quality of a film is partly a measure of the quality of its collaborative talent," and led him to include a description of this director's collaborative practices.[9] Similarly, I do not intend to disregard the director's principal responsibility for the making of his films, thus risking bestowing the same mystique on the screenwriter that was once placed upon the director by exaggerated auteurist criticism.[10] A study of Fellini's cinema that excludes Fellini's vision from the equation would lead to gravely distorted conclusions, even according to its own terms, for the mere reason that Fellini was among the screenwriters of the films he directed. However, in order to preserve the independence of the artists' respective visions and at the same time to go beyond the institutional myth of single-authorship, this book follows a process similar to that described by Robert Carringer as a "temporary suspension of single-author primacy ... to appraise constituent claims to a text's authorship," which is necessary in order to then reinsert the primary author "within what is now established as an institutional context of authorship."[11]

The uneasiness generated by the analysis of literary collaborations in Fellini's cinema is tied not only to the critical institution of the film auteur, but also to the lower value assigned to the screenplay, as well as to the intricate nature of screenwriting practices. The scholarly debate on the literary value of the screenplay has struggled to ascribe legitimacy to the script, owing to its intermediary place, and has grappled with a conception of the script as something hybrid and difficult to classify. For example in the mid-1960s, Pier Paolo Pasolini had approached the world of film-making and defended the artistic value of the screenplay, which in his opinion most scholars failed to appreciate.[12] To Pasolini, the script's constant state of fluctuation from linguistic to visual codes was the cause of its relegation to a subordinate form of art; yet at the same time it was the poetic strength of this literary genre. In retrospect, Pasolini's defence of the cultural and aesthetic recognition of the script can be seen as akin to the idea of the "visual poem" that was elaborated by another and earlier eclectic figure, the scholar and film consultant Sebastiano Arturo Luciani (1884–1950), who in his treatises equated an effectively written script with a text that, while directed at a subsequent artistic realization, namely a film, also had an independent value, like a musical score that can be enjoyed on paper by those who know how to read it.[13] In Luciani's opinion, the value of a script rested in its essentiality, rhythm, and above all its visual force: "all the artistry and all the originality of the screenwriter is revealed in the way in which he *sees* a certain scene or develops a certain situation."[14] Cases such as these, which could be joined by innumerable others, speak loudly of the value actually placed on the script by creative minds.

In addition to the fact that the screenplay has been traditionally held as a less valuable genre, the study of screenwriting is associated with the challenging task of correctly identifying a script's author or authors. Owing to the philological challenges associated with scripts composed by multiple writers, it has become common opinion that attempts to identify with any degree of certainty the contribution of any one screenwriter to a particular film might in most cases lead to no more than hypothetical conjectures. As a consequence, scholars have employed less assertive terms in speaking about the screenwriter's presence in a film, preferring for instance the more suggestive notion of *effect* or *touch* over the more hierarchical and binding one of *influence*. Gian Piero Brunetta explains the meaning he ascribes to the word *effect* by providing a summary of what he calls the "choir" or "genealogical tree" of post-war Italian cinema that extended to many groups or "families" around key screenwriters.[15] Furthermore, Giulia Muscio warns that rewriting the history of cinema based on the screenwriters' contributions can be unwise because of the dearth of evidence and the multifariousness of collaborative practices and can therefore lead to scholarship characterized by Pindaric flights, excessive synthesis, or compilations of anecdotes.[16]

A cautionary stance is certainly a healthy one, but never to the point of preventing the study of collaborative screenwriting relationships altogether. Methodological limitations are greatly reduced when one studies the genesis of confined sections of the history of Italian cinema, such as Fellini's richly documented films where one can fully capitalize on the investigative breadth inherent in a collaborative perspective.

Owing to the cultural prestige associated with Fellini's productions, scripts have been consistently published and often accompanied by ancillary materials, interviews, and commentaries. Most important, though, even if a specific influence cannot be verified, the very fact that two artists are drawn to collaborate on a specific film in itself holds significance, especially from a cultural study perspective based on the broader idea of relationship.

Undoubtedly, collaborations within auteur cinema, such as those examined in this book, have also served the function of allowing producers to recognize the cultural worth and stylistic stability of the authorial package, a fact which can be validated by the sharp contrast between the constant turnover of producers during Fellini's career and the longevity of his screenwriting relationships.[17] However, as the present book documents, these artists developed deeply symbiotic partnerships, merging their respective styles and concerns during long-lasting friendships, as was the case with Pinelli, with whom Fellini first worked during his apprenticeship as a screenwriter. Large group meetings, which were characteristic of Fellini's experience during his early years as a screenwriter at the Lux Film studios, were rather infrequently called during the planning of the films that he directed, an exception being the early phases of *La dolce vita*.[18] The ideas collected were generally formed into a treatment by Fellini's chief screenwriter, who also served in a sense as a secretary and an archivist of notes and was most prominently Pinelli and then later Zapponi. At this point, Fellini assigned specific scenes of the screenplay to different writers before gathering all the pages to begin revising, selecting, and merging them together. This amalgam of authorial input was then further revised and discussed with the writers.[19] Fellini's modus operandi strongly favoured sessions of individual brainstorming, especially when he was conceptualizing the *soggetto* or screen idea, often taking place during drives in the car, since all of his writers, but especially Flaiano, Rondi, Pasolini, Zapponi, and Guerra, were well inclined to the extemporaneous work of the poetic and intellectual counsellor.[20] It was during this early phase of work that the conceptual universes and sensibilities of these creative minds flowed together more freely, warranting a broader contrastive analysis between the artistic and philosophic worlds of Fellini and each of his writers.

Perhaps owing to the overblown rhetoric around Fellini as a solitary genius, there has actually always been a certain prying curiosity by specialized and non-specialized audiences about the vicissitudes of the director's obvious long-term collaborative relationships, such as those with his faithful composer Nino Rota and his wife, the actress Giulietta Masina.[21] Most of the scholarly discussion on Fellini's creative partnerships tends to remain at the biographical level without engaging in close rereadings of the texts and reveals marked difficulty in producing a balanced and complete two-way assessment of the creative exchange because of a limited polarized understanding of the phenomena of collaboration and authorship. Nonetheless, a number of contributions of merit on the subject of Fellini's screenwriters have been undertaken, providing a bedrock for further investigation in the present book, yet knowledge on this topic is still fragmentary and primarily concerned with only the more renowned writers such as Ennio Flaiano, Pier Paolo Pasolini, and Andrea Zanzotto.[22]

While a study such as the above-mentioned example by Robert Carringer, and several other studies that followed, is primarily concerned with providing a strictly technical and economic description of production dynamics, this analysis is interested in the broader artistic significance of Fellini's creative relationships, which are hence understood in their twofold nature: for the meaning they held for the director and for the significance they held for the writers.[23] This study aims at achieving an ample bird's-eye view of Fellini's literary collaborations, allowing then for the tracing of artistic and intellectual nodes at the core of these relationships. The analysis of the genesis of Fellini's films, with its complex human and artistic exchanges, requires equally involved and intimate sources. In addition to analysing variants across different archived versions of the scripts, the films themselves, and the autonomous artistic work of the writers, the investigation integrates interviews, autobiographies, and journals.[24] Among the sources employed in this book, Fellini's *Il libro dei sogni* (*The Book of Dreams*) is one of the most unusual tools utilized to focus on the deeper mechanics of collaborative synergy, thus demanding a few introductory remarks.

To my knowledge, Fellini scholars currently still under-utilize *Il libro dei sogni*, most likely because of its recent publication and its unconventional and hybrid nature.[25] Fellini began to keep a regular nocturnal journal on 30 November 1960 at the suggestion of Ernst Bernhard (1896–1965), a psychoanalyst recommended by the friend and director Vittorio De Seta (1923–2011). The practice of the visually illustrated dream journal came from Carl Gustav Jung (1875–1961), who for about fifteen years, when first developing his theories, documented with meticulous drawings his confrontation with the unconscious; he referred to this dream journal as "The Red Book." In his oneiric journal, Fellini was to record his own dreams to be then discussed with Bernhard, whose interpretations and suggestions are sometimes summarized in the book itself. While initially serving a therapeutic purpose, *Il libro dei sogni* progressively became a bank of ideas from which the director drew for his work. After Bernhard's death on 29 June 1965 while Fellini was filming *Giulietta degli spiriti* (1965, *Juliet of the Spirits*), the director continued to attend to his journal with ever-growing fervour, eventually filling at least two large notebooks, the first dating from late 1960 to the summer of 1968 and the second from early 1973 to 1982, thus spanning three decades.[26]

Fellini's well-known and critically perilous autobiographical ambiguity, which earned him the epithet of "The Great Mystifier" (coined by Pasolini), certainly coincided effectively with the marking of his films within the genre of auteur cinema.[27] However, this characteristic of Fellini's cinema, while appearing at times histrionic and commercial, actually contained treatment of collective myths and was motivated by a sincere exploration of the self. Indeed, the many confessions of both professional and personal uncertainties detailed in *Il libro dei sogni* – which remains one of his most autonomous and intimate creations and may not have been compiled with the objective of publication in mind – reveal the very human and vulnerable side of the director. Furthermore, psychoanalysts have been quick to note that Fellini's dream journal, composed in the first person, embodies the director's search for his creative source as well as his image and development as an artist.[28]

In introducing this new source, Fellini's biographer Tullio Kezich (1928–2009) reminds the reader that the allegorical nature of this text and the characters appearing on its pages are not to be taken as direct representations of real-life individuals but rather as symbolic vehicles used for the dreamer's experience.[29] Kezich's words are in line with a psychoanalytic understanding of the dreamer's process; however, they pose a boundary for scholarly application of this unique text. Nevertheless, when one remembers the obvious yet so easily neglectable fact that *Il libro dei sogni* does not contain Fellini's dreams themselves but only Fellini's interpretation of them, any need to undertake additional or different psychological interpretations readily subsides.[30] Moreover, it would be erroneous to overlook the aesthetic characteristics of *Il libro dei sogni*, in which the autobiographical investigation of oneiric and creative life is recorded and expressed in a hybrid medium that blends the forms of the journal and the comic book. As Fellini recorded his dreams, he also interpreted in verbal and visual poetic language the associations that they evoked for him as well as the meanings that these dreams had for him. Consequentially, my application of Fellini's dream journal is more aesthetical and historical than clinical as it aims to explain Fellini's take on his collaborative relationships, considering Fellini's own interpretation of the dreams according to their stylistic and dramatic structure vis-à-vis their connection to the director's biographical and collaborative context.[31]

An Ambiguous Adherence: Esotericism in Fellini's Work and Collaborations

The traditional literature on Fellini has often confirmed the spiritual quality at the root of his cinema, first in more general terms such as in Bazin's observations of the "ripening" of the characters as ruled by a transcendental logic; in Renzi's emphasis on a child-like perspective that is able to marvel at cosmic mystery; and in Bondanella's underscoring of the director's dominant interest in the irrational dimension of the mind.[32] Adopting innovative and interdisciplinary perspectives, recent scholars have zoomed in on specific aspects of Fellini's cinema, thus discovering the artistic ramifications of such a spiritual quality. For example, John Stubbs demonstrated the way in which the conception of reality as ineffable leads to a "style of excess," namely a baroque accumulation in Fellini's choices in areas such as set design and make-up; Van Order examined the music and sound editing, finding that the recurring "slippage" between diegetic and non-diegetic sources functions as a parallel to the dynamic between fantasy and reality; Andrea Minuz, narrating the way in which Fellini's films aesthetically elaborated issues of Italian national identity, confirmed the modernity of Fellini's type of "skeptical religiousness" in his relationship to Catholicism; and Hava Aldouby, in a recent analysis of the role of painting in Fellini's pictorial discourse, revealed the function of postmodern conceptions and representations in advancing Fellini's romantic quest for reality and his faith in the artist's subjectivity as the source of meaning.[33]

The collaborative perspective that I adopt in this book contributes to the understanding of this director's spirituality, by tracing its evolution within the context of specific literary partnerships, unveiling the ways in which his screenwriters catalysed and challenged his views. Before entering into the study of Fellini's creative relationships, it is important to clarify from the start the nature of this director's spiritual quest and also include an open discussion of his prominent interest in the occult. As will be elaborated throughout this book, Fellini's perspective on esotericism is characterized by an "ambiguous adherence." This phrase was coined by the director himself in a note to the typescript of *Il viaggio di G. Mastorna* (hereafter *Mastorna*) where he expressed, as one of the key motivations to his continued interest in the project, the desire to "address critically (or with an ambiguous adherence) psychic phenomena, spiritualism, magic, rituals, and superstitions."[34] Curiously, even in the finest cases of scholarship, serious analysis of Fellini's obvious interest in paranormal and mediumistic phenomena has been largely avoided. Tullio Pinelli once lamented the critics' difficulty in addressing this characteristic of Fellini's world view with the necessary nuance and balance: they either glossed over it as personal mania of little (or shameful) importance or made a spectacle of it according to the aura of extravagance and madness attached to the authorial myth of Fellini.[35]

A quick glance at the records of Fellini's personal library removes any doubt about the director's fervent interest in matters of parapsychology, the occult, and clairvoyance. The books on these and other related areas, such as religious medieval and Renaissance painters, are numerous and often contain within their pages Fellini's vivacious notations and underlining. In addition, Fellini's personal library exposes his preference for literary authors in fantasy (Frank Kafka, Tommaso Landolfi, Italo Calvino, Edgar Allan Poe, Ernst Amadeus Hoffmann); detective stories and psychological thrillers (Patricia Highsmith, George Simenon, Edgar Wallace); and also science fiction (Isaac Asimov, Ray Bradbury). Rather than being censored or else spectacularized, Fellini's penchant for esoteric literature and his recurrent consultations with mediums should be considered as an expression of a certain understanding of reality and a philosophy of life and art.

Fellini's forays into parapsychology through readings and attendance at seances should not be disregarded or placed within a stereotypical auteurist idea of this artist, where the director inevitably emerges, regrettably, as an irrational or anti-intellectual figure. On the contrary, a sincere and assiduous participation in and the study of phenomena that are considered supernatural suggest a desire to investigate the life of the mind and to understand its potentials and limits.[36] This was certainly the case for a twentieth-century artist such as Fellini, whose perseverance in seeking out individuals who claimed miraculous powers reflected certain human and artistic ambitions, including a romantic desire to extend the artist's capacity to produce meaning even within the most obscure and unfamiliar areas of human existence. At the same time, Fellini, being himself a master of representation and illusion, was well aware of the theatrical and deceitful strategies employed by some of the claimed clairvoyants whom he would meet ("where research cohabits with fraud" as Andrea Zanzotto once said); however, even in such cases, Fellini was probably inspired by the ways in which mediums were able to evoke an aura of mystery around them.[37] It is not surprising then that Fellini's films are qualified by the magnification of what Jacqueline Risset has termed "the beauty of illusion," often afforded by the unreliable point of view of the films' protagonists.[38]

It is well known that Fellini frequented mediums, psychics, and magicians of various types, with sincere curiosity and compassion for the personalities of these individuals, no matter how noble or mediocre they were. Fellini's trust in some of the mediums he met was in some cases profound and long lasting, and he even accepted them as mentors in decisions relating to his work, as is best exemplified by his relationship with Gustavo Adolfo Rol (1903–94), perhaps the most famous and accredited among the Italian channellers and psychics of the time. Three of the major contributors to Fellini's cinema – Tullio Pinelli, Nino Rota, and Federico Fellini himself – all frequented Rol's house in Turin and were apparently greatly touched by the work of this man.[39] The phenomena and words provided by Rol, probably combined with those gathered from the many clairvoyants whom Fellini used to visit, left the director with the sense that the material world was endowed with a liquid and relative quality, a fact that was to him both wondrous and terrifying. Following one of Rol's experiments with cards, Fellini once reported: "I saw a terrible thing that words cannot say ... matter was breaking up, a gray and watery mud that decomposed itself pulsating a disgusting amalgamation where the black clubs on the card dissolved and resurfaced with red veins ..."[40] On another occasion, Fellini underscored the beneficial influence of the medium's work: "Rol's 'games' are an invigorating and comforting spectacle to anyone who may approach him with a true openness."[41] Such a perception is not dissociated from that unique phenomenological instability and openness dramatized by many of Fellini's works and most notably in *Giulietta degli spiriti* and his crucial but unrealized project *Mastorna*, where the protagonist's reality shifts between hallucination, dream, and paranormal experiences.[42] Indeed, *Mastorna*, arguably the director's most personal script and one developed with an unprecedented degree of independence from his principal screenwriters, can here serve as a vivid illustration of Fellini's complex and ambivalent fascination with the spirit world.

The first attempt to realize *Mastorna* took place between 1965 and 1967 after the filming of *Giulietta degli spiriti*, to which it would have been a natural progression, with the alter-ego of the director as the protagonist; however, preparation for this film was marked by a number of incidents, including difficulties in selecting a leading actor, a disastrous lawsuit with the producer, and a serious health crisis, all of which prevented the film from being made. One of these incidents was the death of Fellini's psychoanalyst, Ernst Bernhard, in 1965, which suddenly deprived the film-maker of the cognitive guidance that he felt was enabling him to face and make sense of supernatural events within a quotidian horizon. Bernhard, whose work blended Jungian theories and various mystical Eastern traditions, influenced Fellini and his cinema dramatically through the practice of the dream journal as well as the application of the I Ching, the divination system that the director fully embraced and used as a guide at challenging times in his career.[43] Even later in his career, Fellini never felt secure enough to finally undertake the making of *Mastorna* and to fully explore the theme of the spirit world, as he himself once noted, because of its "aesthetic, fantastic and adventurous nature" which is so "stimulating" and yet "dangerous ... for an artist's creative vocation."[44] Rather, Fellini probably felt like the protagonist in *Toby Dammit* – the short that temporarily replaced his first reconsideration of *Mastorna* in 1968 – who is in danger of losing his head (figuratively in Fellini's case) by challenging invisible forces and attempting to jump over the chasm of the unknown. The possibility of making *Mastorna*, nonetheless, never ceased to resurface for Fellini, especially in the late 1970s, but instead of being realized as a film unto itself, it would be scattered as fragments throughout the film-making that marked the latter part of his career.[45]

Back in 1965, when Fellini first undertook *Mastorna*, he asked Dino Buzzati (1906–72) to assist him in the writing of the script.[46] In the years that followed, Fellini sought help from other writers, though these exchanges resulted only in additional short-lived and inconclusive attempts to fully realize the film. Brunello Rondi mentioned having provided Fellini with a few materials for *Mastorna*, but Rondi also confirmed that this was the one screenplay that the director wrote with a great degree of independence.[47] Tonino Guerra was later invited to work on the script; however, the collaboration was abruptly and quickly interrupted when Fellini's superstitious fears about the project were reawakened.[48] At the end of the 1970s Fellini also involved Andrea Zanzotto in the development of this unrealized project, and in the 1990s he consulted Ermanno Cavazzoni (1947–).[49] None of these attempts, however, was particularly effective in finalizing the script. In the chapters to follow, I will indicate how the moments in which Fellini considered undertaking this major project often coincided with a reconsideration of his team of collaborators, suggesting that he was searching for the creative formula and support to complete it.

At the onset of the ordeal of *Mastorna*, Fellini, adopting his typical preparatory method of research and travel, which he had practised ever since his years as a screenwriter, travelled with Buzzati to seek out and interview individuals across Italy who appeared to manifest extraordinary phenomena and to have first-hand knowledge of the afterlife. This preparation provided, in Buzzati's words, an "indirect psychological preparation" that "gave impulse to the magical charge that Fellini already had inside himself."[50] Buzzati's writings, focusing on the overturning of normal human perspectives in the face of supernatural events and death, resonated very early on with Fellini. The affinity existing between the two artists can be documented by a number of minor cases of intertextuality. While Buzzati wrote the short story "Le tentazioni di Sant'Antonio," Fellini wrote and directed *Le tentazioni del Dottor Antonio*. In both works the protagonist contemplates a familiar background (the clouds in the sky in Buzzati's and the billboard in Fellini's) that gradually acquires a life of its own until it takes on the form of the devil, which in both works is understood as the perturbing element that surprises and confuses the parameters of reality and presents links to the sphere of the erotic; moreover, both give the sensation that Antonio's vision might have simply been a dream.

The most significant case of intertextuality, though, is the novella *Lo strano viaggio di Domenico Molo* (The strange journey of Domenico Molo) published in the *Omnibus* in 1938. Both Buzzati's story and Fellini's script *Mastorna* describe the afterlife as a complex, confused, and fabulous city or circus where the souls of the protagonists find institutions, bureaucratic hurdles, and characters that are similar to those found on earth. Both stories seem to demystify the afterlife experience, conveying an anticlimactic sense of disappointment and even detachment for the hereafter. The souls inhabiting these stories manifest a Dantesque purgatorial sweet nostalgia of their earthly lives; they are uncertain of the rules of their new world and become prisoners in a waiting game for the vessel (a boat, a train, or an airplane) that will take them to a destination that is also unknown and a source of anxiety. Both stories end with the protagonists' return (real or imaginary) to earthly life and are written with the intention of generating a more honest perspective on life through the death experience. While Fellini never completed his film, Buzzati eventually published his orphic tale of the descent to hell, *Poema a fumetti*, which in turn manifests the influence of the work completed with Fellini through its strong ties with the disenchanted and bitter tones running through parts of *Mastorna*.[51]

The model presented for the afterlife in *Mastorna* is, however, more complex than the one in Buzzati's earlier story. The afterlife as described in the script functions as a clear and cruel mirror of earthly life, where people's fears and desires are magnified and rendered more apparent. The limbic space in which the cello player Mastorna finds himself after dying in an airplane crash is controlled by a carefully designed educational system, as spirit doctors, guides, professors, clerks, and guards assist the dead through a personalized journey; for Mastorna, this entails facing many people and situations from his past while recognizing the fact of his actual death, overcoming his limited understanding of sexuality and familial roles, identifying his true identity within an entire life lived with little authenticity, and finally letting go of his hope for reaching an ultimate destination.

At this very point of his evolutionary spiral Mastorna is taken to the head of a mysterious mountain pass where a new journey must now begin. The script's ending memorably encapsulates the idea of life as an infinite journey into the unknown, reiterated by Mastorna's female spirit guide who repeats to him something that another traveller had told her: "And openly I pledged my heart to the grave and suffering land, and often in the consecrated night, I promised to love her faithfully until death, unafraid, with her heavy burden of fatality, and never to despise a single one of her enigmas. Thus did I join myself to her with a mortal cord."[52] This passage belongs to the Romantic version of Empedocles, by Friedrich Hölderin (1770–1843), from his play *Tod des Empedokles* (1978–9, *The Death of Empedocles*) which had previously inspired Albert Camus (1913–60) who had chosen it as the epigraph to his *L'homme révolté* (1951, *The Rebel*).[53] These intense, singular, and absolute words, originally uttered by the Sicilian-Greek philosopher as he prepared to cast himself into the mouth of the Etna after having renounced his role in society, come to Mastorna as a sign of his having reached a climactic point in his journey.

Interestingly, Empedocles's words, filled with humble acceptance of life's mortality and sorrows, can be interpreted either from the point of view of Mastorna, who is now surrendering to an idea of life as a continuous experience of discoveries into unfamiliar territories, or from the point of view of his spirit guide, the woman who is now suddenly seduced by a longing for the warmth and simplicity of mortal life. After having spent the night in a shack, embraced by the spirit guide, Mastorna awakes in the middle of the night and leaves for the high mountain pass. Implying the fact that any idea regarding the afterlife can only be our way of imagining the unknown that lies ahead, the script concludes with the female spirit guide fantasizing about where Mastorna may have gone. Consistent with her rekindled interest in earthly experiences, the guide imagines Mastorna walking through Florence on an early morning in spring, ecstatic at the spectacle of the ordinary simplicity of life, and then entering into a concert hall where he abandons himself to the music of his cello accompanied by the grandeur of the orchestra.

The lyrical abandonment to, and at the same time the satirical detachment from, fixed representations and conceptualizations of the meaning of a soul's life is revealed at the end of this script to be rooted in the deep interlacement of Fellini's heightened openness towards the unknown and his belief in the infinite marvel of the ordinary. The director's interest in the esoteric and mediumistic world was a consequence of his openness – by which the human being is seen as "a creature of unexplored summits and abysses" or, as Fellini understood through one of his last recorded dreams, as a "mystery among mysteries."[54] Along these lines, prompted to clarify his philosophy in more general terms, Fellini once stated: "I believe in everything and my capacity to marvel has no limits. I believe in everything because I want to fully preserve the freshness of my imagination, without tying myself to anything that might impose limitations on it ... [I] believe in the existence of a reality that can be defined 'invisible' only by those who do not have eyes to see it. I am voluptuously open to everything."[55] This was the spirit of enquiry that led Fellini to zealously explore his oneiric life as well as various occult and esoteric phenomena, including attempts to learn more about Mexican shamanism in the company of Carlos Castaneda in 1985.[56]

This particular experience became the subject for another unrealized script, *Viaggio a Tulun* or *Tulum* (1986, Trip to Tulun), written with

Pinelli, who, as we will see, was his grounding storyteller and lifelong companion of spiritual explorations. *Viaggio a Tulun* also stages the ambivalent stance that is so central to Fellini's work and so functional within his collaborations. In fact, through the typical fictional transformation and colouring of autobiography, the protagonist here is a film director who is constantly battling between continuing his journey into the foreign lands of myth and magic and turning back to his more familiar home. Fellini's deeply rooted ambiguous perspective is expressed in the way in which the protagonist abandons himself to (but also downplays and mocks) the experiences encountered, as in the emblematic case of the meeting with a Mexican holy man, a figure who is presented as something "between priest-like and buffoon-like" within an atmosphere that is both "terrifying and silly."[57] Finally arriving at the ancient city of Tulun (or Tulum), the director and his companions in the film are guided by a shaman through an exhausting visionary ritual, which together with a number of inexplicable events leaves them confused as they return home.

From both the script of *Viaggio a Tulun* and *Il viaggio di Mastorna*, Fellini later prepared storyboards for the comic book artist Milo Manara, another creative relationship centred on a mutual interest in magic.[58] While *Mastorna* ends by balancing the quest for the transcendental with an appreciation of earthly simplicity and beauty, *Viaggio a Tulun* ends in the comic-book version by balancing traditional truths with modern doubts, and lofty esotericism with more mundane eroticism. Clearly, the director's comical and demystifying bent is a consequence of his faithfulness to the wisdom that is potentially contained in the most plain, simple, and earthly aspects of life, where the inebriating possibilities of the spirit world are constantly lowered and rediscovered within human standards. This dynamic coalesces with the idiosyncratic mixture of awe, anxiety, and satire that infuses the occult rituals and gurus in many of his films.

The pervasiveness and centrality of Fellini's interest in esotericism can be extended, as a common denominator, to his non-screenwriting collaborations, the most prominent example being the one with Nino Rota, who often accompanied Fellini during his visits to Rol and who was also absorbed by matters of esotericism.[59] Indeed, when considered within a broader collaborative network, the study of the genesis of Fellini's cinema also reveals a cross section of an unorthodox spiritual sector of the culture of twentieth-century Italy. Throughout the chapters of this book, however, the discussion will touch on

Fellini's peculiar, ambiguous adherence to matters of esotericism only in as much as it explains, and is in turn clarified by, his screenwriting collaborations.

The Structure of the Book

It would be tempting to organize a study on collaborations by using a quantitative slant and assessing the amount of influence that each collaborator had on Fellini throughout his career. It would, however, be an ingenuous way of proceeding since the phenomenòn of mutual inspiration cannot be reduced to quantitative criteria, owing to its varied and magmatic nature. Rather, as the narrative of this book intends to show, collaborations can be better understood through the study of artistic relationships viewed in both a case-by-case and an interconnected fashion. Quantitative claims about the writers' influences would risk levelling the insights that are painstakingly reached regarding the complexity and uniqueness of each of Fellini's creative partnerships. It is precisely in the individual folds of each of these examinations that the most interesting and possibly the most valuable contributions are to be found.

As this book is not a traditional auteurist monograph, it does not present a comprehensive analysis of all of Fellini's films; however, it discusses various movements from his cinema that illustrate specific collaborative dynamics. The chapters of this book are, for the most part, studies of collaborative dyads, and each is devoted to a particular relationship between Fellini and a major screenwriter. The final chapter addresses Fellini's more unstructured work with a number of poets who worked as writers and consultants to the scripts.

Chapter 1 focuses on Fellini's longest lasting collaboration with the tragic playwright Tullio Pinelli and investigates their common spiritual interests, as well as the way in which the director asserted his idea of cinema in contrast to Pinelli's style, in *La strada* (1954), *Le notti di Cabiria* (1957, *The Nights of Cabiria*), and *La dolce vita* (1960), as well as in their later collaborations on *Viaggio a Tulun*, *Ginger e Fred* (1986, *Ginger and Fred*), and *La voce della luna* (1990, *The Voice of the Moon*). In chapter 2, I examine the ways Fellini and Ennio Flaiano mutually inspired each other in developing a peculiar form of satire in *I vitelloni* (1953), *La dolce vita*, and *8½* (1963), but also the ways they disagreed regarding the public representation of authorship and in their understanding of epiphany. Chapter 3 analyses the role played by Bernardino Zapponi, who replaced Pinelli's and Flaiano's roles in 1968, in the genesis of the idiosyncratic adaptations *Toby Dammit, Fellini Satyricon* (1969, *Fellini's Satyricon*), and *Il Casanova di Federico Fellini* (1976, *Fellini's Casanova*), as well as the diaristic films *Roma* (1972, *Fellini's Roma*), *Block-notes di un regista* (1969, *Fellini: A Director's Notebook*), and *I clowns* (1970, *The Clowns*). Chapter 4 addresses a breadth of topics central to Fellini's collaborations with poet screenwriters such as Brunello Rondi, Pier Paolo Pasolini, Tonino Guerra, and Andrea Zanzotto (1921–2012). I describe the ways in which Brunello Rondi informed the philosophical discourse of films such as *La dolce vita, Prova d'orchestra* (1978, *Orchestra Rehearsal*), and *La città delle donne* (1980, *The City of Women*). I attempt to untangle the complex and profound dialogue between Fellini and Pasolini that unfolded across decades both within and outside their work on *Le notti di Cabiria*. I also assess Fellini's collaboration with Tonino Guerra on films such as *Amarcord* (1973), *E la nave va* (1983, *And the Ship Sails On*), and *Ginger e Fred*, tracing how the poet contributed to the reclamation of a mythical corporality and origin. The summoning of primordial maternal archetypes is a central theme in my discussion of Zanzotto's contribution to *Il Casanova*. Within many of these relationships, until now largely uncharted, Fellini continues to act as inspirer, but also, and novelly so, as the receptive mind at the other end of inspiration, receiving and metabolizing the activity of the writers who accompanied him behind the scenes.

Chapter One

Tullio Pinelli

It has been suggested that the friendship between Federico Fellini and Tullio Pinelli moved along tracks that ran so deep and were so hidden that they often remained unknown to the artists themselves.[1] In the 1930s and post-war years Pinelli enjoyed fame among literary circles, whereas Fellini won the praise of readers of the Roman satirical magazine *Marc'Aurelio*. Pinelli, twelve years Fellini's senior, had a more classical and literary education, while Fellini's background favoured popular culture, especially comics, radio, and music-hall variety shows. Despite their differences they discovered that they had common artistic interests and sensibilities, even from their first meeting in 1947 in Rome at a newsstand when, as the legend goes, they bumped into each other while reading the opposite sides of a hanging newspaper. As Pinelli recalled, they found that they "immediately talked in the same language," and a few hours later they were already discussing an idea for a script smacking of magical realism – the story of a man who slowly realizes that he can fly and who finally leaps out of his window.[2] The flirtation with transcendence, magic, and the supernatural would become a constant theme in the films that marked their collaboration.

Originally from Turin, Pinelli had moved with his family to Rome in 1942 after his hometown was heavily bombed, interrupting his practice as a lawyer, and took on a position at Lux Film, where he was asked to write a number of screenplays per year and to suggest novels that could be adapted into films.[3] Lux Film was a film production company owned and operated by the industrialist Riccardo Gualino (1879–1964), who, along with the musicologist Guido Gatti (1892–1973), had the objective of linking profit to a program of acculturating cinema by strengthening its connection with the highbrow literary world.[4] Tullio Pinelli, who had competed for the position at Lux Film with two other writers, Vitaliano Brancati (1907–54) and Elio Vittorini (1908–64), who eventually became distinguished novelists in post-war Italy, met the Lux Film's objectives of moving within the circles of the intelligentsia of the day.[5]

Working together as screenwriters, Pinelli and Fellini became known as one of the most talented and effective teams in Italy. From 1947 to the early 1950s they co-wrote a large number of scripts for directors such as Alberto Lattuada (1914–2005), for whom they wrote *Senza pietà* (1948, *Without Pity*), *Il mulino del Po* (1949, *The Mill on the Po*), and *Il brigante di Tacca del Lupo* (1952, The bandit of Tacca del Lupo); Pietro Germi (1914–74), for whom they wrote *In nome della legge* (1949, *In the Name of the Law*) and *Il cammino della speranza* (1950, *Path of Hope*); and Roberto Rossellini (1906–77), for whom they wrote *Il miracolo* (1948, *The Miracle*), *Francesco, giullare di Dio* (1950, *The Flowers of St Francis*), and *Europa '51* (1952, *The Greatest Love*).[6] In the preparatory phases of many of these films they undertook a series of picaresque journeys, "rendering," as Pinelli stated, "into a fable a reality they had discovered" and strengthening another common element of their friendship: the flair for adventure.[7] Their partnership was so solid that when Fellini was asked in 1951 to take on a full, independent directing job for *Lo sceicco bianco* (1952, *The White Sheik*), he proposed that Pinelli co-direct the film, though, Pinelli's demeanour was not made for the chaotic and crowded world of the set.[8]

Like the hermit character Ireneo of his one-act play *Lo stilita* (1937, The stylite), Pinelli preferred to watch the world from a distance.[9] In *Lo stilita*, a play bordering on the absurd, a merchant ventures into the desert to begin living as a hermit on top of a column, accompanied by a scribe; however, while the merchant finds himself unfit for such life, the scribe sees it as a coherent choice for himself. The play has been read as a denouncement of fascist society, but more distinctly it appears to be a statement regarding the writer's need to step out of worldly events in order to see them more clearly.[10] While Federico Fellini moved on to the role of director, Tullio Pinelli remained the writer and as such continued to work on plays and short stories.[11] He also continued to work as a screenwriter for several directors such as Dino Risi (1916–2008), Liliana Cavani (1933–), Vittorio De Sica (1901–74), and Mario Monicelli (1915–2010), but especially for Fellini, with whom he scripted every film from *Luci del varietà* (1950, *Variety Lights*, co-directed with Alberto Lattuada) to *Giulietta degli spiriti* and, after a pause of about twenty years, *Ginger e Fred* and *La voce della luna*. Pinelli and Fellini also collaborated on a number of never-realized scripts such as *Moraldo va in città* (1954, *Moraldo in the City*), *Le libere donne di Magliano* (1955, The free women of Magliano), *Viaggio con Anita* (1957, *A Journey with Anita*), and *Viaggio a Tulun*.

Tullio Pinelli has been viewed as the most acquiescent and accommodating of Fellini's screenwriters. The biographer Tullio Kezich likes to praise Pinelli for his immunity from the "syndrome of the unhappy writer."[12] In reality, Pinelli did not always yield silently to Fellini's authorial propaganda. In one of his letters to Fellini, Pinelli reproaches the director for having inadequately mentioned his writing import during a press conference for *Il bidone* (1955, *The Swindle*): "You can't avail yourself of the collaboration of an author and then behave as if he had done nothing, or worked only as typist."[13] Even though Pinelli was certainly less contemptuous and proud than some of the director's other collaborators, his engagement with the films was not less involved or pivotal. In an interview Pinelli stated, "It is absolutely true that Fellini put much of himself in all the characters of his films; but this is just as true for his collaborators, by measure of the common ground they shared with him as men and authors," and then added, "It is as author that I must remind others that many of the fundamental themes of my theatre have significantly influenced, through my work at the scripts, the films of Fellini."[14]

Tullio Pinelli's playwriting was enthusiastically received by prominent critics such as Silvio d'Amico, he was awarded an important recognition at the National Drama Competition in 1947 as best up-and-coming playwright, and his plays were successfully staged in various cities, most notably *La pulce d'oro* (1934, The golden flea) and *I padri etruschi* (1940, The Etruscan fathers).[15] Pinelli's plays are typical of the metaphysical Catholic theatre, where representation is challenged by the attempt to stage the psychological and metaphysical complexities of human reality. Not unlike the works of the more famous Ugo Betti (1892–1953), Tullio Pinelli's plays explore the motivations and consequences of evil, thus focusing on intimate themes such as guilt and everyday redemption, often through allegories. Fittingly, in 1955 Achille Fiocco included Tullio Pinelli along with Ugo Betti, Diego Fabbri (1911–80), Riccardo Bacchelli (1891–1985) and others in his study titled *Correnti spiritualistiche nel teatro moderno*.[16] Pinelli's religious interests were inherently linked to the tragic atmosphere of his plays, which set the works apart from those of other young authors of his generation. In *Sessant'anni di teatro in Italia*, published in 1947, the critic Baldo Curato declared enthusiastically, "We must welcome with sincere appreciation a young author such as Pinelli, who has been capable of bringing to the stages of our theatres an atmosphere and a sense of tragedy that is extremely rare nowadays."[17] It was precisely the tragic and Christian tones of Pinelli's mature work that eventually entered into Fellini's early films along with other specific concerns, stylistic elements, and motifs.

Dominique Delouche (1931–), Fellini's assistant director between 1955 and 1960, opened his *Journal d'un Bidoniste* with the following dedication: "To our friend Tullio Pinelli, whose shadow cannot be dissociated from Fellini's face." Even though Pinelli was quite outspoken about the connection between his writing style and Fellini's films, there has never been a scholarly attempt to systematically evaluate the extent and nature of his contribution. Pinelli, and his tragic dramaturgic approach to the script, was a presence against which the director defined his more mature non-literary and comedic form of cinema. Films such as *La strada*, *Le notti di Cabiria*, and *La dolce vita* document the results of their synergy, which also entails the blending of Pinelli's more orthodox Christian point of view and Fellini's eclectic form of spirituality. Moreover, in order to understand their enduring interest in matters of esotericism as well as the growing distance in their approach to the script, one has to examine their later collaborations on *Viaggio a Tulun*, *Ginger e Fred*, and *La voce della luna*.

Neutralizing Tragedy: A Pattern from *La strada* On

It is indeed striking to observe the degree to which Fellini largely avoided throughout his career the representation of violence and death. In the few existing tragic scenes from his films the camera shot is softened with great discretion, as for example the scene in the Villa dei Suicidi in *Satyricon* that was filmed with the utmost tactfulness, and the bombing of San Lorenzo in *Intervista* (1987, *Fellini's Intervista*) where the whole war is synecdochically compressed into the image of the woman running under a tunnel for help. As it happened, when working with Pinelli on films such as *La strada*, *Le notti di Cabiria*, and *La dolce vita*, Fellini was often engaged in exorcizing the violent and tragic tones that characterized this writer's dramaturgic style. The collaborative dynamics analysed below speak to Fellini's earliest improvisational attempts to manifest his comic leanings and non-narrative approach to film-making, which became dominant as Fellini's fame and vision matured and which eventually required him to make a complete break with Pinelli.

Thanks to the available variants of the scripts, the film *La strada* accommodates a detailed examination of its conceptualization and is a good case study to understand the ways in which Fellini's and Pinelli's artistic sensibilities merged and conflicted. Both artists spoke of having met one day in the early 1950s, excited about a new idea for a story that they were imagining. When they remember how they debated on who voiced his idea first, their statements contradict each other in curious ways as they both claim to have been the first one to verbalize the idea to the other.[18] Ennio Flaiano did not have a large impact on *La strada*, especially in its inception and early stages, and he played the role, as Pinelli once said, of a distant and sometimes hostile critic.[19] As Pinelli recalls, while Fellini was away filming *I vitelloni* and travelling with Flaiano, he was left alone for several months to write a first draft of the screenplay:

> We spoke at length about the idea and the characters, inventing them together; but in the end I wrote everything myself: the scenario, the treatment, the screenplay, the dialogue (as the opening titles also confirm). It is through writing that a creation takes shape. Therefore it surprises and saddens me when the characters of Zampanò, Gelsomina and Il Matto, and their adventures now famous around the world, are attributed only to the director, because it is through the scenes and dialogue I wrote that they came alive. Honestly, though, I don't know how the film would have turned out from this same script if it had been placed in the hands of another director, no matter how talented.[20]

Certainly the universe of street artists had always been a major interest to both. Fellini would state that he had been entertaining the idea for a film on itinerant circuses and on the mysterious travelling vendors and artists who, during his childhood, used to descend from the mountains to the town of Gambettola, where his family used to spend the holidays.[21] Pinelli had already demonstrated his interest in the topic with his 1935 play *La pulce d'oro* (and continued after *La strada* with *Il ciarlatano meraviglioso*, dated 1967).[22] Pinelli even remarked once that during one of his trips from Turin and Rome, travelling a mountain pass, he had seen a real life Gelsomina and Zampanò: "During one of these trips, on a very steep uphill drive, I saw Zampanò and Gelsomina ... There was a large man pulling a cart as if he was a horse. The cart was covered by a tarp on which a siren was painted, and at the rear there was a woman pushing."[23]

The couple's characteristics, disposition, and dynamics already forecast those in the film, and even a detail such as the drapery with the siren eventually appears in the film's motorized version of the cart. Furthermore, Pinelli's play *La pulce d'oro*, published about ten years before, contains the idea of a young woman being forced to leave her home to follow a nomadic charlatan, which is similar to what occurs in *La strada*. Here one can also find the sense of excitement for a life on the road, combined with the nostalgia for the home left behind, as experienced by Gelsomina. In this farce, built on the understanding of the inseparability of illusion from reality, there is a travelling charlatan named Lupo Fiorino who stops by an inn; he carries with him a cage in which, he says, he keeps a flea that is able to turn whatever it bites into gold. The cage falls open and the insect, according to Lupo, climbs under the skirt of the innkeeper's daughter. Lupo convinces the innkeeper that it would be safer for the girl to spend the night in his bedroom. When the father realizes he has been deceived, he decides to murder Lupo. A violent struggle ensues, but the murder is not carried to its completion; rather, after several twists, the father allows the girl to leave with the nomadic con artist.

Tullio Pinelli gladly laboured at a first draft of the screenplay of *La strada*, developing it with coherence and lyricism and further inspiring Fellini's work.[24] The Lilly Library of Rare Books (LLRB) holds the copy of the treatment that Pinelli wrote independently after his exchange with Fellini (hereafter *LS1*).[25] The same archive holds what seems to be Pinelli's first draft of the screenplay with numerous and significant editing done by Fellini's hand (hereafter *LS2*).[26] In addition to these manuscripts, the final version of the screenplay, published in 1955 by Bianco e Nero, is also worth mentioning (hereafter as *LS3*). In comparing these versions of *La strada*'s script to the film, while also keeping in mind Pinelli's theatrical adaptation completed in 2000 with Bernardino Zapponi, one can properly frame Pinelli's place in the genesis of this film.

The earliest version of the script (*LS1*) contains key elements of Pinelli's writing style. Therefore, the changes undergone by the versions of the script and in relationship to the final film product document differences between the styles of Pinelli and Fellini. In the opening of the script, quoted at length below to give a sense of Pinelli's writing style, settings and events are used to underscore spiritual dynamics, a typical trait of almost all of Pinelli's plays.

A bolt of lightning cracks the heavy black clouds, lingering between sky and earth. Then the thunder comes to the silent countryside, a sudden explosion that rolls in the distance beyond the houses on the periphery of the town.

It begins to hail.

White grains fall here and there and bounce off the ground, increasing in size and intensity until they become an otherworldly resounding storm that envelopes the ancient and half ruined aqueduct, the shacks that lie against it, the small gardens set in between huts. The iron roofs emit a deafening rumble; the leaves and flowers are hit by shocking and sudden blows, and lift themselves back up mutilated; and the earth is being covered with white while the rain forms impetuous and roaring streams that invade every place, dragging with them small dams of round grayish icicles.

And suddenly, the storm magically disappears. The same powerful hand that had brought it has dispersed it and dragged it somewhere else; and from under the light that falls from the broken and fleeting clouds, everything reflects lucid and trembling glimmerings. The air is now transparent and full with the vibrations of the rainbow, and in it emerges, at the end of the alley that runs along the high wall of the decayed aqueduct, something black. It is a man walking slowly, dragging a cart covered with an unsecured drape. It seems that the man has detached himself from the heavy and black earth because of the water.

He walks looking at the huts leaning against the old walls; he is trying to orient himself and find among them a particular one. The cart follows him, jolting on the uneven road; and the large leather strap that crosses his squared chest presses with every jolt against his stocky neck, against a neck baked by the sun and crossed by wrinkles where the dark dust of the roads has nested itself permanently throughout the years.[27]

After a storm Zampanò emerges as an ominous and dark creature of the earth, embodying its instinctual violent force. The outburst is a prelude to the eruption of Zampanò's violence later in the story. Humanity and nature constantly mirror each other, thus conveying an allegorical significance to the events. The allegorical subtext of the description was, at least in this case, destined to remain on the page, since, in spite of their beauty, passages such as, "And suddenly, the storm magically disappears. The same powerful hand that had brought it has dispersed it and dragged it somewhere else ..." did not transfer easily into film.

Pinelli's characteristic allegorical use of settings and landscapes can be easily traced in his plays, as for instance in *I padri etruschi*. The play narrates how Velca, a greedy, evil, and irresistible woman who marries a much older man to acquire his possessions, refuses the genuine love of the young Tarquinio; owing to her husband's impotence, Velca convinces Tarquinio to impregnate her, but when Tarquinio reveals to her husband his love for Velca, she has him killed and spends her life mad with grief and guilt in the wilderness. Not only are the ancestral passions behind the characters' actions reflected and amplified by the sinister and occult presence of the ancient Etruscan tombs, but also the natural landscape is often a prelude and accompaniment to the characters' inner turmoil. At the opening of the first scene all is clearly inscribed in primitive ineluctability: "The thick and massive walls, the barbaric gleaming of the elegant copper amphora, the muskets hanging on the walls, and above all the primordial blue sky, revealed the world of a very ancient and primitive people."[28] Once the fate of Tarquino is written, Velca's final conflicting dialogue with him unfolds against a backdrop with tones of desolation and death: "A vast plain, deserted and silent, scattered with solitary oaks. As far as the eye can see, the land is covered by wild yellow and gold blossoms amidst short grass. It is sunset. Enormous flaming clouds send reflections the colour of blood across the entire sky."[29] During the writing of *La strada*, Fellini evidently understood that the use of landscape for psychological resonance was a key element of the story and, thus, he originally integrated and translated it visually whenever he could. For instance, when expressing the change in Gelsomina before and after the death of Il Matto, the film shows first sunny and bucolic vistas followed by wintry and desolate landscapes. Fellini's preference for the subjective shot, typically considered only within a cinematic discussion on the innovation of the neorealist stylistics, possesses its roots also in the metaphysical theatre of Tullio Pinelli.[30]

While Fellini shared and appreciated a stylistic element such as the lyrical use of landscapes with Pinelli – which pertains to their common artistic pursuit of psychic depth described more in detail below – the tragedy of Pinelli's writing was largely incompatible with the director's vision. The majority of Pinelli's plays are dramas in which the characters experience destructive crisis, often involving violence, and murder, elements that are far removed from Fellini's sensibility: "The tragic ending is really inherent in the development; it is an inevitable conclusion in my opinion. In my stories there is always the presence of death. He who goes out looking for a home, and stubbornly looks for it, dies in the street. He who tries to save his fiancé on the rubber boat drowns himself ... Death is part of everything for me. I cannot conceive a story without a tragic ending."[31]

Pinelli himself stated that Fellini was opposed to the murder of Il Matto from the start, and Fellini apparently complained that such violence was not subject matter for his direction.[32] In spite of this, Pinelli insisted that the murder was the motor of the entire story of *La strada*. Fellini was eventually persuaded to keep this scene, but he did his best to soften it, as the final filmic product manifests, where the director managed to turn the murder into an accident. In *LS1*, Zampanò is described as a furious beast when, upon discovering Il Matto drunk and defenceless in a remote area, stabs him to death. Here, Zampanò's "homicidal furore" and his "knife soiled with blood" vividly attest to Pinelli's initial idea for this scene. There is even a moment when it seems that Zampanò will also kill Gelsomina.

> Zampanò jumps like a tiger between spots of sunlight and shadow ... Now Gelsomina has found Il Matto. She has found him face down in the grass, sprinkled with red, his mouth wide open, his eyes clouded. Zampanò has just stood up and looks at the lifeless body lying at his feet. He has not yet realized that Gelsomina has come running out from the bushes. Gelsomina is still; everything in her is still: blood, heart, eyes, thought.
>
> Everything in her is utter terror that paralyses even her desperation.
>
> All of a sudden Zampanò turns and sees her. The murderous fury that possesses him and the madness of blood push him towards the woman who has discovered him. Gelsomina sees him running towards her with the knife in hand soiled with blood; her knees weaken. She emits a shriek and falls down, losing her senses. Zampanò stops just above her.
>
> Hallucinating and panting, he stares at the girl stretched out at his feet and does not hit her.[33]

Later, in the *LS2* and *LS3* versions of the script, Zampanò's animalistic violence becomes less dramatic. Without a knife and without the attack against Gelsomina, Zampanò's killing is depicted increasingly as the unfortunate result of an accident, an unpropitious misjudgment of force.

Pinelli's predilection for the tragic is expressed in other cases scattered throughout the scripting of *La strada*. For instance, *LS1* contains a scene in which Zampanò and an accomplice enter a house, tie all the women to the chairs, and rob them of their valuables. The scene, which was eventually deleted, is particularly harsh both for the violence demonstrated in the wild and almost mythical fight between Zampanò and the dog guarding the property and for the sheer terror experienced by Gelsomina.[34] The relationship between Gelsomina and Zampanò becomes progressively less brutal as the script moves from the first version to the film. In *LS1* not only does Zampanò explicitly consider killing Gelsomina after murdering Il Matto, but he also mistreats Gelsomina with greater cruelty. In the first version Zampanò mercilessly beats and rapes her. What follows is the rape of Gelsomina in this early version of the script:

> Gelsomina slips through the space between the cart and the wall; she throws herself into the darkness of the countryside. It is a desperate run on the soggy earth in the blackness; behind her there is the terrifying acceleration of the steps and the heavy breathing of the man, moving closer and closer. A run without end and out of breath. When Zampanò plunges against her and grabs her, Gelsomina feels as if she has been running for an infinite time. She gasps, and the hoarse scream that she lets out dies right away under the tempest of blows she receives. She fights back instinctually, and feels only the violent beating of the man who surrounds and suffocates her. She feels herself falling, the man pressing on top of her; and this time she screams out of an ancestral and mysterious instinct, struggling even more wildly in a terror never felt before. She bites and scratches. This is a fight against a relentless and brutal strength that immobilizes and annihilates her. Her screams are even more hoarse and extend through the nocturnal solitude of the fields.[35]

In his comparison of *LS1* to the later versions of the screenplay and to the film, Peter Bondanella has also noted this variant. However, Bondanella's auteurist analysis does not consider Pinelli's contribution to *LS1*.[36] In the chilling passage concerning Gelsomina's rape her fear and struggle are described in detail; in the later drafts of *LS2* and *LS3* the event is expressed only distantly and indirectly with the figure of Zampanò looming above the entrance of the caravan, followed by ellipsis: "Gelsomina, pushed from the outside by Zampanò, enters the caravan; she lies on the rags, curled up and hiding herself inside them. In the light from the back door appears the large figure of Zampanò, who climbs behind her ..."[37] The film itself hints even more vaguely at the possibility of Zampanò sexually exploiting Gelsomina.

The version of *La strada* that Pinelli prepared for the theatre in the 1990s together with Bernardino Zapponi provides further confirmation of his original idea of the story in terms of, as Fellini once wrote, a *"favola feroce"* (a ferocious fable).[38] In contrast to the film, the play is incidentally told by a fakir, another sort of street artist and one who is certainly more equipped to bear the sufferings that the story entails and who begins by narrating, "How it ended I don't know, but I know how it started."[39] The play returns to its original tragic tone in several instances: by suggesting more clearly Zampanò's sexual abuse of Gelsomina, by including Gelsomina's fear of being raped by Zampanò, and by returning to a more violent representation of Zampanò's murder of Il Matto. Moreover, the ending of Pinelli's play adaptation, when a peasant woman tells Zampanò about Gelsomina's last days, undergoes a greater dramatic crescendo because the spectacle about Gelsomina's pitiful state of delirium, grief, and death is actually shown. Instead, the film has the viewer imaging the final moments of Gelsomina's life while a maid narrates them to Zampanò from behind a sheet that she is hanging out to dry.

The progressive softening of the tragic quality of Pinelli's initial story of *La strada* shows Fellini's attempt to render every character, including Zampanò, more likeable and to focus more on the magical aura of Gelsomina's whimsical nature by emphasizing her childlike, amusing, and bizarre behaviours rather than the tragedy of her situation. This occurs visibly in the film, as the following scenes, some of which were not scripted, are presented: Gelsomina's ritual to predict the rain, her imitation of a tree, her witnessing a child burying a pet, her surreal meeting with a solitary horse that is quietly trotting in the night, her meeting with the three musicians who are walking towards the town's festival, and her clumsy fall into a hole during a tense and dramatic conversation with Zampanò. For its being endowed with a similar special sensibility, the character of Ivo Savini (Roberto Benigni) in *La voce della luna* has been associated with that of Gelsomina, although the function of this characteristic in *La voce della luna* has been explained by Millicent Marcus as an alternative route away from the self-enclosed discourse of consumerism and contemporary media culture.[40] This penchant for subversive and playful mediumism, along with Fellini's general tendency to let Gelsomina carry on with her clownish acting, represents the more genuine fruits of Fellini's sensibility. To confirm this aim, the folder in which the scripts are contained shows evidence of the direction Fellini's mind was taking the story; Fellini's amusing and graceful cartoon sketches include those of Gelsomina as a clown rather than a Christ-like figure, peeking out with her curious, large eyes from behind a drop curtain.

Fellini's struggle with Pinelli's tragic narratives is not only traceable in *La strada* but also evident in *Le notti di Cabiria*. The idea for the film itself came from a crime report about a prostitute, the Sicilian Antonietta Longo, who, during the summer of 1955, was found stabbed and decapitated near the lake of Castel Gandolfo.[41] In the film the eerie setting of Cabiria's finale becomes that of the volcanic and legend-filled lake of Nemi near Rome. It was Ennio Flaiano who had written a short piece on the way in which the media had distorted this event to the point of glorifying the killer and denigrating the victim, and had brought the news to the attention of Fellini and Pinelli.[42] Pinelli was particularly struck by the event and felt further justified in having the protagonist, Cabiria, die at the end of the story.[43] In the film the protagonist is shadowed by the imminent danger of death (just as in *La strada*, owing to the looming presence of Gelsomina's dead sister, Rosa, another element that Fellini worked to minimize).[44] In *Le notti di Cabiria* the expectations of the audiences of the time were set on a tragic trajectory owing to the aforementioned sensational crime news as well as the foreshadowing of the opening scene in which Cabiria is thrown into a river by a man who pretends to be her boyfriend. However, in Fellini's hands, the film's ending becomes one of the greatest celebrations of the joy and will to live ever seen in cinema.

In preparation for the filming of *Le notti di Cabiria*, Fellini, sometimes accompanied by Pinelli, Pier Paolo Pasolini, or Ennio Flaiano, or at other times by his set designer Piero Gherardi, observed locations and met with prostitutes, homeless people, and various individuals living or working on the streets of Rome at night. Fellini was usually disturbed by the stories the prostitutes told him about the gruesome murders by a serial killer called "the hammer," yet he became curious when he heard the story about a man who at night drove through the city distributing goods, clothing, and medicine to the poor. Fellini eventually found the man's address and arranged to accompany him, together with Tullio Pinelli, during one of his nocturnal tours.[45] This meeting was important to both Fellini and Pinelli because it helped them to discover a hidden world, a kind of new biosphere, teaming with touching and surprising characters. The man, Tirabassi, also known as "L'uomo col sacco" (The Man with the Sack), was included in the screenplay, and the scene was shot; however, it was later censored, and only in recent editions has it been reinserted into the film. According to Kezich, Cardinal Giuseppe Siri, who secretly screened the film to help the director prepare for possible opposition from the Vatican, found the independent charitable enterprise of "L'uomo col sacco" not convenient to the Church's image because it was operated outside of the Church's authority.[46] This character was a true revelation for Pinelli, and he followed him for several years after the film had been completed. Pinelli finally did justice to the example of Tirabassi in the 2004 theatrical adaptation of *Le notti di Cabiria*, where he turned him into an allegorically Christ-like character. Upon meeting Tirabassi, Cabiria expresses her admiration in silence towards the saintly sacrifice of the man, his unprejudiced goodness, and the significance of his life and work, and her shame for the shallow life that she is instead leading.[47]

Again, Pinelli's theatrical adaptation provides a way to identify the scenes and elements that he deemed important in the story and to find more examples of his tragic orientation for *Le notti di Cabiria*. Pinelli's play, even though not going so far as to have Cabiria killed as he had once conceived, carefully constructs the character of Oscar, her deceiving admirer, who is shown as a coherently evil character. In the film Fellini had preferred to keep the motivations of this character ambiguous, keeping open the possibility that his initial intentions and admiration for Cabiria were honest. Pinelli's play, instead, shows Oscar intentionally disguising himself as Cabiria's dream husband, whom she believes to have first seen on the illusionist's stage. Eventually Oscar tricks her into falling in love with him, and then she sells her house and belongings for their future together. Pinelli deliberately changes a few small incriminating details with respect to the original screenplay – most importantly at the end of the play when Oscar admits, "My name is not Oscar," a statement that unveils the fact that he has been weaving a scam around Cabiria from the very beginning and simply lacks the determination to carry his cruel plan to its murderous end.[48] Both the ineluctable logic and the Christian vision of Pinelli's narration require a clear definition of characters. Fellini instead did not believe in a Manichaean vision of humanity, as the absence of purely evil characters in his films testifies. Through Fellini's lens, by virtue of what Pasolini calls his "undifferentiated and undifferentiating love," the spectator is moved to pity characters like Zampanò and Oscar; it is not clear where their evilness ends and where their goodness begins, or vice versa.[49]

Tullio Kezich makes a parallel between the character of Steiner (Alain Cuny) in *La dolce vita* and Fellini's friend Luigi A. Garrone, the unsuccessful writer whose painful and lonely death Fellini had witnessed in a hospital several years before; however, the chief inspiration behind these characters belongs to others.[50] A more fitting biographical source for Steiner would instead be the suicidal Cesare Pavese (1908–50), a childhood friend of Tullio Pinelli and his brother Carlo, to whom they had written letters in an attempt to help him find respite in the Christian faith. Remaining though within the textual domain, Steiner is most fruitfully compared with the character of the writer Pietro Rovere in Pinelli's play *Lotta con l'angelo*, who is also dissatisfied with his material achievements and with his failure to properly respond to God's call for martyrdom, and he ends up killing himself and his wife. During an interview Pinelli provided an enlightening description of Steiner:

> [Steiner] is an anticipation of what happens every day. This episode is entirely mine. I suggested and wrote it. Unfortunately, the evening at Steiner's house has been rewritten and is completely different from what I had done, resulting in one of the worst episodes of the film. However, I said this to Federico, "Be careful because here you did something that communicates that the person kills himself because of the type of friends he has, and naturally so." At the beginning, though, it was different. Steiner had to kill himself because of desperation, out of happiness. Someone who arrives at the apex of happiness, of life's sweetness, with a beautiful, faithful, and loving wife, with his beautiful children, knows that he has reached a dead end and therefore kills himself and his children. It is not an isolated event. It is truly what is happening now on an immeasurably larger scale. This is an exceptional episode in the film; it is not in the same tone as the other parts; it stands out. In my opinion it is one of the most farsighted moments on what is happening now.[51]

Steiner represented for Pinelli the intellectual affected by a "desperation from happiness," who is materially realized but spiritually dissatisfied. Indeed, as it had happened with other characters such as Zampanò and Oscar, Fellini wished to render Steiner's mad despair and tragic actions more comprehensible and accessible. As Pinelli mentioned above, this move was accomplished through the party scene where Steiner is surrounded by rather shallow friends and intellectuals, an episode that clouds the deeper reasons behind the character's desperate actions and therefore the significance of his crisis.

Brunello Rondi, another of Fellini's instrumental screenwriters, must have understood the incompatibility between Pinelli and Fellini when it came to dramatization. In describing the episode of Marcello's father in *La dolce vita*, he spoke of a "traditionalist sediment," "noble but heterogeneous," "an element belonging to an old dramaturgy that remains abstract within the chaotic and aggressive tone of the film."[52] Furthermore, Brunello Rondi acutely explains how Fellini overcomes the literariness of the episode of Marcello's father by releasing a charge of "sympathy and good-hearted fun" that interjects into the film "a sudden *vitellone*-like complicity between father and son."[53] As will become clearer in a later chapter, the character of Steiner was actually the seat of authorial conflict not only between Fellini and Pinelli but also between Pinelli and Rondi, a fact that might explain why, in a letter to Rondi about Steiner, Fellini failed to mention Pinelli's original ideas.[54] To make the matter even more interesting, Pier Paolo Pasolini also wrote his version of the sequences entailing Steiner, whom he named Mattioli, making him originally from Emilia-Romagna and an ex-student of Roberto Longhi (1890–1970), as was Pasolini himself.[55] However, as far as the friction between Pinelli and Fellini is concerned, the episode of Steiner attests to the growing difficulty they were encountering in maintaining the delicate balance between tragedy and comedy.

Nearly three years after *La dolce vita*, Fellini would vividly dream of Tullio Pinelli's "exaggerated, outdated and not-valid writing" that was connected to a blatantly erroneous characterization of Giulietta/Gelsomina as a cruel being. The dream was recorded in the summer of 1963 and is associated with the beginning of work on *Giulietta degli spiriti*, the film that marked the end of Fellini's long partnership with many of his collaborators, including Pinelli, who surfaces in this dream as an artistic antagonist (see figure 1).

The image depicted represents Gelsomina, the protagonist of *La strada*, who "in order to seem different and cruel" plunges into the depths of a river to feed a defenceless puppy to a crocodile. Fellini's record begins as follows: "A drawing of the film I am planning on doing (*Giulietta degli spiriti*) to show myself that the things Pinelli wrote are not valid. Everything appears exaggerated, unreal."[56] The dream resembles a mental simulation of a shooting test for a sequence that exemplifies what Fellini feels is Pinelli's no longer bearable, tragic narrative. It must be remembered that Giulietta Masina, with her ability to

Figure 1. Fellini's rendition of a dream with reference to Tullio Pinelli, 20 August 1963

convey a fable-like transmutation of reality through her acting, satisfied a deeply rooted element within Pinelli, who also scripted her part in *Fortunella* (directed by Eduardo De Filippo, 1958).[57] Therefore, in this dream Fellini is apparently reclaiming his own perspective on the actress, and condemning Pinelli's rendition of Giulietta from *La strada* on as being essentially incompatible with his comical and lyrical bent.

The dream explicitly portrays Pinelli's storytelling as unnecessarily dramatic and violent. Without any explanation, Giulietta is suddenly driven to the malicious act of obsessively pursuing the annihilation of an innocent puppy, a cruelty that summons the presence of a large crocodile resting at the muddy bottom of the river. What follows in the dream of 1963 is a chain of events that entails a series of transformations, which in turn seems to be an enigmatic take on the relationship between literature and cinema: "The crocodile may have swallowed the dog in a single bite, but it's no longer a crocodile but a toad, dead, desiccated and closed between the pages of a book." After being reduced to a toad, a less menacing and destructive equivalent of the crocodile, the monster is absorbed as a dry leaf into the pages of a book, thus revealing its association with the sphere of literariness and in turn strengthening its link to the dramaturgy of Tullio Pinelli. The alchemy of the dream eventually leads to nothing: "Another nasty toad appears and devours the first, then finally eats itself with one bite of its jaws, what's left? Just the mouth, spread horrifyingly wide, then even that disappears."[58] Placed within the context of the collaboration between Fellini and Pinelli, this dream could be indicating that in 1963 the director is clearly starting to perceive the dramatic and tragic formulae of Pinelli's writing as sterile, a "self-devouring" creative dead end. Indeed, tragedy, at least in the traditional narrative form practised by Pinelli, brings about the type of definite closures that were incompatible to the director's style. At the onset of *Giulietta degli spiriti* the experience of *La strada* is inevitably brought back to Fellini's mind, and the dream expresses his anxiety towards Pinelli's tragic vision.

A Metaphysical Fellowship: Transcending Christianity

Interest in mysticism and the supernatural is a hallmark of Pinelli's plays throughout the 1930s and 1940s and beyond. The scholar Vito Pandolfi noted the following about Pinelli: "The sense of mystery and the anxiety, even if unconscious, for an otherworldly truth always pervade his more explicitly human works." The writer Ernesto Laura said of Pinelli: "It is a characteristic of Pinelli to surround things and persons with a magical and enchanted halo, but only faintly suggested."[59] It is important to acknowledge that Fellini was indeed the ideal director for Pinelli's work and that this playwright had struggled for many years to find a director capable of representing the metaphysical tone of his work. Pinelli himself said, "The collaboration with Fellini was unique and personal. Compared to the other films I worked on, in Fellini's I feel more of an author and I recognize myself better."[60] On this note, it must be observed that the renowned critic Silvio d'Amico, in reviewing a 1943 theatrical rendition of Pinelli's *Lotta con l'angelo* by director Giorgio Venturini, highlighted the director's difficulty "to express scenically the mystical obsession of its protagonist."[61] The fact that Pinelli had already developed such interest in the supernatural well before the beginning of his work with Fellini is yet another clue to the weighty influence that the playwright must have had on Fellini from the very beginning. Pinelli was the only writer with whom Fellini wrote *Un'agenzia matrimoniale* (*Introduction Agency*) – part of an episodic film coordinated by Cesare Zavattini called *L'amore in città* (1953, *Love in the City*) – wherein the existence of a werewolf is accepted as common and natural, thus leading to grotesque and unusual circumstances. Across Fellini's entire career Pinelli was his chief partner in scripting stories relating to the supernatural and to the exploration of transcendence.

   In all the early drafts of *La strada* there is a scene that takes place after a wedding, in which a farmer shows the animals to Gelsomina in the suspended and half-lit space of a stable. She is drawn to a trembling ox that she is told is mad because it sees ghosts at night. Gelsomina identifies with the poor beast because of her own fears of the night, and she begins to wonder about death and tries to look into the animal's mad eyes in an attempt to discover something about that mystery: "She looks into the ox's eyes, looks in the direction of the ox's eyes, as if hoping to see what the ox 'sees,' she is afraid."[62] The scene continues as Zampanò arrives and Gelsomina assiduously and explicitly interrogates him, with little success, about his beliefs regarding the existence of ghosts and the nature of the afterlife. The conversation between Gelsomina and Zampanò on this subject highlights Zampanò's materialism as he values money over any abstract consideration. Obviously, this part must have been an important one because it is present in various versions of the screenplay and was certainly dear to Pinelli; he included it again in the text of his later stage adaptation.[63] The scene was also important to

Fellini, who wanted to use it to emphasize Gelsomina's growing awareness of human mortality and therefore clarify her interest in the strange animal that in her eyes becomes a mediumistic rather than simply a "crazy" creature.[64] In the final film product the "mad ox" sequence was visually condensed into the scene with Osvaldo, where Gelsomina expresses the same type of interest towards a creature who is, like her, considered different and crazy. Osvaldo, who incidentally goes from being paralytic in the screenplay to being mentally different in the film, attracts Gelsomina's attention, and for a moment she attempts to empathize with him, to see, as happened with the mad ox, what he sees. Fellini's direction truly exploits Gelsomina's visit to Osvaldo in generating an otherworldly atmosphere of suspense; Osvaldo's room catches Fellini's interest from the early stages of the scripting process.[65] On set, the room is transformed into a large space that Fellini has filled with peasants' work tools that have been turned into mysterious-looking geometrical toys, sinister lights, and sacred images.

From the very beginning, Fellini's relationship with Pinelli was based on a common search for a non-dogmatic and non-institutional, yet personal and quotidian, transcendence that could be found within or outside Christianity. Both artists shared leanings towards the fantastic and the magical, as shown by their mutual projects concerning the lives of saints and mediums, and more explicitly in their attendance at the paranormal manifestations of individuals such as the doctor and medium Gustavo Adolfo Rol. Pinelli relayed his admiration for Rol and explained that the medium had provided him with the proof of what he already believed to be true: "the existence of these magic powers, so called-magic, or in other words of this supernatural world that in part is tied to religion and in part is not, a concrete existence that can reveal itself even through religion."[66] What differentiated Pinelli from Fellini when it came to the realm of the supernatural was that, while Pinelli framed the miraculous precisely within a Christian context, Fellini had, as Pinelli himself acknowledged, a "visione molto panica" that was characterized by a more general, almost pagan, sense of religious apprehension.[67] Pinelli expressed how Fellini could not conceive everyday life separate from a supernatural or hidden dimension, sometimes placing his total trust in those who claimed a special rapport with the afterlife, while Pinelli described himself as being somewhat more rational and cautious.

Tullio Pinelli's interest in the supernatural was always framed within a religious context, definitely Christian in nature. The character of Pietro

Rovere in Pinelli's play *Lotta con l'angelo*, previously also discussed in connection with Steiner in *La dolce vita*, experiences a final salvation in similar ways to Zampanò. The comparison between the ending of this play with the script of *La strada* provides a sample of his Christian world view and how it interacts with what the writer called Fellini's *visione panica*.[68] Pinelli's play *Lotta con l'angelo* ends with the dialogue between Pietro, who has just killed his wife, and his favourite son, Davide, who does not stop believing in his father's capacity to save his soul:

PIETRO: (*stares at Davide in silence. Then with a terrible tone*) So. May this horror remain as your only memory of me. It will help you to overcome the flesh, when you will be tempted to deny martyrdom. (*Pause*) I have rejected it, and I descend to the eternal suffering.

DAVIDE: No. Not yet.

PIETRO: It is just horrible. But from the bottom of the abyss, I will see you with our brothers' angels, close to Him. My son. (*Pause*) You will see Him by his side for all eternity.

DAVIDE: (*murmuring*) God of mercy.

PIETRO: Glory to Him.

DAVIDE: Hope. Save yourself.

PIETRO: It is not right.

DAVIDE: Do you still love Him?

PIETRO: I will make hell tremble, singing glory to Him.

DAVIDE: (*murmuring*) If you love Him, the enemy cannot pass.

PIETRO: (*murmuring*) God the Father! God the Father!

DAVIDE: (*almost speaking into his ear*) You are saved. Do you still love Him?

PIETRO: (*with a whisper*) To death.

DAVIDE: You are saved. (*Pause. Slowly he stands, his eyes staring at Pietro Rovere, who still lies on the couch with his eyes cloudy, wide open, and turned to the sky*).[69]

Let us juxtapose this passage with the finale of the early version of *La strada*.

Zampanò has stopped and is listening. He listens to what he has never listened to before: silence.

A sudden shiver shakes him from head to toe. It is a shiver of terror. And after the terror comes the fear of a never-before-experienced feeling of emptiness. It is not the fear of hunger or of jail or of another man; it is the fear of emptiness.

His knees weaken. Zampanò crouches down on the sand. As if hit by a concrete and terrifying illness, something he had never felt before, Zampanò struggles against something that is being painfully born out of his bestial soul: angst.

In the evening the rustling of the waves repeats itself continuously, and Zampanò, for the first time in his life, cries.

A woman was born and has died for this.

The dawn on the sea is like the beginning of the world.

Zampanò sleeps profoundly on the sand. He does not rest as he always used to, twisted on himself, as if in an animalistic instinctive defence: his limbs rest open and abandoned, with the serene faith of a child's sleep.

His face is calm and human.[70]

Not only does this passage show a clear Christian interpretation of Gelsomina, another trait of the theological nature of Pinelli's storytelling, but also the rebirth of Zampanò is made obvious by the highlighting of the "beginning of the world" and the luminosity and peacefulness of the scene. In a later variant of the script, Fellini's handwritten marks gradually change the script into its filmic, objectified, and visual language and also leave Pinelli's explicit Christian themes open to question.[71] Finally, in the film, the director translates *La strada*'s finale according to his *visione panica*, expressing Zampanò's transformation into a human being with feelings through the act of crying; moreover, Zampanò's sudden awareness of the night sky suggests his realization of his solitude in the infinite cosmos. The results of this collaborative dynamic led a critic such as André Bazin to place emphasis on the existential, rather than Christian, tone of the film's ending where Zampanò's "mass of muscles" is reduced to "its spiritual evidence ... Not through remorse ... but through the overwhelming and incomprehensible sorrow that can be the only sensation of his soul ..."[72] It is likely that the blending of Pinelli's Christian religiosity with Fellini's looser form of spirituality played an important role in the creation of films that were able to reach a wider audience, an audience in the 1950s and 1960s that was possibly looking for more modern and existential forms of Christianity. It follows that Bondanella's definition of La strada as a film "dominated by the director's personal mythology" seems reductive, if not misleading, for the very mechanism of allegory, which has been discussed at length in relation to the film *La strada* and with reference to the Christian symbolism of the characters in general, is clearly representative of the theatre of Tullio Pinelli.[73] Furthermore, the ahistorical and religious sense that characterizes *La strada*, as several scholars have pointed out in emphasizing the use of parable and symbolism in the film, is but a symptom of the weighty presence of a playwright such as Pinelli in the creation of this film.[74]

After a pause of about twenty years in their collaboration, Fellini eventually asked for Tullio Pinelli's assistance again on other occasions and always when working on stories centring around the theme of the supernatural – but also in the case of *Ginger e Fred*, starring Giulietta Masina.[75] Around 1984, Fellini and Pinelli were discussing a project inspired by the life of the medium Eusapia Palladino (1854–1918). This fact can be deduced from the exchange of letters between Fellini and Pinelli regarding materials received from the occultist writer and journalist Paola Giovetti Tenti.[76] Fellini and Pinelli had already directly dealt with the topic of mediumism in *Giulietta degli spiriti*, and earlier still when exploring medium-like behaviours in Gelsomina in *La strada* and in connection with the unrealized project called "La piccola suora" (The little nun). The latter had come from reading the true story of a nun, in a manuscript found in a convent during the making of *La strada*; with her spontaneous and innocent miracles the nun had attracted the attention of the Inquisition and eventually died in distress under the pressure of sceptic questioning.[77]

Later Pinelli and Fellini discussed another possible project along these lines. In a letter dated 1986, Pinelli proposed an idea for a film based on a novel by Thomas Mann (1875–1955), *Joseph und seine Brüder* (1943, *Joseph and His Brothers*). He assured the director that the story would express the combination "of divine and human, of illusion and intuition, of carnal and human love and prophetic and mystical visions" and that the story would give rise to extremely fascinating images such as "the great deserts. The sacred places. The 'cities' ... The magical or religious rituals for Baal, Ishtar, Ashtarti, etc. The endless herds. The caravans with camels, donkeys, oxen ... The Bedouins plunder. The Kings of the cities and their Priests."[78] However, 1986 became instead the year during which they worked together on the esoteric *soggetto* of *Viaggio a Tulun*, which was based on Fellini's trip to the Yucatan the previous year to meet with Carlos Castaneda (1925–98) and explore the world of Mexican shamanism. This project called for a screenwriter like Pinelli, who brought his passionate curiosity about metaphysical and miraculous phenomena but also the promise of constructing an effective narrative around a rather inconclusive and confused mystery.

Their last work together, on *La voce della luna*, which was the director's final feature film and one inspired by the novel *Il poema dei lunatici* (1987, *The Voice of the Moon*) by Ermanno Cavazzoni, allowed once more for Pinelli's and Fellini's mutual desire to search the realm of the beyond. This desire is best exemplified by the scene in which the protagonist looks for a hole in the walls of a country cemetery in order to peek into the afterlife and communicate with the spirits. Inevitably, though, the collaboration on *La voce della luna* was fraught with disagreements, which are nonetheless very instructive in clarifying the growing gap between their approaches to the script.

Nothing but Images: *La voce della luna*

Since the beginning of his work in cinema, when Fellini was a screenwriter in team with Tullio Pinelli for Lux Film and for directors like Roberto Rossellini, Fellini favoured imagining the visual make-up of the film rather than narrating and writing, leaving much of the screenwriting work to Pinelli, especially the dialogues:

> As screenwriter I used to suffer a great deal. I think I have been an awful collaborator with the director. I used to imagine the scene cinematographically from the very start, meticulously suggesting all the details of a situation. Already then, I used to think that dialogue was not very important in cinema: the tie worn could have been more important than the lines spoken ... There is a moment, in every film, where I sense the insufficiency of the screenplay, the uselessness of proceeding on the literary level. Therefore, I open my office and I begin to call people ... [Pinelli] always wrote more than I did when we used to work as a team. His solid dramaturgic preparation allowed him to solidify the scene with a good dialogue. Yes, Pinelli is truly a talented screenwriter ... A film is the work of an author where everyone collaborates ... the screenwriters before everyone else.[79]

Fellini's predisposition towards the visual became ever more pressing as the years passed, affecting and shortening the literary phase of conceptualization and anticipating Fellini's work in casting, set design, and shooting. With *La dolce vita*, Fellini, as a result of his interest in psychological journeys, began to favour a Picasso-like decomposition of the narrative structure. During the years after *Giulietta degli spiriti*, with Bernardino Zapponi the script resembled a collection of images and atmospheres. Fellini's own artistic ambitions, which led him to increasingly disregard the dramaturgic aspect of cinema in a quest for a visually self-sustainable cinema, are better understood when examined in terms of his relationship to the script. In fact, studying the story of Fellini's collaborations with his screenwriters, consisting of a rather heterogeneous group ranging across a wide spectrum of cultural hierarchies and genres, also means describing Fellini's love-and-hate relationship with the written and literary aspects of cinema.

The break in the creative partnership between Pinelli and Fellini during the completion of *Giulietta degli spiriti* was not caused by an incompatibility regarding interests in supernatural and paranormal phenomena, as was more the case with Ennio Flaiano; rather, their conflict resided in their approaches to film narrative. Tullio Pinelli was well aware of Fellini's genius as a director but sometimes feared the risks that improvisation on the set entailed for the films' planned message. These concerns lasted until *Giulietta degli spiriti*, when, as Pinelli recalled, their mutual understanding increasingly faded as Fellini's films became progressively linked to images as "an end in themselves," "no longer anchored" to the characters, the story, and the situations, as they had been in the period leading up to *La dolce vita*.[80] Fellini's vision of the human psyche and also of cinema changed dramatically under the influence of the psychoanalytic theories that opened him to consider the abyssal complexities of the human mind. Pinelli stated that he believed such "psychoanalytic experiments" were harmful to Fellini in that they eroded the solidity of his sense of self and placed him at the mercy of a fragmented vision of the psyche, which was in turn exacerbated by the chaos inherent in modern society. Pinelli lamented the excessive fragmentation of Fellini's films from the mid-1960s onwards, a type of experimental narrative, which according to him was better suited for documentary-like projects such as *Roma* and *Intervista* but was not the proper way to design a feature film.[81]

As revealed by the dream of 1963 described earlier in the chapter, Fellini was indeed beginning to grow restless about the tragic style of Pinelli. Yet, as can be noted in a later dream, Pinelli's presence reemerged from time to time in Fellini's mind with auspicious tones as a protecting and guiding intelligence that allowed him to safely enter the open sea of imagination. Pinelli, like other important collaborators in Fellini's work, represents a point of reference and an anchor in times of crisis of the inspiration. This is evident in the following excerpt from a letter written by Fellini to Pinelli during their years as screenwriters at Lux Film: "In certain moments of discouragement your dear, sharp, and serene expression, your open, reassuring, and joyful smile keep me company and I am trustfully waiting for you."[82] Tullio Pinelli also appears in another dream that probably occurred sometime during the winter of 1977, where he is no longer an antagonistic presence but appears as a guide to the director's inspiration (see figure 2).[83]

In this dream a couple of turtles swimming down a canal to reach the open sea are guided by two stingrays that, thanks to their special sensitivity, understand that the journey cannot continue, and turn back (the horizon above the sea is indeed covered with ominous black clouds). Fellini draws himself on the riverbank, looking at another man seated on a chair, who is identified by graphic clues as Tullio Pinelli.[84] As Fellini's dream interpretation in this particular case is primarily conveyed by his visual choices, the image indicates a parallel between the team formed by turtles and stingrays in the water and the one by the director and the writer on the land. Consequentially, the open and stormy sea is connected to the realm of artistic creation and exploration, a pattern that happens also in other dreams, as for instance in the entry recorded sometime in the fall of 1980 where the director is shown looking out from the shore to a muse figure who is standing in the waves, while a tyrannous double-self yells from within a puppet theatre for him to come back to the more drudgery aspects of his profession.[85] Suggestive of the writer's grounding and stable narrative work, in the 1977 dream Pinelli is portrayed as a silent and wise witness seated on the bank, firmly rooted to his chair, to whom Fellini looks for precious guidance as he faces lack of inspiration. Nonetheless, typical of their relationship, Pinelli's presence also reminds the director of the challenging disparities between them, and the dream ends with the turtles retreating and fading away, and once again a crocodile appears in the canal. This time the large reptile gradually becomes smaller and less menacing until it eventually enters like a curious and waddling "Walt Disney puppet" into office spaces. The image of the crocodile, also found in a previously discussed dream in connection with Tullio Pinelli's tragic writing, suggests that Fellini is here envisioning a way to neutralize and transform his writer's tragic bent through light-hearted playfulness.

The last film they worked on together, *La voce della luna*, manifests a growing separation between the centripetal and traditional force of Pinelli's plot and characterization and the centrifugal and experimental force of Fellini's mass of visual motifs. Fellini's last film may

Figure 2. Fellini's rendition of a dream with reference to Tullio Pinelli, winter? 1977

be appreciated for its fluidic and dream-like quality and for its cogent critique of consumerism and contemporary media culture. In fact, one of the chief reasons Fellini was attracted to Cavazzoni's epic tale set in the Po Valley, where wells become sources of both revelation and delusion, was its ability to stage the mechanisms of fantastic invectiveness, a literary characteristic that functionally merged with Fellini's polemics against postmodern life and the cinematic reclaiming of the power of subjectivity and creativity.[86] It is probably for this reason as well that *La voce della luna* is not only Fellini's last film but also, at the level of film-making, the moment at which his improvisational and set-based directorial style reaches its climax.

During the scripting of *La voce della luna*, Pinelli saw in Ermanno Cavazzoni's novel the possibility for a modern Don Quixote-esque tale of wise folly and wished to elaborate a complex tale along those lines; however, Fellini was impatient with the slow and meticulous writing process that Pinelli believed was necessary and eventually decided to begin filming even though Pinelli insisted that the plot was not mature enough. In the face of Pinelli's resistance, Fellini responded that he no longer worked as he once did in the old days and that now he simply improvised on the set.[87] This behaviour is confirmed by another of Fellini's screenwriters, Gianfranco Angelucci, who described how in *La voce della luna* Fellini made use of his unstructured directorial style to the fullest extent: distributing lines to the actors at the last minute as they were undergoing make-up; concealing the film's ending or overall meaning from the troupe, including the actors; and reinventing the screenplay and dialogue almost entirely during filming and, even more so, during editing.[88]

Apparently both Pinelli and Fellini were in the end displeased with the fact that the film lacked a cohesive story, and to the writer's dismay Fellini eventually reproached him for allowing him to begin filming prematurely.[89] It was Pinelli's opinion that even though Fellini's improvisation at times reached sublime results in *La voce della luna*, it also faltered in the tired repetition of scenes and motifs already explored in previous films: "What had happened during *Giulietta degli spiriti* was repeated more seriously during *La voce della luna*, yet differently; in the first case we did not have violent conflicts, because at the time we had not yet understood the distance that had come between us. Fellini continued working on a folly made up of nothing but images. In *La voce della luna* there is nothing but that."[90] Exhibiting abundant differences between the shooting script and the continuity script, *La voce della luna* may indeed demonstrate the risk of redundancy, in themes and visual solutions, and the inclusiveness that a non-narrative approach to film-making brings, especially when combined with a director who seemed to have lost some of his youthful artistic energy.

Chapter Two

Ennio Flaiano

Fellini's first recollections of Ennio Flaiano date back to 1939, when their paths crossed as Fellini began his work with the popular magazine *Marc'Aurelio* and Flaiano was working for the literary periodical *Omnibus*. While *Marc'Aurelio* was a publication containing a variety of comic sketches and light pieces about Rome's celebrities, *Omnibus* was a politically dissident journal and showcased essays on the arts and history. A group of young and unbridled artists – Stefano Vanzina (alias "Steno," 1919–88), Cesare Zavattini, Ettore Scola (1931–), and Gioacchino Colizzi (alias "Attalo," 1894–1986) – formed around *Marc'Aurelio*. Flaiano's circle was instead composed of established journalists, writers, and artists such as Leo Longanesi (1905–57), Mario Pannunzio (1910–68), Vincenzo Cardarelli (1887–1959), Mino Maccari (1898–1989), Mario Soldati (1906–99), and Alberto Moravia (1907–90).[1] Between these two groups, loosely representative of low- and highbrow cultural spheres, and in retrospect also of the relationship between cinema and literature, much cross-pollination of ideas took place. Flaiano himself, as Fellini recalled, would occasionally wink at him from the other side of the cultural fence.[2]

Throughout his career Flaiano preserved an anarchical and transgressive stance towards current political and literary trends. Together with other writers like Alberto Moravia, Leonardo Sciascia (1921–89), and Vitaliano Brancati, Flaiano went beyond what had become a fashion for naturalism, by treating the category of reality critically. Flaiano's critical relationship to neo-realism was another of the elements that united him with Fellini because both men investigated the unreliability of perception.[3] Being ten years older than Fellini, Flaiano lived through the 1930s as a young man and participated as a second lieutenant in the Ethiopian campaign (1935–6). From this experience, which resulted in his early repudiation of fascism, came his first and only novel – the winner of the first prestigious Strega Prize in 1947 – *Tempo di uccidere* (*Time to Kill*). It is the story of an Italian officer who accidentally kills an African native woman and, as a result, sets out on an odyssey through a desolate human and natural landscape, often unsure of what is real and what is hallucination, to come to terms ultimately with the weight and consequences of his actions. In corresponding with director Jules Dassin (1911–2008) about the possibility of adapting *Tempo di uccidere* for the screen, the writer was said to be willing to accept all the changes deemed necessary, on the condition that the film saved the novel's tragically ironic essence.[4] The core of Flaiano's work is certainly characterized by an acutely dramatic ironic quality, the expression of an "intimate form of survival beyond tragedy" and a "form of accepted defeat," as the critic Goffredo Fofi keenly put it.[5] Often placed within paradoxical and surreal situations, Flaiano's characters are stripped of all hypocrisy and self-delusion until their human limits are fully displayed to the reader, a dynamic that could be located somewhere between "playfulness and disaster," as the title of one of his books suggests.

The image of the fantastic bird *avalovara*, an icon of Brazilian literature, the body of which comprises innumerable other tiny birds, has been used by Maria Corti in order to encapsulate the way in which Flaiano's oeuvre is organically made up of aphorisms, journal entries, notes, and thoughts.[6] Along these same lines, Giorgio Moser, one of Flaiano's directors, once said: "Flaiano desired to write stories with open endings and with a multiplicity of points of view. He wished to bring together as a mosaic several small episodes through faintly suggested themes and to leave the task of interpreting them to the spectator. This ... was the type of cinema that Flaiano created, especially with Fellini."[7] The opus of Flaiano is very heterogeneous and experimental in terms of genre, including novels, plays, short stories, novellas, and anthologies of aphorisms and anecdotes.[8] For this reason, and owing to the apparent spuriousness and sparseness of his writings, the critics of his time generally ignored Flaiano after his initial success with the novel *Tempo di uccidere*, which possibly explains the writer's heightened sensibility towards public recognition. As it happened, while an overly dramatized and traditional plot structure was one of the elements of friction in the collaboration between Fellini and Pinelli, this was not the case with Flaiano, who, without doubt, was at home with Fellini's progressively more fragmentary tendencies. Flaiano's preferences for epigrammatic and fragmented narrative forms is a reflection of his intention to deconstruct the protagonists of his stories, a pattern that Gian Piero Brunetta noted in connection with the writer's "effect" on some of Fellini's most famous films of the late 1950s and early 1960s.[9]

Flaiano's activity in screenwriting was almost entirely concentrated in the 1950s and resulted in the contribution to fifty-eight titles spanning diverse genres, including documentaries, comedies starring Totò, so-called *maggiorate* comedies, political and historical films, and auteur cinema. In many of these instances Flaiano acted more as a consultant than as a writer and did not consider himself artistically involved with the final product. This was not the case, however, with a number of works that fell under the category of art film, in which he brought to the foreground his deeper aesthetic and philosophic concerns. In a letter to the director Luciano Emmer, Flaiano once wrote: "The truth is that I can very well make screenplays in bad faith if they are for films in which I am not interested or that are simply part of a professional game. When we start talking about a true film or about art, then I think a little about myself too ... the art film must respond exactly to the idea I have of art and of truth."[10] This was certainly the case with his contributions to some of Fellini's most famous films, where authorship often and not surprisingly became a point of contention between writer and director.

That mutual understanding that crossed the low and high cultural divide and had first attracted the two at the end of the 1930s resulted in a fervid, intense, and turbulent collaboration throughout the 1950s. Flaiano first joined the team of Fellini, Pinelli, and Lattuada as an external collaborator to the screenplays of *Luci del varietà* and *Lo sceicco bianco*.[11] It was during the making of *I vitelloni*, when he and Fellini travelled and worked congenially, that Flaiano began to take a more central role in the conception of the story. Leo Longanesi even proposed that Flaiano turn *I vitelloni* into a novel.[12] A year later Flaiano was disappointed by *La strada*, finding the general idea faulty to the extent that he threatened to interrupt his work on this film. He criticized the "peculiar obscure atmospheres" and "the affectation of its characters" and insisted that "the too beautiful fable may have come down to earth, and its symbolism may have melted into the plot."[13] With the exception of *La strada*, Flaiano maintained quite successfully the role of key screenwriter for *Il bidone*, *Le notti di Cabiria*, *La dolce vita*, *Le tentazioni del Dottor Antonio* (1962, *The Temptations of Doctor Antonio*), *8½*, and more confrontationally for *Giulietta degli spiriti*. Flaiano also collaborated on an important unrealized screenplay, *Moraldo va in città*, a story that was supposed to become the sequel to *I vitelloni* and that emphasized the autobiographical character of the provincial young man journeying to Rome, the type of character that is also found in *La dolce vita*.

During their collaboration Fellini and Flaiano mutually inspired each other in expressing a compassionately satirical perspective on humanity, honestly examining it in its grotesque aspects, limitations, and delusions. The experience of Rome, the city that had attracted them both from their respective Adriatic provinces, is a central theme in their work together, serving as both the magmatic heart of humanity as well as a surrogate for the promise of the exotic. Goffredo Fofi wrote that Fellini's and Flaiano's perspectives came together in a "sort of generous scepticism – which is still today one of the reasons that Fellini's work is so fascinating and vital."[14] The following pages confirm this dynamic, documenting it in its various textual ramifications; however, they also show how Fellini and Flaiano increasingly disagreed on whether the outcomes of epiphany – within the context of the journey to and through Rome, the encounter with femininity, or the creative pursuit – should be disillusionment or self-realization, and whether emphasis should be placed (if at all) on the transformative potentials of the spiritual and magical themes in their films. In fact, it is by placing this chapter within the broader context of Fellini's screenwriting relationships that the unique quality of "generous scepticism" is found in several moments of his cinema, as well as by studying a number of other collaborations rooted in and shaped by the director's passionate and yet ambiguous position towards the miraculous.

Frivolously Yours: The Public Dispute over Authorship

The roots of the friction in the artistic partnership of Fellini and Flaiano, which would eventually be interrupted in 1964, lay in a combination of authorial conflicts and philosophic differences. A retelling of the roller-coaster nature of their relationship can serve as a way to explain the differences that existed at the level of authorship, before going on to examine the elements of conflict and affinity at the level of artistic objectives and sensibility. Flaiano quickly began to feel resentment towards Fellini for the way in which he often and carelessly forgot to give credit to his writers during interviews and press releases. Regarding Flaiano's frustration with Fellini, the screenwriter Suso Cecchi d'Amico said: "Fellini truly put Flaiano's patience to the test, declaring to everyone that he [Fellini] worked without a script and that he arrived on the set with only a small piece of paper the size of a bus ticket in his pocket upon which he had sketched a few ideas. Brazen. Indeed he had scripts, at least until the last years."[15] Fellini would even have to later rectify the meaning of a few comments regarding the making of his films, as for instance the statement that he had released in 1954 to the magazine *Il Mondo*: "Besides being the director of the film, I also want to be the author of the scenario and a collaborator on the screenplay. In this case, it is silly to ask who is the author of the script. It would be like asking a poet if he is the author of his verses or if it is the paper and the ink he uses."[16] Fellini's amendment arrived in the form of a letter to the same magazine about a month later on 23 February: "Frankly, reading it again, this statement seemed immodest and unjust towards my collaborators who deserve merit. I am referring to Ennio Flaiano and Tullio Pinelli, who have co-written the scripts of the films I directed or those that I am about to direct. I consider meeting these two writers the greatest fortune of my career as director."[17] However, as an author of the screenplay, Flaiano reluctantly swallowed the original unflattering and reductive simile, which suggested that the screenwriters were lifeless instruments to be commanded by the hand of the director.

Flaiano's resentment exploded a year later during the making of *Il bidone* when Fellini did not invite him and Pinelli to the press conference and apparently did not even mention their names. Eventually, on 24 April 1955 Flaiano wrote the director an indignant letter in which he denounced Fellini's disloyal "propaganda system" that aimed to present the director as the "only writer responsible."[18] This is only the first accusation of megalomania that Flaiano made against Fellini. Incidentally, the film *La decima vittima* (1965), directed by Elio Petri (1929–82), for which Flaiano was one of the scriptwriters, sets the residence of the egomaniacal protagonist played by Mastroianni in a "Lungotevere Fellini" (a naming that was actually discussed years later by the city's administration), perhaps alluding to the director's dreams of grandeur. In 1955, Flaiano spoke out especially because *Il bidone* was still only a screenplay and therefore it was not – at least not yet, and in the most obvious sense – strictly Fellini's invention. He reminded the director that if it were not for his two writers, *Il bidone* would not exist, since it had been he and Pinelli who had defended the film when Fellini was thinking to abandon it. Flaiano declared that he felt saddened and betrayed. As a result, he announced the end of their friendship and collaboration and to his final farewell added the painful opinion that according to him, Fellini had inherited the vanity of Rossellini but nothing of his genius.[19]

In spite of their temporary falling out, the partnership was re-established for the writing of *Le notti di Cabiria*, even though Flaiano received another blow to his ego with the arrival of Pier Paolo Pasolini as collaborator to the screenplay, in addition to Brunello Rondi. As Flaiano's letters and statements show, Flaiano had a strong feeling of antipathy towards both of them, and the dislike was reciprocal, as evident from Pasolini's correspondence with Flaiano and by Rondi's diminishing of Flaiano's screenwriting in Fellini's films as "negative" and "lacking any real inventive contribution."[20] Nonetheless, the collaboration survived, reaching a peak of synergistic fervour during the writing of *La dolce vita* and *8½* and continuing until 1964 when their working relationship came to an abrupt end. Significantly, the drop that finally made the glass overflow occurred during a dispute about the public representation of authorship in the eyes of the media. This dispute was born from an article written by the journalist Sergio Saviane (1923–2001), renowned for his acrimonious remarks, in *L'Espresso* on 24 May 1964. In this article Saviane voiced his discontent in regard to Flaiano's absence from a television show that was dedicated to Fellini's work and hosted by Sergio Zavoli (1923–). Saviane also added that Flaiano's testimony would have helped to demystify Fellini's genius. In his article Saviane asked Fellini to apologize to Flaiano and grant him the recognition he deserved as the author of his screenplays. Saviane was not the only one taking Flaiano's side. The cartoonist Bruno Rasia, for instance, drew some vignettes in which he depicted Flaiano as a victim of Fellini's creative thefts. In one vignette a gigantic Fellini is tenderly holding a puppet Flaiano in his arms and saying, "Ennio ... You had a beautiful idea, now I am going to tell it to you!"[21] The dispute created by Saviane's article brought into the open all the unresolved tensions between Flaiano and Fellini as well as those existing between Fellini's other collaborators. This situation led Pinelli and Rondi to write letters to *L'Espresso* to provide a more accurate depiction of the type of teamwork that existed behind Fellini's films and to remind the public that the collaborators also had a place in the inventive process.[22] It is not clear what angered Flaiano the most at this point – whether it was the fear that Pinelli considered him responsible for Saviane's article or the fact that Rondi had publicized himself, within the context of the debate, as the most important of Fellini's writers; perhaps he simply took the circumstance as a pretext to conclude his painful relationship with Fellini. Whatever might have been the ultimate reason for this angry parting of the ways, Flaiano wrote his goodbye to Fellini in a letter:

7 June 1964

Dear Fellini,

As you can see, I am finding out with some delay about the article by
Saviane in the *Espresso* and about Pinelli's justifiable protest, and Rondi's
entertaining letter. You know me well enough that if I am writing you, it is
not to tell you I haven't had a hand in this – and you know this very well –
but only to make sure you've noticed the comical side of all this. Well, I
would have written to the newspaper myself, but I didn't know anything
about it until yesterday evening; and now, frankly, I don't think it is a good
idea to reopen the issue, since Rondi has clarified everything. For Pinelli,
however, it is a different matter. I am sincerely sorry that he might have
believed I was the mastermind behind this, and I will write to him.

Saviane said only one correct thing – and that is that our collaboration is
over. If there were any doubts, Rondi's letter has removed them all. It was
fun to read it, almost as much as the sixty pages that he wrote for *Giulietta
degli spiriti* – those that we threw away. Let's hope that during the shooting
he will write some good dialogue. Our reputation is at stake.

Goodbye, dear Fellini. Frivolous friendships end frivolously. Nonetheless, what does one say in such cases?

"Goodbye and good luck"

Ennio Flaiano[23]

As was observed in the previous chapter, Fellini's team changed drastically after *Giulietta degli spiriti*. Embittered by the controversy, Fellini
did not feel motivated enough to try to appease Flaiano this time. Instead he took this as an opportunity to let him go.

Rome, 12 June 1964

Dear Flaiano,

I never had doubts about the frivolity of your friendship, but what can
we do about it, this is how you are and even the letter you wrote me is
frivolous. For me, everything was fine just the same. The collaboration
has ended? I am sorry about it. It seemed to me that deep down you too
had fun working with us, and my films did not lead to such unsuccessful
results as often occurs with the other directors with whom you work.

Dear Ennio, goodbye and good luck to you too, frivolously,

Federico[24]

Indirectly, a month later Fellini also made a final statement about the
condition of the relationship when the Rizzoli production organized

a trip to Los Angeles for the Academy Awards ceremony and Flaiano received a coach seat instead of a first-class seat like everyone else did. According to Kezich, Fellini did not have any say in this decision, and it was therefore very likely the doing of the production company, reflecting its desire to minimize or distance Flaiano in some way.[25] However, the event and the gossip that followed infuriated Flaiano. In one of Fellini's dreams, a few months later, the producers Dino De Laurentis (1919–2010) and veteran director Alessandro Blasetti (1900–87) are depicted as the cruel and irresponsible guards of the cage of a large leopard. Fellini, under the claws of the fierce cat, wonders whether or not he will survive, and his gaze goes out to the spectators, hoping for an answer or aid. In the crowd is an "extremely hateful, unfriendly" Flaiano, busy with his usual activity of vitriolic criticism.[26] Fellini's ex-collaborator is considered here as distant and not the least bit interested in the director's artistic fate. Moreover, Flaiano's depiction here is in tune with Fellini's descriptions of him as someone who is the prisoner of his own excessively bitter and satirical persona.

In spite of these more or less vain conflicts, Fellini and Flaiano still found many points of affinity between them and reasons to continue to express their mutual appreciation. Gradually they resumed communication and eventually came to reanimate their friendship, sending letters to express their admiration for their respective accomplishments. Flaiano celebrated *La dolce vita* after watching it again, and then *Satyricon*, while Fellini communicated how he had devoured in two nights the two tales contained in *Il gioco e il massacro* (1970) that Flaiano had sent him.[27] Their communication was also resumed by the need to make decisions about the publication and adaptations of a number of their screenplays.[28] As additional proof of their regained friendship, Fellini received books as gifts from Flaiano with warm dedications: "To Federico e Giulietta / with the old friendship from Ennio Flaiano Milan, March 1970"; "To Federico, from an even more adolescent Ennio than usual – with affection."[29]

In 1970 after Flaiano had suffered from a stroke and relocated to a boarding house on Via Isonzo near Corso d'Italia and Fellini's office, they began spending time together again. Flaiano wrote to Aldo Tassone, emphasizing his change of attitude towards Fellini: "I made peace with Fellini and I see him often – for breakfast in some trattoria. We enjoy each other's company."[30] After the death of such an instrumental screenwriter, Fellini's longing for Flaiano heightened with his desire to continue developing the successful series of films that hinged on the Mastroianni character. Fellini's awareness of the vital role that Flaiano had had in the success of his films is rendered obvious by a dream entry dated 30 December 1973 (see figure 3).[31]

About a year after Flaiano's death, the ex-collaborator returns to Fellini in a dream as the pathetic image of a devout and zealous writer, a bit older and out of shape, dressed in a heavy coat and working at his table, quickly filling pages and pages with writing. Interestingly, in this dream Flaiano is writing a script about his own life, which is supposed to be Fellini's next film, thus saving the director from his current inspirational stagnation. In the dream Fellini wants to find a worthy assistant for Flaiano and is concerned that Flaiano is working too hard at the script and sacrificing himself for the story. In addition to Flaiano's obvious importance as a collaborator in a very pragmatic and material sense, this dream, alluding to a film based on Flaiano's own life, speaks of the screenwriter's personal involvement with Fellini's films and in particular with his contribution to the films' stories and characters through his own experiences and memories. The episode from *8½* in which a child is punished at the boarding school for having been discovered with La Saraghina is inspired by Flaiano's own biographical elements blending with Fellini's in a film. Part of this episode belongs to Flaiano's memories: it was Flaiano who spent some time at a similar religious school in Fermo, rather than Fellini who studied at a public school in Rimini.[32] It follows that just as the stories in films such as *La dolce vita* and *8½* are products of multiple writers, even the often-emphasized autobiographical nature of these films is the product of a dialogue between collaborators and not merely a result of Fellini's monologue. It is reasonable to conclude that a consideration of Flaiano's artistry and life could be fruitfully integrated into the auteurist scholarship that has described *8½* as the mirror of Fellini's spiritual autobiography, an objectification of Fellini's own melancholic artistic temperament, or as the play between the chaos of Fellini's life and the order of artistic form.[33]

Significantly, all throughout his career Fellini continued to find in his dreams a feeling of nostalgia for a dedicated and vigorous collaborator such as Flaiano, especially at difficult crossroads in his work. On 21 January 1975 Fellini recorded a dream dealing with his feelings about Flaiano's state of inactivity and inexplicable disappearance (see figure 4).

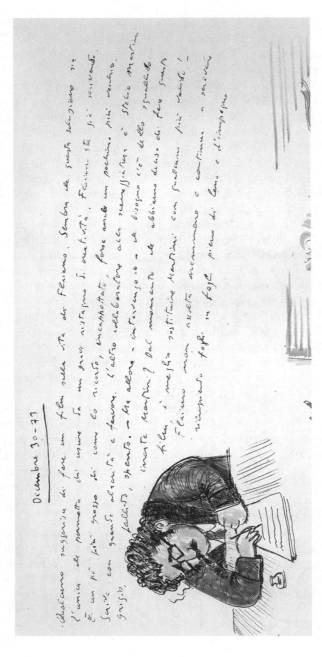

Figure 3. Fellini's rendition of a dream with reference to Ennio Flaiano, 30 December 1973

Figure 4. Fellini's rendition of a dream with reference to Ennio Flaiano, 21 January 1975

Fellini made a grey drawing showing the writer lying paralysed, wrapped up like a mummy, while a clownish hospital attendant arrives to carry him away. The image is dominated by the question "Who has made Flaiano disappear?" The text accompanying the drawing explains that someone has stolen Flaiano's paralysed body from his apartment just before the hospital attendants could take him away and lock him up for good in the hospital.[34] Another journal entry, dated 3 November 1980, reveals Fellini's unconscious desire that Flaiano could have helped to save him from his predicament with *Il viaggio di Mastorna*.[35] Coincidentally, at this time Fellini was working with the journalist Beniamino Placido (1929–2010) on a memoir interview that also touched on the relationship with Flaiano. Placido himself is also present in this dream and nonchalantly and indirectly proposes a story to Fellini that could address the topic of death in a "simple style" that Flaiano would have liked. This dream occurred when Fellini had just completed *La città delle donne*, a film that offered a way for him to incorporate many of the elements from *Mastorna* while protecting himself from his esoteric drive; the theme of a journey through death was replaced by a journey through the feminine universe. Both film projects sublimated the desire to continue down the path that he had begun with *I vitelloni*, *Moraldo va in città*, *La dolce vita*, and *8½*, all of which identified with Mastroianni as protagonist and with Flaiano's central contribution. It is to these films, juxtaposed with other samples of Flaiano's independent work, that one must turn to understand the stylistic and philosophic elements of friction and synergy between the two artists.

The Self as Monster: Satire and Compassion in *La dolce vita*

Flaiano, in whom Fellini appreciated many qualities including a "comical and bitter humanity," was a writer who "found himself in harmony" reading classical Roman satirists such as Juvenal, Martial, and Catullus.[36] His appreciation and support of Fellini's satirical bent was enduring. This is visible early on, at the time of *Luci del varietà*, when Flaiano praised Fellini's courage in depicting the usual characters of the variety theatre with a new antisentimentalism, presenting them in all their shortsightedness.[37] This point of affinity remained vital until the end, as evidenced by Flaiano's enthusiastic reaction to *Satyricon* that he eloquently expresses in a letter: "I saw your *Satyricon* and it impressed, marvelled, startled, and, deep down, delighted me. Nothing is missing. I will dream of it often and gladly. I know that certain solutions could be reconsidered, but you achieved the essential: the continuous drama of monsters, that is, of ourselves. The spectators who exit the theatre saying, 'I did not like it' seemed as if they themselves were exiting from the reality portrayed on the screen."[38] The film seemed to achieve in Flaiano's mind a level of cosmic irony, capable of encapsulating the timeless heart of the Italian experience. In his raving review of the film he calls it a "history of Italy imagined in a dream," rekindling in us the understanding that "you can't live fifty years in Italy without being touched by it, and at the end, surprised."[39] As the pages below will document, Flaiano's satirical perspective blended powerfully with Fellini's, generating the pensive and compassionate humour as well as the sharply critical lens on societal mores that characterize films such as *I vitelloni, Il bidone, Le notti di Cabiria, La dolce vita, 8½, Le tentazioni del Dottor Antonio,* and *Giulietta degli spiriti,* in which scholars have traditionally detected a Pirandellian "unmasking operation."[40]

Flaiano's writings often contain anecdotes involving Fellini and himself as protagonists. Within the broader context of their exchange these pages further exemplify the nature of their common satirical perspective. In one of these anecdotes, Flaiano narrates their meeting with a tragically ridiculous woman in a Roman café sometime in 1956:

> The woman, withered by a precarious life, made up quite badly, enters a dairy store on Via Tuscolana. Her make-up, mixed with a look of sleepiness on her face, makes her seem like a beaten Pierrot. The front of her hair is bright and shiny, while the back is as curly and opaque as an Assyrian beard ... She thinks out loud to attract Fellini's and my attention ... She plays with her web-like purse and with her scarf, then sighs and hums. We notice that she has a mangy grey dog on a leash that seems more like a mouse than a dog ... Fellini and I use the excuse of the dog to start a conversation ... Finally she leaves ... while Fellini and I laugh slyly. Later, the thought of her saddens us. We make several hypotheses with the questions: Who is she? How did she arrive at her present state? How does she live? What about that unwavering self-confidence? In these women, solitude is mantled with decorations and continuous and vain demands for attention, as also happens with those rafts adrift where the survivors' shirts are hoisted, making them appear almost festive to sea birds.[41]

Humour combined with reflection generates a compassionate irony. In this instance, rather uncannily, life apparently staged for Fellini and Flaiano a case that was similar to Luigi Pirandello's famous exemplification of what he called *sentimento del contrario*. In explaining the transition from laughter to sentiment, from comedy to humour, Pirandello describes an old woman who stands out as ridiculous and laughable in her attempt to appear younger than she is; however, when further thought is given to understanding her story and motivation – namely, her need to secure her hold on her younger husband – the same woman becomes a tragic character.[42] Obviously Fellini's and Flaiano's satirical perspectives stemmed from a deeply felt and essentially philosophic humour, which was akin to the kind practised and theorized by Pirandello.

In another of Flaiano's narratives, he and Fellini are visiting an eccentric character who claims to be an important and persecuted magician, with the excuse of finding information about a missing woman. While the two artists laugh at the man's "uncouth and ridiculous ceremony," they are inevitably struck by the man's ability to correctly guess the woman's name and location.[43] Flaiano initially describes the magician as a typical man with unusual powers, who is desperately seeking acceptance by society. Gradually this encounter helps Flaiano to reach awareness of the fact that magic and scepticism are two inseparable human phenomena, where the latter justifies the former and renders it "less monstrous"; Flaiano thus imbues his ironic representation of the psychic with a new sense of empathy.[44]

In a letter to Tullio Kezich, Flaiano once said that the common ground uniting him and Fellini was "the attention and the tolerance towards the actions of man, including our own, or the compassion for our destiny."[45] Furthermore, the writer had a true appreciation of the relentless and faithful "search for himself" that Fellini carried in his work, including his more obscure and irrational aspects.[46] Flaiano confirmed this point of affinity in speaking about the direction of Fellini's work: "From 'White Sheik' to today [1959], Fellini has not *transformed* but clarified himself and freed himself from much dross. The conflict between life and dream, expressed with farcical tones in the first film, has always been present in the other films, until it took on a precise and dramatic form in *La dolce vita*."[47] Fellini's and Flaiano's "repudiation of vulgarity even when talking about vulgarity," noted by Goffredo Fofi, essentially originates from this type of compassionate satire towards the self, accepting and understanding of all that is human, even that which appears monstrous.[48] In their view, mediocrity and virtuosity were no longer two opposite polarities but different shades of grey.

Flaiano's treatment "La notte porta consiglio" for the film *Roma città libera*, directed by Marcello Pagliero in 1946, is a case study that helps us to understand Flaiano's transcendence of the categories of good and evil, as well as realism in its intersection between neo-realism, noir, and surrealism. Here, a series of characters who are revealed only by their social categories (the Thief, the Young Man, the Young Woman, the American, the Midget, the Distinguished Mister, et cetera) become unknowingly entangled in a complex network of criminal schemes and passions. The surrealist bent, pertinent here to his work with Fellini, can be traced in the character of the distinguished old man, who has been struck with amnesia and whose image appears reflected and deformed in the mirrors of a café as his identity is fractured, but also in the gro-tesque couple formed by the drunken American soldier and his midget impresario. It is not surprising that Flaiano and Pagliero were close to such surrealist artists as Jean Paulhan (1884–1968), Raymond Queneau (1903–76), and Jean Cocteau (1889–1963). It has also been noted that in his contribution to comedies orbiting around Totò, Flaiano laboured to insert surrealist elements into mainstream films.[49] In a scene from *Roma città libera*, the Distinguished Mister (a spectacular Vittorio De Sica), beaten and overwhelmed by life, sings his own kind of existen-tialist blues on a nightclub piano. His song speaks of "the clear, fresh, and serene mornings when we are young," and "of evil, of suffering, of the iniquities accomplished by man," but says also that hope is made visible through evil and that from it something new can rise. All must live, even the evil-spirited because they may learn to love life, but with freedom.[50] As it happens, in Flaiano's story, evil is understood as a tem-porary state of ignorance, and every man should be granted the right to err. Consequentially the confusion between right and wrong that per-meates the story is to be accepted as a natural state of things. The direc-tor, Marcello Pagliero, focused instead on this ideal of freedom, a choice that was linked to his decision to substitute Flaiano's title, "La notte porta consiglio," with a title that directly reminded him of Rossellini's *Roma, città aperta*, in which Pagliero, the year before, had played the role of the Resistance leader Manfredi. As the film's title indicates, Pagliero continued to carry the flag of freedom that Rossellini had first hoisted, but it is infused with Flaiano's unique humanistic and compassionate satire that also serves as a tool to probe the psyche.

Flaiano's protagonists expressed from early on an extraordinary hon-esty about their own weaknesses as well as the weaknesses of others, yet maintaining the anti-rhetorical grace of the understatement that qualifies Flaiano's writing. The evil-spirited characters inspiring the Distinguished Mister's song, who have the right to learn to love life, can be recognized in the characters that Fellini wrote with Flaiano's help. One of them is Augusto (Broderick Crawford), the swindler of *Il bidone*, a film to which Flaiano felt deeply attached as an author.[51] In spite of his inveterate inclination to scam even the poorest and the most unfortunate, Augusto is allowed to move through his experiences, alternating between success and humiliation, love and selfishness.

The lost souls of *La dolce vita* are also granted their complete right to go through life freely without being the objects of judgment. When Marcello Mastroianni, who played the protagonist Marcello Rubini in *La dolce vita*, visited Fellini and Flaiano in Fregene during the summer of 1958 while they were beginning work on this film, he asked to read what the two had written so far. As the legend goes, all they had for him was a drawing of an underwater landscape filled with strange marine creatures.[52] This anecdote, though likely humorous, is not devoid of significance. In Flaiano's diary of that period, published posthumously in a volume entitled *La solitudine del satiro* (*The Via Veneto Papers*), the nightlife of Via Veneto – the central Roman setting of *La dolce vita* that Fellini reconstructed almost entirely in his studio – is depicted and understood through an extended maritime metaphor: "Now that summer is coming, it's plain as day that this is no longer a street, but a beach. The cafés, which overflow onto the sidewalks ... have, each one of them, a different type of umbrella for their tables, like the ones at the seaside establishments at Ostia ... Proceeding with little forward thrusts, automobiles glide like gondolas towards the theater, and the public takes in the fresh air that drifts hither and thither with the indolence of seaweed and the false confidence of choir-singers."[53]

The world of Via Veneto was the focus of Flaiano's "indiscrete lenses" in the short articles that he published in the late 1950s in the magazine *Mondo*; in particular, the Roman nightlife with its vices and characters always fascinated him. This compassionate satire, linked to the acceptance of the human *monstrum* rooted deep within the psyche, is a common thread that united Fellini and Flaiano. In *La dolce vita* this attitude finds its highest expression, and the shortcomings of humanity are observed with a detached and almost scientific point of view that does not accuse and does not exclude sentiment and empathy. In this way *La dolce vita* grieves with its characters as they are observed within the unflattering but very human narrative of their individual and collective lives. The ideas of honesty, detachment, and compassion surfaced in a letter written by Flaiano on 8 February 1969, in which he amicably acknowledged what the film had meant to him:

> Dear Federico, yesterday I watched *La dolce vita* again ... I fell into the film as if I had never seen it before ... I believe that it remains your most enduring work because of the charge of compassion and angst for a world that is leaving its tracks and rushing towards a moment of desperation; but also for the film's great narrative freedom and for the strength and the irony of its detachment that have saved you from any self-gratification. You were discovering at the time a reality that others were not seeing, and you told it all, with its possible future developments.[54]

This perspective is functional in the act of generational confession that according to Flaiano is performed by *La dolce vita*:

> Fellini's film [*La dolce vita*] was born from this desire to tell ourselves how things went for our generation, we who had believed it possible to resolve spiritual matters in the same way we had been resolving economic matters. Emptying the glass, we saw that in the bottom there was a worm. Each of us reacted according to his nature: some swallowed the worm too, some threw away the glass, and some vomited. I continued to vomit, but without recrimination. All that I have left is the freedom to understand and the comfort of loving my fellowman for what he has shown himself to be, without judging, with the certainty that desperation is not only in our own soul but in everyone else's and that it comes from far away.[55]

Flaiano drew inspiration from the friction between the human impulse towards absolutes and their limitations, aiming in his desecrating writing for a cultivation of immunity from self-glorifying illusions. Fellini's satire, even though it was a fundamental element of his poetics and style and was deeply ingrained in him with his background as a caricature artist, was not tragic and pessimistic, but it accentuated the potentials of epiphanic moments. As explained in the pages below, the endings that Fellini single-handedly created for *Le notti di Cabiria* and *8½* communicate luminous surprises and the rejuvenation of the self rather than the religious contrition of Pinelli or the bitter smile of Flaiano.

A Light in the Night: Negotiating Epiphany from *I vitelloni* to *8½*

In the midst of struggles with the producer De Laurentis resulting from the first failed attempt to make *Il viaggio di Mastorna*, Fellini expressed the desire to reconcile with Flaiano, while understanding the incompatibility existing between their two respective perspectives. A large drawing, radiating with warm colours, fills a page of *Il libro dei sogni* dated 22 November 1966; it shows Fellini and Flaiano walking towards each other in a moving yet awkward attempt to embrace one another (see figure 5).[56]

The image emphasizes the difference in height between the two figures, which was a real fact, but here also a symbolic one. The drawing represents Flaiano, his study, and the objects surrounding him as peculiarly small, and the tall figure of Fellini must arch his back in order to move towards the writer. To understand the significance of the director's perception of Flaiano's creative universe as metaphorically characterized by "low ceilings," one must contrast their differing positions towards matters of the spirit.

Ennio Flaiano, like Federico Fellini, moved to Rome in his twenties from the Adriatic coast, though not from Emilia-Romagna's riviera but from farther south, from the port city of Pescara in what was then Abruzzi-Molise. This common experience of migration to the big city has often been considered an important ingredient of their affinity. The weight of this "provincial adventure" has often been noted as an element in the development of their personal relationship, also reflected in their common "genial and amateurish eccentricity."[57] Furthermore, the contrast between the province and the city, and Rome in particular, stands out as a pervasive theme in both Fellini's and Flaiano's work. Flaiano and Fellini knew first hand the hopes and pains in the life of a young man from the province who is struggling to integrate with the competitive and closed journalistic society of the metropolis. They had been enchanted by the vibrant milieu of the city and by the amazing array of humanity that could be met there. Both artists knew exactly what it meant to grow up in the Adriatic provinces. In seaside towns such as Rimini and Pescara, life's rhythm alternated between the frenzied influx of tourists in summer and the desolation and loneliness in winter when the towns' youth took refuge from the fog and boredom by sitting in cafés and fantasizing ridiculous adventures to pass the time. The fact that the Second World War dramatically changed the Rimini and Pescara that Fellini and Flaiano had once known gave them due cause

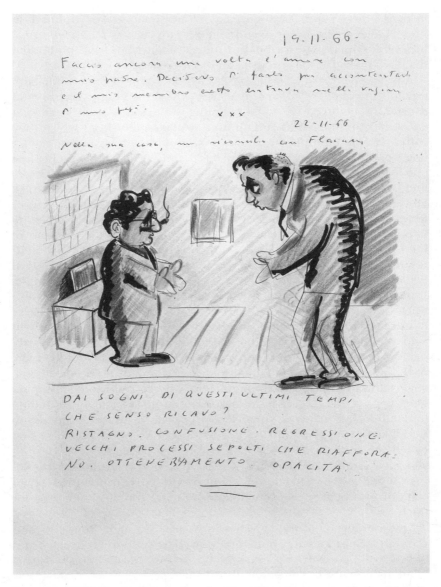

Figure 5. Fellini's rendition of a dream with reference to Ennio Flaiano, 19 November 1966

to revisit these towns through memory and imagination captured on film. However, the locations chosen for a film such as *I vitelloni* do not include Rimini or Pescara, but include places such as Ostia and Viterbo that better recalled the atmospheres of the past.

Also, Rome, and in particular its nightlife, would remain for both artists a universe unto its own, a place where the young artists could constantly be exposed to stimulating adventures and surprising encounters and, most important, to a vantage point from which they could observe multiple facets of humanity. One can again turn to "La notte porta consiglio" for an earlier example of Flaiano's excitement about Rome's nocturnal cosmos, where radically different characters and lives crash into one another with astonishing and moving results. However, in Flaiano's poetics – and not only because this is a noir film – these meetings all lead to the knowledge that everything in life is ruled by chance, as the close-up on the pair of dice at the end of the film explicitly suggests. "La notte porta consiglio" also exemplifies the importance and pervasiness of the motif of the night found in Flaiano's creative work, as other titles also make obvious. For example, *La notte* (1961), which Flaiano wrote together with Tonino Guerra and Michelangelo Antonioni (1912–2007), follows an intellectual in crisis, as *La dolce vita* did a year before, to portray the upper-middle-class world ridden with ennui and decadence, though this time set in Lombardy instead of Rome. An early and memorable example of the wonders of the Roman nightlife in Fellini's cinema is found in *Luci del varietà*, suggesting Flaiano's contribution. Here, Checco Dal Monte (Peppino De Filippo), after having been locked out of his apartment for failing to pay the rent, follows a surprising trumpeter in an exotic adventure through the city at night. He then meets characters who seem to step out of the realm of fables: an American jazz musician, a crazy gunslinger, and a Brazilian singer. It is because of the fertility of the Roman nightlife that Checco, who is at first faced with the prospect of solitude and poverty, regains new inspiration, courage, and hope for the future.

The journey of Moraldo-Marcello to and through Rome, to and through the murky sea of humanity, as well as through life's many rites of passage – the entrance into society, the discovery of creativity, the relationship with the other sex, as told in a series of memorable films such as *I vitelloni*, *La dolce vita*, *8½*, and later *La città delle donne* – was destined to become one of the most famous examples of a modern epic. This cycle was never fully completed by Fellini, and some of its phases remain only in the unrealized scripts of *Moraldo va in città*, *Viaggio con Anita*, and *Mastorna*.

I vitelloni was written almost exclusively by Flaiano and Fellini, and in it the contrast between city and province plays an important role. While Pinelli's name is listed in connection with the treatment that is archived at the Lilly Library of Rare Books (LLRB), only Flaiano and Fellini signed the screenplay. The version of the treatment archived at the LLRB indicates Pesaro as the chosen town for the story, a geographic compromise between Rimini and Pescara and between the two artists' experiences of them. *I vitelloni* also presents other forms of compromise between writer and director. The film both satirizes and aligns with the point of view of the young men, a complexity that has led critics to speak of the ideological inconsistency and contradiction in this film.[58] When one considers the fact that the script bears the imprint of Flaiano and that it is then transformed by Fellini's direction, the real causes of such inconsistencies become clearer. The double perspective of this film observes the young men's lives both critically from without and with complicity from within. Flaiano's perspective is expressed by the narrator, another and more aware male character, who knows first hand the life of the youth depicted in the film. The narrator's voice does not complement the visual text with additional details but takes the liberty of being redundant, as is evident when first introducing the main characters. These characteristics have been described by Maria Sepa, who interprets the ironic stance of this voice and its dialogue within the visual text of the film as Flaiano's typical anarchic touch and as the screenwriter's judgmental attitude that challenges the director's moral indulgence.[59] Indeed, Fellini is pursuing a visual lyrical empathy, which is likely motivated by the fact that the young characters in the film come to stand for man's existential issues at large; an emblematic example is the sequence showing the dark silhouettes of the young men on the deserted winter beach.

Critics have noted traces of developing characters that resemble those of *I vitelloni* in Flaiano's own writings and the way in which the writer progressively arrived at "fashioning a character who posits difficult questions to himself and about society and who leaves his hometown in search of the new and the different in an effort to expand the parameters of his thinking."[60] According to Flaiano the word *vitellone* is a deformation of *vudellone* (large gut), indicating a son who, while being fundamentally unproductive, enjoys indulging in excessive eating.[61] In Fellini's perspective, the *vitellone* represented a more abstract state of idleness, which he explained as his tendency to dwell in a state of in-between, of being satisfied by an unsolved mystery: "What is autobiographical is the story of a kind of call that pierces the torpor of the soul and wakes me. I would very much like to stay in that state, in those moments when the call reaches me. I feel, then, that someone is knocking at the door and I don't go and open it. Of course, I shall have to make up my mind to open it, someday or another. Basically, I must be a spiritual *vitellone*."[62]

Incidentally, the protagonist Moraldo – with whom the director identifies, as is signalled subtly by his editing choice of dubbing him with his own voice in the finale – is the most mystical among the *vitelloni*; he wishes to experience the extraordinary as he dreams of distant places while looking at the stars in the company of the minor yet symbolic character of the train station attendant. The treatment archived at the LLRB contains details about Moraldo's readings that confirm this aspect of his personality: among his favourite authors are prominent figures of esotericism such as Èdouard Schuré (1841–1929) and Desiderius Papp (1895–1993).[63] Undoubtedly, the intellectual restlessness of Flaiano's type of *vitellone* merged with the spiritual tenseness of Fellini's, synergistically generating the unsettled and unsettling picaresque character of Moraldo-Marcello. Flaiano quickly understood the coexistence of realism and transcendence in Fellini's cinema, a dynamic in which the writer knew he played an important balancing and grounding role. Even the books that he sent to the director as gifts betray this perspective. For Christmas of 1954 Flaiano sent Fellini a book about Pieter Brueghel the elder, Leo Bruhns's *Das Bruegel Buch*, and in 1955 he sent him Giulio Carlo Argan's study of *Fra Angelico*. These two very different Renaissance painters likely represented to Flaiano cases of the other world and the sacred being grounded in a heightened attention as evidenced in crudely and mundanely rendered details.[64]

To the youth of this imaginary Adriatic town in *I vitelloni*, Rome appears as the ultimate object of their fantasy, competing at the level of exoticism with places like Brazil. When Fausto and Sandra return from their honeymoon in Rome, Fausto is sporting a mustache, a sign of a change representing a rite of passage, and he amazes everyone by setting up a record player in the middle of the street and improvising a dance that he and Sandra had learned at a Wanda Osiris show. This surprising dance is the effect of Flaiano's and Fellini's imagination of Rome, perceived as a surrogate for an epiphany experience. Ultimately, however, it is the protagonist Moraldo, thanks to the idealistic nature already expressed by his esoteric interests, who eventually has the courage to escape from the repetition of provincial life, leaving for the foreign and mysterious place known as Rome.

After *I vitelloni*, Fellini and Flaiano continued their story of the urbanized provincial in the never-realized script entitled *Moraldo va in città*.[65] At the end of this story the protagonist is exhausted and depressed after his adventure in Rome, where he witnessed the unhappiness of people from various social strata and realized his inability to identify with any of the social groups and lifestyles he observed: the bourgeoisie of his girlfriend, the upper class of his controlling and decadent mentor, or the aimless and self-destructive behaviour of his bohemian friends. Unlike the events of *La dolce vita*, but similar to the situation experienced by the female protagonist at the end of *Le notti di Cabiria*, Rome, with its variegated and surprising life force, rescues Moraldo and instills in him a desire to go on:

> Moraldo is alone. He watches the battered, little black Fiat move away and rattle down the street. Now Moraldo advances toward the city, slowly at first, and then at a quicker pace. An irrational exuberance comes over him little by little.
>
> The lights around him now seem gay. And the faces, the faces of the crowd that walks alongside him, they now seem less hostile. A dark-haired girl walks by him with her opulent hair bouncing in waves on her shoulders. She gives Moraldo a flashing smile.
>
> Farther on, a boy in shirtsleeves rides his bicycle past Moraldo. The boy whistles a song ... Two young lovers come toward him. They hold tightly to each other as they walk ... A baby cries. Voices of women intermingle ... Life, life, with its inexhaustible, unforeseeable treasure of encounters, chance events, people, and adventures.
>
> Moraldo walks briskly among the people, smiling at everybody.[66]

For Fellini, Rome represented the mysterious capital of the exotic, with the promise of adventure, and the repository of life's creative blood, the locus of epiphany. In his diaristic film *Roma*, Fellini indulges in the human and aesthetic stimulation provided by the city, the heart and essence of which can never be fully grasped and exhausted. Flaiano also acknowledged Rome's exotic lure, but for him the city was the journey's dead end, as is amusingly illustrated by the story of his alter ago, the alien protagonist of *Un marziano a Roma*, which was first staged in Milan in 1960 under the direction of Vittorio Gasman

(1922–2000). Here, the alien's initial excitement does not last long, and soon he begins to realize that the interplanetary encounter will not lead to the great transformations for which he had hoped. Soon the alien begins exhibiting the symptoms of a satirical mind by writing epigrams in Flaiano's style and through his experience will gradually come to discern the dangerous illusion that hides and lurks behind the veil of the exotic. The alien closes the play, singing a refrain from a song that was first voiced by another character in the play named the Exiled King of Arcadia who knows all too well the ironic game of representations and projections based upon a sense of otherness: "So deep is the bliss / of a sleeping town! / It lies in the obscene and severe poses of an Oriental woman. / The man who descends into these waters, will not – will not set sail again!"[67] For Flaiano, Rome is equated to an Asian woman, emblematic of the exotic, a never-ending well of foreignness, but also an abyss that swallows the traveller and renders the continuation of his journey impossible and useless. In an earlier and shorter version of *Un marziano a Roma*, dated 1954 (the same year as *La strada*), Flaiano imagines a meeting with Fellini at the site of the landing of the alien spacecraft. The director is dishevelled and in a state of prophetic rapture:

> Around seven I met my friend Fellini, pale and devastated by emotion. He was at the *Pincio* when the spaceship landed, and at first he thought he was having a hallucination. When he saw people running and yelling and heard sharp orders being shouted from the spaceship in a somewhat cold, scholastic Italian, Fellini understood. Immediately stampeded and stepped on by the crowd, he woke up without shoes on, his jacket in shreds. He wandered around the park like a dolt, barefoot, trying to find any exit whatsoever. I was the first friendly face he met. He cried while embracing me, shaken by an emotion that was communicated to me soon enough. He then described the spaceship to me: a saucer of enormous dimensions, yellow and bright like a sun. And the unforgettable rustling, the rustling of a silk foulard, upon its landing! And the silence that followed that moment! In that brief instant he felt that a new period was beginning for humanity. The prospects are, he tells me, immense and inscrutable. Maybe everything: religion and laws, art and our very lives, will soon appear to us illogical and meager. If the solitary traveller who descended from the spaceship is really – and by now after the official communiqué it would be foolish to doubt it – the ambassador from another planet where everything is known about ours; this is a sign that "things are more simple" elsewhere. The fact that the Martian came alone proves

that he possesses means of self-defence that are unknown to us and such knowledge that could radically alter our system of living and our conception of the world.[68]

The entire passage is a satire of Fellini's overly active imagination and hopeful dreams for a miraculous transformation of the human being into something more than human. Fellini assails Flaiano with a wave of enthusiastic expectations that the alien's arrival will completely revolutionize human thinking, bringing people to a simpler and deeper understanding of the universe, and fostering new powers (humorously, a few lines later, Flaiano also hints at the hopes for increased erotic and seductive powers). To make his satire of Fellini's belief in magic precise, the Fellini character even ascribes to the landing a sound similar to that of a "rustling of a silk foulard," which is the very sound effect, a subtle and sibylline blowing of the wind, that returns in almost all of Fellini's films to connote the mysterious presence of the beyond. Of course, though, *Un marziano a Roma*, is the story of how nothing, not even the landing of an alien, can change the human mind, and that of Italians in particular. Fellini's divinatory enthusiasm is placed at the very beginning of the short treatment, in contrast to the pessimistic ending, which instead better embodies Flaiano's views.

Flaiano's disillusioned perspective was expressed in connection with the writer's experience on the set of *Le notti di Cabiria* during the shooting of the sequence of Cabiria's pilgrimage to the sanctuary, a sequence in which any hope of salvation is indeed shattered by a falling back to earthly limitations. In one of Flaiano's collections of short narratives, *Una e una notte* (1959), he included a piece that captures his mood and reflections during the day of shooting at the sanctuary with Fellini:

> Certain places, he thought, give a sensation of an impasse; we cannot explain it to ourselves, but we feel that it is our duty to understand, and therefore we think about the experience repeatedly ... The truth is that nothing made sense, everything was fake, and we had to be satisfied with this fact ... The crowd had not come there for faith, nor had they been moved by hope in a miracle. Still, something happened because, within a group of other extras who had been asked to call out loud for a miracle, a woman shouted that she wanted it for real. Her poor and ragged face, wrinkled by a continuous life of common pleasures and sufferings, was wetted by true tears and stood out in the crowd for that desperate shout.

Nothing else happened, and shortly afterwards the crowd silently packed into the cold courtyard already lapped by the moon. The cashiers called the extras to their tables and paid them.[69]

This short narrative points to Flaiano as the chief instigator of the sense of void that dominates the sanctuary sequence of *Le notti di Cabiria*. More important, the final passage of Flaiano's story, where the protagonist comes to grips with the sense of a void arising from the ancient and stern landscape around the sanctuary, after having witnessed a false and yet heartfelt pilgrimage, reveals much of the philosophic framework of Flaiano. This is the very perspective that would later powerfully influence *La dolce vita*, a film in which any redemption from the cycle of moral decadence and from a stifling spiritual vacuum is painfully absent. In a letter dated 4 July 1960 to the critic Filippo Sacchi, Flaiano expressed his resentment at the scant recognition that he had received for *La dolce vita*: "I waited some time to write you to see if another film critic besides you had noticed my presence in the film 'La dolce vita.' I was waiting in vain."[70] Indeed it is in this film that Flaiano's world view, in which the occurrence of a miracle is recorded with a bitter smile of disillusionment, is more clearly felt. Brunello Rondi, who, philosophically speaking, is situated at the diametrically opposite side of the spectrum in Fellini's team, and, as we will see, functionally so, confirmed this dynamic when he said that Flaiano "devalued mystical elements typical of Fellini's art."[71]

The character of Sylvia in *La dolce vita*, the unattainable American actress played by Anita Ekberg (1931–), and especially her famous sequence in the Trevi Fountain, owes much to the poetic world of Flaiano. This character resembles very closely the enigmatic feminine characters of Flaiano's literary world, most notably the African Mariam from *Tempo di uccidere*, who is unintentionally killed by an Italian solider. In the novel, when the man first lays his eyes on her, she is bathing innocently in a pond and stimulates in him the following thoughts: "She perhaps still knew all the secrets which I had rejected without even examining them like a paltry legacy, in order to content myself with boring trite truths. I looked for knowledge in books and she had it in her eyes, which looked at me from two thousand years away like the light of certain stars which take that time to be picked out by us."[72]

Similarly, Sylvia, who exhibits a special empathy for stray cats and dogs, enters into the Trevi Fountain and starts to bathe as if she were in a beautiful waterfall alone in the wilderness, as if inviting Marcello to participate in a spontaneously hieratic ritual. After a moment of astonishment, Marcello follows her into the fountain and seems to have suddenly found a way out of his limited world; he says to her and himself: "Yes, she is right! We got it all wrong! All of us got it wrong! Still, it's clear, is it possible you still do not understand, that we do not understand? (*he shouts*) I am coming too!"[73] In the script, but not in the final cut of the film, Marcello responds to Sylvia's call to him from the fountain by quoting a poem by Jules Laforgue (1860–87) stressing hope in the reawakening effect of instinct: "Dans le jardin de nos instincts, allons cueillir de quoi guérir" (in the gardens of our instincts let us collect what heals).[74] Later Marcello will lose himself in a pantheistic celebration of Sylvia: "You are all things ... you are everything ... You are the first woman of the first day on the earth ... You are Eve ... You are mother, sister, you are lover, woman ... You are an angel ... the devil ... the Earth, the house ... Home."[75] In Flaiano's stories these types of magical and unsettling feminine characters maintain an ironic effect, as the male protagonists' sense of sharing in their sacred world is only a temporary illusion, their world and language remaining inaccessible.[76] Even though it may be true that Brunello Rondi originally suggested to Fellini the idea of having an American actress bathing in the fountain, after having seen the photographs of Anita Ekberg bathing in the fountain the summer before, Flaiano's disenchanted imprint appears here and confirms his deep involvement in the development of this scene.[77]

While Flaiano underscored the inability to communicate with the world of myth, Fellini attempted to express such communication plastically and exploited the opportunity to represent the mythical aura of Sylvia. Interestingly, Flaiano may have worked here with an awareness of this collaborative dynamic because, as has been noted by Stefano Stoja, when typing the final version of the sequence at the Trevi Fountain, Flaiano did not mention the name of the fountain and described it as seen from the inexperienced point of view of Sylvia, thus handing over a scene scripted in such a way as to make space for the director's work in expressing her innocent ecstasy.[78] In fact, in spite of Marcello's pathetic attempts to reach her blissful dimension, Fellini inevitably emphasizes the durability and the authenticity of her magic aura. The complementary synergy of Fellini and Flaiano rendered the night sequence between Marcello and Sylvia as one of the most unforgettable in the history of cinema, as the protagonist's yearning for the woman's mythical dimension matches the director's own pressing desire for transcendence. It is this particularly fortunate conflation of the two different visions and the contradictory aesthetic forces that contribute to making this famous sequence unforgettable.

A character similar to Sylvia returns a few years later in *Le tentazioni del Dottor Antonio*, a short film on which Flaiano also collaborated. This time the delusion associated with the feminine character becomes even more accentuated, though stemming from the moralistic thinking of the male protagonist (Dottor Antonio, played by Peppino De Filippo). Also in line with the satirical examination of human contradictions, previously identified as one of the elements of affinity in this collaboration, Dottor Antonio is a ridiculous and pitiful individual who, in his attempt to repress his sexual desires, turns women into demons and begins an imaginary battle that ultimately leads to the destruction of his own mind.

Moving from the stern and fatalistic Freudian type of psychoanalysis found in the sinister farce of *Le tentazioni del Dottor Antonio*, Fellini gave in to the regenerative psychology of Jungian psychoanalysis, claiming with *8½* the reawakened energy of symbols and erecting a monument to the imaginative power of the psyche. The film *8½* marks the last phase of the collaboration between Fellini and Flaiano, as the growing authorial conflict and the distance in vision between them reached a culminating point in the handling of the film's ending. Flaiano had written and agreed with a finale where Guido is with his wife in the dining car of a train that is speeding quickly through a poignantly desolate and dark countryside, an ancient landscape made up of bright houses, silhouettes of mountains, statuary horses, and barren fields upon which the light from within the train casts its shadows. Suddenly Guido is overtaken by the peaceful vision of all the important people in his life seated at the tables in the car and smiling at him. After a moment in which Guido feels exhilaration and gratitude and a desire to connect with his wife, the intangible intuition dissolves, and he desperately attempts to communicate his fleeting epiphany to his wife, while looking into the camera.[79] Flaiano's imprint on the scripted finale of *8½* is validated by an earlier journal entry, in which he had recorded the feeling of awe and solitude communicated by the vision of a stark and timeless countryside that is experienced fleetingly from within the protected and bright space of a train car. "Once, there on the Padanian plain, the train stopped on a steel bridge. At that moment, the sun was disappearing at the edge of the flat countryside, and the lights went on inside the third-class compartment. I was alone, my heart overflowing with emotions never experienced before and with a comforting melancholy:

as I was eating the food I had brought with me for the trip, I started crying. I was very young and I could not bear, at the time, the disconsolate warnings that a landscape full of experience gladly dispenses to those who take the time to look at it."[80]

For Flaiano, *8½* ended in the relentless sound of the train heading forward into the night, with desperate hope. Fellini considered various endings for *8½*, but finally, even though the night-time finale taking place in the train had already been shot, he opted to shoot the film's conclusion in full daylight, in the open air within the magical and cumulative circle of the circus-mandala. Incidentally, spheres and circularity become increasingly a hallmark of Fellini's work, with connections to what much scholarship identifies as the baroque characteristic of his cinema. As if to emphasize this, spherical shapes often appear at the end of Fellini's films, differing in emotional tone and poetic significance: the ball of *Toby Dammit*, *Roma*'s insistence on the Coliseum and the circular highway around the city, the demolition ball of *Prova d'orchestra*, the tunnel of *La città delle donne*, and the moon of *La voce della luna*. Fellini's later films also seek circularity in their narrative structures as well: *Satyricon* begins and ends with ancient murals; in *Roma* the search for Rome's core is circular; *Amarcord* follows the circuit of the year's seasons; and in the last moments of his life the protagonist of *Il Casanova* returns to his Venetian origins through dreams.[81] According to a Jungian interpretation of the finale of *8½*, the mandala is directly connected to the cumulative stylistic tendency of Fellini's cinema.[82] Fellini's increasing tendency towards accumulation was against Flaiano's artistic sensibility, as he stated in his customary vitriolic manner: "[Fellini's] art, which Pasolini defines as neo-decadent, needs symbols, and to avoid erring, it must spice up every entrée, enrich all its sauces. I eat light."[83] On another occasion Flaiano recommended that "a story dominated by the irrational and the fantastic requires a plain style."[84] As will be elucidated in another chapter, Pasolini's definition of Fellini's art draws a parallel between Fellini and the poet Giovanni Pascoli (1855–1912) and does not base the parallel on lavishness. However, it is interesting to note the way in which Flaiano interprets the category of decadent in terms of an overly enriched style, a fictitious inspiration, and a gushy artistic ecstasy, all elements that seem to point not to Pascoli but rather to the poet Gabriele D'Annunzio (1863–1938), also from Pescara, a figure against whom so many nineteenth-century Italian writers fought for political, moral, and artistic reasons, and from whom they tried to distance themselves. Owing to the antipodal position between Flaiano's ironic and demystifying stance and the auto-celebratory and nationalistic voice of D'Annunzio, it is possible that some of the animosity Flaiano must have harboured for D'Annunzio may have transferred into his perception of Fellini.[85]

Flaiano could not fully conform to Fellini's desire to emphasize the celebration of epiphany and even the possibility, in the midst of the most hopeless confusion, of magically reacquiring peace, wisdom, and youth. Flaiano sarcastically wrote, "With Fellini I suspended the collaboration after *8½* when he converted to magic, an area in which I am not competent."[86] Fellini's esoteric and psychoanalytical interests dramatically exacerbated the already very entrenched point of contention relating to the public representation of authorship. In essence, for Fellini, the night of the human life is not always pitch black; it may be randomly lit by flashes of enigmatic truth, not unlike the hypnagogic images that are found so often in Fellini's *Libro dei sogni*. Fellini reorders Guido's "Great Confusion" – the title that Flaiano had in mind for *8½* – into a harmonious and playful dance.[87] The temporary and illusory utopia that Flaiano intended is turned by Fellini into a fully fledged celebration, a new film in itself – the type of art that, for its inventive visual freedom, Fellini would pursue for the rest of his career and without the assistance of Flaiano.

Chapter Three

Bernardino Zapponi

When Fellini's initial team of screenwriters dissolved in 1965, his career creatively stalled for about three years until 1968 when he began an intensive collaboration that lasted more than ten years with the eclectic and lesser-known writer Bernardino Zapponi. Fellini's new screenwriting partnership coincided with an artistic rebirth and redirection of his cinema. Critics did not recognize Bernardino Zapponi's writing, unlike Pinelli's and Flaiano's work, a fact that Fellini most likely appreciated after his intense artistic and authorial negotiations with Pinelli and Flaiano. In a number of caricatures Fellini expressed in a satirical manner his fondness for Zapponi's low profile as a writer. Zapponi is presented sitting behind a fantastically oversized typewriter, optimistically typing away on an enormous sheet of paper while exclaiming, "I am writing a great book!" In another caricature Zapponi is shown labouring uneasily on the script for *Il Casanova* while the somewhat snobbish and literary-minded ghost of the Venetian stares over him.[1] Interestingly, Zapponi's lowbrow status as a writer and his proficiency in the popular genres of horror, science fiction, mystery, and eroticism appealed to Fellini's increasingly dominating authorial and psychoanalytical interests and galvanized his already natural inclination for popular culture.

Having worked for the satirical newspaper *Marc'Aurelio*, though during different years, both Fellini and Zapponi shared an affinity for comics and saw eye to eye when brainstorming visual sources for their films. In his recollections Zapponi often indicates this common interest. For example, he recalled that the interior of the late 1930s house where the young journalist stays in the film *Roma* was based on the style of the comics of Attalo, one of the senior artists of *Marc'Aurelio*. Zapponi also enthusiastically retold the story of the visit by Lee Falk (1911–99), the creator of the comic book *Mandrake*, to the set of *Roma* and brought to mind the vividly colourful Rome depicted in the comics of Guy Peellaert (1934–2008) as being a source for this film. Later, concomitant with their work on *La città delle donne*, Zapponi suggested a number of erotic-comic-book artists, such as Irving Klaw (1910–66), John Willie (1902–62), and Eric Stanton (1926–99), who all illustrated sadistic and perverse feminine figures.[2]

Unlike a writer such as Pinelli, Zapponi explained his storytelling style by contrasting his predilection for cinema over theatre and for lowbrow rather than highbrow modes of representation and tradition: "I don't have much interest in theatre. My dialogue is very cinematographic, in the sense that it must always take into account the reality of scenes, and then the dialogue follows. I tell about a family seated at a table, imagine the scene, and then come up with what they might be talking about."[3] Zapponi's novel *Passione* (1974, Passion) – the tragicomic story of a homosexual relationship between a Roman mechanic and his apprentice – forcefully documents the cinematographic characteristic of Zapponi's writing style, strongly favouring descriptions and action scenes over dialogues. This cinematographic quality was ideal for Fellini, who from the mid-1960s on saw himself more and more as a painter than as a storyteller and was ready to challenge traditional canons and forms of narration, turning screenwriting into an exercise of pure visual improvisation and brainstorming.

Zapponi's earliest experience as a screenwriter was in 1951 for Mario Soldati's film *È l'amor che mi rovina* (Love is ruining me). When he met Fellini, Zapponi was collaborating on two other collections of short films – *Le streghe* (1967, *The Witches*) and *Capriccio all'italiana* (1968, *Caprice Italian Style*) – during which his path also crossed with several high calibre artists such as Vittorio De Sica (1901–74), Luchino Visconti (1906–76), Pier Paolo Pasolini, Cesare Zavattini, Stefano Vanzina, and Mario Bolognini (1922–2001). It was the collaboration with Fellini that fully launched Zapponi's career in cinema and led to the scripting of a number of movies with other accomplished directors, especially Dino Risi (1916–2008), Tinto Brass (1933–), Mauro Bolognini (1922–2001), and Dario Argento (1940–), who were often on the fringe of social mores and intermixed artistic prestige and popular genres.[4]

When working with his screenwriters, Fellini always preferred a light-hearted and free-flowing atmosphere, avoiding the sense of doing "serious work" that could have stifled the imagination necessary to develop characters and situations.[5] In relation to his sessions with Fellini, Zapponi recalled: "It is like playing pool: one thing hits another, and new ideas, suggestions, iconic and visual references are born … Slowly we start to take notes, which in turn begin to articulate in the form of episodes."[6] Incidentally, dreams recorded in Fellini's journal in 1968 strongly suggest an increased desire for a heightened playfulness in his work, connected to the figure of Bernardino Zapponi. For example, in March 1968 Fellini recorded a dream, also noting the intention of sharing it with Zapponi in order to use it for a film, which is illustrated by the drawing of an airplane formation flying in an "extremely luminous atmosphere" towards an unknown destination and purpose, and "bearing light, abstract children's constructions."[7]

Zapponi's eclectic background also included the direction of a richly idiosyncratic and entertaining quarterly magazine *Il Delatore* (1958–65); a pseudo-psychoanalytic study of the mind of inquisitors, *Nostra signora dello spasimo* (1963, Our lady of agony); and a collection of short stories called *Gobal* (1967), which initially inspired Fellini to contact him. As it happened, Fellini and Zapponi worked together on a series of very experimental film projects. Their collaboration began with the short film *Toby Dammit*, which was largely inspired by Zapponi's own short stories. Throughout the 1960s and 1970s their new creative approach to screenwriting – influenced by Zapponi's prior experiments with collage-style publications – was applied to idiosyncratic adaptations such as *Toby Dammit*, *Satyricon*, and *Il Casanova di Federico Fellini*, as well as to the diaristic films *Roma*, *Block-notes di un regista*, and *I clowns*. Except for *Amarcord*, written by Fellini and Tonino Guerra, and the occasional assistance given by Brunello Rondi, Zapponi remained Fellini's principal screenwriter for about fifteen years. His authorial flexibility, descriptive writing style, and interest in the unconventional use of the psyche complemented Fellini's increasingly detached relationship towards the script and his search for a heightened exploration of the irrational, consequentially inviting the neo-baroque and postmodern interpretations that critics have emphasized in Fellini's cinema of this period.

The Script as Collage: The Unbound Notebooks of the 1970s

Before fully embracing his work in cinema, and meeting with Fellini, Zapponi collected eccentric fiction, essays, and surreal and satirical illustrations by cartoonists such as Roland Topor (1938–97), Mino Maccari, and Maurice Sinet (1928–) in his own magazine *Il Delatore*. The publication was active between 1958 and 1965, with provocatively titled issues such as "Il sadismo" (Sadism), "Il cattivo gusto in Italia" (Tackiness in Italy), "La follia" (Folly), "Dizionario del gergo della malavita" (Dictionary of Criminal Jargon), "La morte" (Death), and "I travestiti" (Transvestites). The narrative form in *Block-notes di un regista*, *Roma*, and *I clowns* owes much to the eccentric and fragmentary types of thematic research that Zapponi had undertaken since the late 1950s with *Il Delatore*. Zapponi's magazine investigated themes in the form of collages that placed in continuity, and at the same level of importance, low and high cultural domains, as well as historical documents, short narratives, drawings, photographs, and jokes, in what seemed to be a homemade method of psychoanalytic ethnography. In the introduction to his book on the Inquisition that was published as early as 1963, Zapponi described his approach as being different from "a treatise of rigid architecture" and being like "an impressionistic *collage* or ... documentary," a position that foreshadows the experimental documentary forms later undertaken with Fellini.[8]

In Zapponi's and Fellini's hands, the genre of the documentary is transformed into a mélange of the diaristic and the mockumentary. Here, as in their adaptations, they sought a point of origin and a perspective that would be open and could generate the greatest amount of associations and suggestions. Zapponi's description of the way in which Fellini once proposed to begin their work on *Roma* exemplifies their perspective: "He [Fellini] would say, 'I want to shoot from the helicopter, to see from high up as clouds form above Rome, and to film these large masses of every colour gathering, breaking apart, unravelling.' Then he would continue: 'The *Ponentino*. How is this famous wind born? Where? That's it, I would like to catch it from its start, to follow it making its way to Rome. I would like to film people who feel it coming over them, in the most varied places and situations: in the cafés, in bed, on the street.'"[9]

In this brainstorming phase, the city of Rome – which functions here as the source text to be excavated, deconstructed, and psychoanalysed – is introduced through an experience, the perception of the arrival of a summer breeze called *ponentino*, an apparently insignificant yet startling quotidian event that overrides all rhetorical and formulaic associations and representations of the Eternal City. The actual film has a different beginning, which still continues to neutralize stereotypes of Roman history and culture by means of a diametrically opposite strategy; here Rome is introduced from a spatial and temporal distance, through the filter of childhood memories of growing up in the northern province of Romagna, therefore emerging in fragmentary icons both fabulous and ridiculous in tone. *Roma* is permeated by the search for an intimate urban space, a subtext, the city's secret that reveals itself only to careful observers who have been long exposed to the city's image and life. The version of the script of *Roma* that is archived at the Lilly Library testifies to Fellini and Zapponi's collage approach to scripting these experimental documentaries. The scripted sequences of *Roma* are bound separately, signalling their independence from one another, and like the colourful notebooks of a child, they are heavily intermixed with drawings.[10] There is no story to be found, but there are instead collections of unusual faces, sets, and situations. At this phase of Fellini's career the script had become a *zibaldone*, an apparently disorderly notebook of heterogeneous content, which finds its best filmic counterpart in *Block-notes di un regista*. It has been noted that Fellini's storytelling approach in a film such as *Block-notes* allows him to use film-making as a strategy to gain new insight into his own personality; his notebook approach to the script is unfettered by the etiquette of presentability since it allows for the inclusion of "the bad along with the good, the silly with the sublime."[11] In essence, the experimental procedure applied to a film such as *Roma*, which the critic Aldo Tassone called a *fantadocumentario*, is not separate from the one employed for *Satyricon* and *Il Casanova* and which could likewise be termed *fanta-adattamenti*.[12] In these projects the referent, the original text, is only a pretext or subtext of the film.

The mingling of the object with the subjectivity of the interpreter was a general trend in many arts in the late 1960s and 1970s. This trend also involved the social sciences, especially cultural anthropology, where researchers began to include in their analysis their own point of view for a more honest representation of the Other. For example, when it comes to cinematic adaptations of literary texts, as early as 1964, Pier Paolo Pasolini pursued dialogical and experimental approaches, first in *Il vangelo secondo Matteo* and then in his Greek tragedies and medieval works of the mid-1970s.[13] These types of adaptations are connected to the movement that sprang from the ideas of Antonin Artaud (1896–1948) concerning a "Theatre of Cruelty" (first appearing in *La Nouvelle Revue Française* in Paris in 1931), which asserted a need for a new theatre that would be able to capitalize on all its plastic expressive potentials and free itself from the ancient tyranny of the script. Among the Italian artists who fought hardest for a more personal theatrical representation was actor and director Carmelo Bene (1931–2002), who in 1967 played the role of Creon in Pasolini's *Edipo Re* (*Oedipus Rex*). According to Bene, the performer has the responsibility to recreate and challenge literary texts, in particular of well-known classics such as *Amleto* and *Pinocchio*, and in the process to demolish the limitations of institutional modalities of representation, knowledge, language, and selfhood itself. In his volcanic performances Bene revolutionized the idea of the actor through his practice of *"macchina autoriale,"* by which he did not recite a script but traversed and recreated it, "discovering" as the critic Jean-Paul Manganaro wrote, "the suspended and unknown instant of the story, unveiling its unthinkable facets, what can not be understood in it."[14]

Even in its most enigmatic and repulsive conjunctions, Fellini's *Il libro dei sogni* is an example of the director's intuitive grasp on the cultural milieu of his times and a source that provides the unconventional but poignantly heuristic confirmation of nodes central to the present textual and contextual analysis. A dream dated 16 January 1968, coincidentally the year of Carmelo Bene's directed film *Nostra signora dei Turchi* (Our lady of the Turks), associates, unsurprisingly, Bene's performances with the approach to film-making that Fellini had begun undertaking with Bernardino Zapponi: "Coming down a rope, Carmelo Bene (just like in his production of *Pinocchio*) acts haphazardly for Giulietta and me. The madman doesn't realize he's shitting on himself copiously. Giulietta looks at me, perplexed and shocked. Carmelo Bene, satisfied by his performance, leaves the stage, collecting part of his shit as if it were a suitcase. Bernardino Zapponi and I are covered with his feces; our underpants are full of it. We absolutely have to wash up. Bernardino proposes going to his house, but I insist on my office. We head for Via Francesco Crispi 30, shocked and covered with shit."[15]

In this dream Fellini, Giulietta Masina, and Bernardino Zapponi are among the spectators of a play by Carmelo Bene, which Fellini apparently saw and which shares similarities with Bene's *Pinocchio*. Even though this seemingly unflattering and perplexing dream could invite a variety of psychoanalytic interpretations, the journal entry documents how Fellini himself links the unrestrained and anti-dramatic production of the *"macchina autoriale"* and the equally unrestricted and probing inventiveness that he is undertaking with Zapponi at this time. Fellini senses that he and Zapponi are entering a phase of unbounded, unplanned, and self-indulgent abandonment to creation, of which Carmelo Bene represents a possible model; their blossoming new collaboration and approach to scriptwriting surfaces in this dream as the director's disquieting but pressing desire for creative innovation.

According to Zapponi's recollections, the practice of screenwriting with Fellini increasingly acquired in these years a peculiar divinatory and gypsy-like quality: "We detested desks; we worked in cafés, at home, everywhere, in a very flexible and free fashion. We discussed sequences, we searched for images, we invented the sets and always thought a little beyond reality, searching for that extraordinary level that would have given the right colour to what we called *la sconosciutezza* [the unknown]."[16] Their trips served the purpose of meeting individuals and exploring places related to their projects, and so they restlessly moved from Zapponi's home to Fellini's office, from restaurants to cafés on the outskirts of Rome, especially in Ostia. During their brainstorming sessions Zapponi and Fellini searched mostly for images and atmospheres linked to the central indefinable idea. Therefore, in spite of what Zapponi called Fellini's "coquetry" in publicizing a reduced importance of the script in his work as film-maker in the later years of his work, the script's function had simply changed towards a more free-flowing accumulation of ideas, a collection of themes and motifs to be elaborated visually at a later stage.[17]

Popular Culture and Neurosis: *Toby Dammit* and Beyond

Zapponi's psychoanalytical-anthropological perspective, marked by a belief in the power of art to explore and explain the deformations of modern man and his lifestyles, was a major trait of his affinity with Fellini. Zapponi's book about the torture systems of the Inquisition, *Nostra signora dello spasimo*, aimed at an understanding of the mental pathologies that characterized the inquisitor and was motivated by the idea that such pathologies continue to exist today in many forms of sadism. Here Zapponi concludes: "The life of Italians is unhappy because only a few are free inside: freedom is not a physical state but a spiritual civilization, from which we are still very distant."[18] Unsurprisingly, Zapponi's early interest in mental pathologies would eventually lead him to collaborate with the horror film-maker Dario Argento on his highly acclaimed *Profondo rosso* (1975, *Deep Red*) in developing a way to cinematically explore the murderer's point of view.[19] Indeed, Zapponi's intrepid nature in exploring controversial points of view exceeded Fellini's, as happened for instance with homosexuality, a topic to which Zapponi had dedicated an issue of his magazine *Il Delatore*.

Zapponi had proposed the topic to Fellini in two instances: the case of his already mentioned novel *Passione* and the case of a *soggetto* for a film entitled "Storia d'amore" or "L'effeminazione," in which a man becomes a transvestite to satisfy the absence of the woman who has left him. Fellini, however, rejected both of them, even though the latter was considered for some time as a short to be paired with another short directed by Ingmar Bergman (1918–2007). The discussion on Fellini's relationship with Pier Paolo Pasolini presented in the next chapter offers an opportunity to further clarify the director's reticence towards directly addressing the theme of homosexuality in his films.

The "infernal" atmosphere that is perceivable in Fellini's cinema from 1968 to the end of the 1970s, especially in films such as *Toby Dammit*, *Satyricon*, and *Il Casanova*, owes much to Zapponi's leanings for "horror genre, Poe's tales, ghosts, gothic, and dark and sinister atmospheres," which characterized his writings as a product "somewhere between the *Grand-Guignol*, the dark novel, and the vampire movies" but at the same time satisfied Fellini's longing for the unrealized hereafter of *Il viaggio di Mastorna*.[20] The preference for horror permeated Zapponi's understanding of *Satyricon*, in which fear is generated by the uncanny and strange representation of human beings, because, as he once said, "people are viewed as in another dimension from ours, a dimension of dream and also nightmare."[21] Furthermore, according to Zapponi, the Casanova created by him and Fellini is "a character who lives permanently in a mortuary dimension, made of beds that resemble coffins, of funereal apparitions, of old women, in the putrid greenish colour of Venice."[22] Even when asked to speak about his participation in *La città delle donne*, Zapponi recalled his favourite scenes as those in the more sinister setting of the cemetery of the memories of Katzone's sexual conquests.[23] Interestingly, this is the atmosphere that Brunello Rondi termed "funereal" and complained about as the main reason for his increased distance from Fellini's work, beginning with *Satyricon* and lasting for most of the 1970s, with the exception of *Prova d'orchestra*, the musically based film written without Zapponi. Referring to films such as *Satyricon*, *Roma*, and *Il Casanova*, Rondi said: "[Fellini] started a very peculiar phase ... that I would define as mortuary-funereal, in which Fellini has revealed a vision of the world that is extremely sombre and rather unpopular, in spite of the sparks of genius that it contains."[24] Speaking of his different idea on how to adapt Petronius's *Satyricon* and the reason he (apparently) decided to have his name removed from the authors of the script, Rondi added, "I believed that ancient history could have been addressed with a great love for life, a formidable and playful radiance that instead Fellini's evidently repudiated."[25]

Toby Dammit, the first film on which Fellini and Zapponi worked together, was influenced by Zapponi's short story collection *Gobal*, which Fellini read sometime in the summer of 1967 at the suggestion of the writer Goffredo Parise (1929–86). At that time, Fellini had been invited by a French production company to contribute a short film to a collective project inspired by Edgar Allan Poe's collection of stories, *Histoires extraordinaires* (1968, *Spirits of the Dead*). The metaphysical mystery stories contained in Zapponi's book *Gobal*, titled after the name of a non-existent island, resonated with the Poesque qualities that Fellini admired in that they told of the vicissitudes of individuals who become pawns to forces greater than themselves and which they could not understand. The film *Toby Dammit* eventually blended some of Zapponi's stories with one of Poe's lesser-known stories, "Never Bet the Devil Your Head: A Tale with a Moral." Fellini was so interested in a few of Zapponi's stories from *Gobal* that he initially proposed one of them, "C'è una voce nella mia vita" (There is a voice in my life), to the producers as a substitute for one of Poe's stories. In spite of the director's insistence, the French production company refused, and predictably so, and Fellini was forced to choose a story by the great American writer instead. After much deliberation on various possibilities, including another story by Poe, "The Premature Burial" – all of which were rejected because they required extremely expensive sets – Fellini and Zapponi turned to "Never Bet the Devil Your Head."[26]

In this short piece Poe, after a long introduction, narrates the anecdote of a man who since childhood has practised the bad habit of repeating the expression "I'll bet the devil my head." As it happens, in the story Toby repeats this saying once too often and with particular emphasis before attempting to jump a stile in a covered bridge. His head, caught on an invisible wire, is severed, and the devil, disguised as a cordial old man, collects it and then disappears. The narrator, who wept at the poor man's funeral, sends the funeral bill to the Transcendentalists, with whom Toby had become associated, but they, greedy and heartless, refuse to pay and force the narrator to sell the body for dog food. In Fellini's film the character of Toby (played by Terence Stamp) becomes an English actor, a sort of *poète maudit* character also standing in as a surrogate for Edgar Allan Poe himself, who, in exchange for a Ferrari, has been hired as the protagonist in a murky film project that chaotically blends artistic and philosophic ambitions with popular genres. Toby is now haunted by the vision of a ghostly child playing with a ball, who at the end, after the actor's unsuccessful attempt to speed over a fallen highway bridge with his new car, collects the man's severed head.

This is the first time in Fellini's career that horror tales have come within his radar. It is possible that Zapponi's leaning towards metaphysical horror tales correlated with the director's leanings at this time after the unsuccessful attempt to make *Mastorna*. Also, owing to the meta-cinematographic quality of Fellini's *Toby Dammit*, a parallel can be observed between Toby's ingenuous betting against the devil and the director's endeavour to address the afterlife openly and directly in *Mastorna*, thus sneering at the superstitious fears he harboured on the project.

Aided by the influence of Zapponi, Fellini was now intensively pondering his relationship with popular genre films, and this new perspective is satirically expressed through the character of the priest who is acting as an artistic consultant for Toby's film. During his monologue to the actor, the priest introduces the nature of the production as "the first Catholic western ... A western interpretation of the evangelic myth of redemption ... Christ's return in an abandoned frontier land" and then proceeds by explaining that "certain formulaic cinema can express a sublime poetry through elementary and naked images, which are eloquent in virtue of their poverty ... something between Dreyer and Pasolini, and certainly with a pinch of Ford, as my friend Roland Barthes would say." Apparently, Fellini went as far as shooting a sequence with a film troupe that showed Toby dressed as a cowboy – footage that was cut (and that, if found, would be the only existing explicit case of a Fellinian western). Testifying to a minor authorial conflict between Fellini and Zapponi, the scene was allegedly cut under pressure from Zapponi, who was evidently more purist than Fellini in terms of genres and found an isolated western sequence to be excessively extraneous within a film dominated by a sinister atmosphere. The writer remembered this episode fondly as an example of the influence he had had on the director during their first project, which was, as will be documented below, so closely linked to his own stories.[27]

In noting the crisis of representation expressed by the second phase of Fellini's work, the critic Christopher Sharrett has argued that films such as *Toby Dammit*, *Satyricon*, and *Il Casanova* are in themselves attempts to debunk the prestige of high culture by approaching it derisively from the point of view of pop culture. Fellini's collaboration with Zapponi, a writer who belonged to a lowbrow area of culture, confirms Sharrett's perspective and indicates how such a goal was achieved at the level of conceptualization and writing. The debunking of cultural tradition and representation is carried out by the undertaking of genre (such as the horror genre for *Toby Dammit*) and by the approach of these films to adaptation that, as Sharrett says, "reveals the paucity of the source, the kitschiness of 'big ideas' from literary history."[28] Sharrett's study is, however, an example of the way in which scholars have been assessing Fellini's films from this period without taking into account the work of the film's screenwriter, therefore remaining blind to the film's immediate artistic context.

Zapponi's writing was endowed with a Kafkian quality that allowed for the coexistence of the ordinary and the extra-ordinary, an element that was certainly appreciated by Fellini, who was also extremely fond of the work of Franz Kafka.[29] Brunello Rondi testifies to Fellini's fascination with the Bohemian writer by explaining: "Fellini adores Kafka's allegorical strength and his fables filled with angst and sorrowful tormented morality."[30] A distorted perception is present in all of Zapponi's stories, linked to the subjective point of view of protagonists affected by neurosis or other mental disorders. In Zapponi's short story "C'è una voce nella mia vita," observation and hallucination are placed at the same level and cannot be easily distinguished. The story is based on the repetition of verses from the poem "La voce" contained in the 1903 collection *Canti di Castelvecchio* by the poet Giovanni Pascoli. The following verses are employed from Pascoli's poem: "There is a voice in my life, / I hear it as it dies away; / a tired, lost voice, / with the quivering of a beating heart. // A demanding and yearning voice. / It grasps at the frail chest / to say many, then many things, / but its mouth is full of dirt."[31] The passage is repeated obsessively and ominously throughout the story as part of the message that the protagonist receives from a mysterious woman speaking to him through a broken telephone. The protagonist, who admits from the onset that he is neurotic, gradually makes his way to an apartment towards which he feels inexplicably drawn. Eventually, upon entering into the room, he finds the dead body of a woman, as well as a group of police officers who have been directed to the same place by an unidentified phone caller. In a surprise ending, the protagonist is revealed to be the killer, who, owing to his detachment from reality, has forgotten about his deed and has been drawn back to the site of the murder by the mysterious voice on the telephone.

The ending maintains the ambiguity of whether the voice was that of the victim's ghost or of the killer's guilty subconscious. Since in Zapponi's story the voice could have had a psychological or a paranormal source, the story opens to the theme of the ambiguity between psyche and spirit, an ambiguity that was very dear to Fellini, as can be seen, for instance, in *Giulietta degli spiriti* where the question of the source of Giulietta's visions, mental or paranormal, is left open to interpretation. Naturally, from a cinematic point of view, Fellini was excited by the prospect of playing with the point of view of a protagonist who experiences life as a gallery of mysterious and ambiguous signs.

Fellini was also interested in another of Zapponi's stories, "L'autista." It is the tale of a chauffeur who develops an obsessive and fetishistic rapport with the beautiful black car of his rich aristocratic employers. As the car assumes human status in the chauffeur's mind, he begins to enjoy abusing it. In a crescendo of madness, the chauffeur – who is also suffering from nightmares about his obsession with the car and his sense of social inferiority – fulfills his wish to destroy the car by pushing it off a cliff. This story is told through the distorted point of view of the man, who goes through an experience not unlike that of the protagonist of Fellini's previous short film, *Le tentazioni del Dottor Antonio*, in which a priest becomes possessed by an erotic billboard and loses his mind. The obsession that the actor in *Toby Dammit* has for the Ferrari also recalls the fetishism of the chauffeur from the story "L'autista," as well as Zapponi's thoughts regarding the connection between Eros and machines. In *Nostra signora dello spasimo* Zapponi expanded on the mental pathologies and repressions to embrace the problem of man's erotic (and masochistic) subjugation to machines. Zapponi wrote, with some overgeneralization, of people's relationships with cars, thus prefiguring the Autista's and Toby's obsessions: "The car is a phallic symbol, but it certainly is also a feminine symbol because it receives; one enters into it and sits folded almost in a fetal position. In this way the mother becomes the image of the dominating mother who drags the child where she wants. The fight of man to impose his will upon the machine is what makes driving exciting, a sort of furious love battle. Usually he who is obsessed with high speeds does not have a satisfying sexual life. They are mature individuals who need a stable relationship. Many tragic accidents could be avoided if the driver's licence exam would include a psychoanalytic session."[32] In Zapponi's stories, lugubrious cityscapes are often seen from a speeding car, and this also happens in *Toby Dammit*. In another of the stories from *Gobal*, "I cinesi," the protagonist functions as an eye scouring through endless arrays of degraded human and urban landscapes.[33] Similar elements from Zapponi's narrative merge into the film's ending, where Toby Dammit drives recklessly through the night streets of a small hill town and arrives at a collapsed highway bridge. In this final sequence, parallel to the ending of Poe's story, Toby attempts to speed with his Ferrari above the chasm but decapitates himself against a metallic wire, and his head is finally taken by the sinister child-devil who has been hunting him from the start.

The assessment of Fellini's corrections appearing on the earlier draft of *Toby Dammit* that is archived at the Lilly Library of Rare Books indicates the director's attempt to render the child-devil less of a concrete presence and more of a nightmarish vision, closer to the suggestive Pascolian voice that intermittently surfaced like a memory in Zapponi's "C'è una voce nella mia vita."[34] In this version of the script, a scene in which the child-devil is floating above the traffic, as if chasing Toby's car when he leaves the airport, is deleted; the child's appearances are then limited to the first vision at the airport and again at the end. Such changes emphasize Fellini's preference for maintaining ambiguity between the paranormal and the psychological. Furthermore, the script shows Fellini's increased use of visual solutions over dialogue, both through the presence of his drawings on the script and also by the crossing out of three pages of dialogue from the finale.[35]

Besides revealing the authorial interplay between Fellini and Zapponi, *Toby Dammit* was also a laboratory in which a new approach to literary adaptation was created, and marks a watershed in the evolution of Fellini's career. The multifaceted nature of *Toby Dammit*, amalgamating multiple textual sources, is the result of a peculiarly invective relationship to the source text and to the script. Zapponi explained the approach to the adaptation of Poe's story as "a very complex operation of appropriation," looking to Poe's writing for stimuli rather than a scenario, a type of "twin neurosis," recreating the story from the inside. What follows is Zapponi's explanation:

> The concrete nature intrinsic to the camera, showing saltpetre dripping from the walls and the skulls piled up, risks substituting the true nightmarish quality of the author-actor, which is obviously unpredictable, with its most vulgar nightmare images. The reader of the story is situated "inside" Poe; the camera lens can only be outside of it ... Transferring Poe onto the screen is possible only through a very complex operation of

appropriation since it is not simply possible to superimpose the structural pattern of cinema on his stories; the rhythm and the articulation do not coincide. Cinematographic suspense establishes its own laws; almost a music, which is not Poe's dodecaphonic music. Poe cannot provide scenarios, but only stimuli; he can only set into action within the mind of the director a mechanism that might produce a twin neurosis. Poe can influence with his distress the author of the film by suggesting visions, ideas, nightmares, and people to him. He can install a creative process in a receptive mind.[36]

Such approach equates to the looser form of adaptation classified as recreation or as analogical adaptation, in which the source text is metabolized into an essential psychic node acting as a point of departure for a very different text.[37] Fellini, confirming his penchant for generating a satirical iconography of the creative process, drew a caricature of Zapponi, showing him at work on the script of *Toby Dammit* as his typewriter is catching on fire under the looming portrait of Poe.[38] Shortly afterwards, Zapponi and Fellini called upon the "twin neurosis" approach to adaptation, when working from the elusive text of *Satyricon* by Petronius Arbiter (ca AD 27–66) as well as later on from the twelve volumes of *Histoire de ma vie* (*The Memoirs*) by Giacomo Casanova (1725–98).

Fellini and Zapponi's approach to adaptation inevitably gave way to the accumulation of a vast body of characters and sets and heavily contributed to the neo-baroque quality that Pasolini associated with Fellini's later films. Already, when writing about *La dolce vita* in 1960, Pasolini had sketched an analysis of "Fellinian language" as based on the fundamental principles of "phonetic self-indulgence" and "semantic dilatation," which express themselves in the choices of mise en scène and cinematography. Pasolini also interjected a revealing comparison with the writer Carlo Emilio Gadda (1893–1973) to highlight that a similar baroque and pastiche style was linked in Gadda to a rationalistic credo, while Fellini's style was linked to an irrational one.[39] Pasolini's intuition of Fellini's baroque style as a result of Fellini's emphasis on the inexpressible was then embraced by future scholarship in Fellini studies. For example, according to John Stubbs, Fellini's fundamental conception of reality as ineffable requires a never-ending accumulation of details, a process that expresses itself through the layering of the sets, the contrasts of colours and characters, and the extravagance of the costumes. In referring to Fellini's "style of excess," Stubbs spoke of Fellini's objective to amplify the evocative potential of the cinematic image, especially in terms of mise en scène, by filling the frame to the brim with as many evocative suggestions, emotional contrast, and cues as possible.[40]

Italo Calvino (1923–85), with whom Fellini had discussed the possibility of collaborating on a film about the world of Italian folk tales, also spoke of Fellini's style in terms of baroque mannerism, as an expressionistic visual accentuation that germinates from and revolves around one original idea. The discussion spurred by Pasolini complements Calvino's statement that baroque mannerism derives its fertility from the impalpability of the root idea.[41] It can be concluded then that Fellini's objective was to communicate a sense of reality's complexity and that his baroque cinematographic language was nothing less than his elaboration on the perception of life as enigmatic, as something exceeding the artist's (and the spectator's) imagination, which is of course rooted in the director's overarching quest. In the case of Fellini's adaptations, by adhering primarily to what we might call "spirit of the text," Zapponi and Fellini found in the literary text a metaphor for the ineffable. By so doing, they were also able to recreate the text almost entirely, moving in parallel to it in an equitable dialogue that permitted the maximum space for new imaginings.

For this reason, the texts that Fellini and Zapponi considered for adaptations were those that Zapponi himself called *grassi* (fat), which "continue to grow within the imagination of their adapters."[42] Among these books were works such as Dante's *Divina commedia*, Collodi's *Pinocchio*, and Ariosto's *Orlando Furioso*.[43] The choice of adapting Petronius's *Satyricon* was motivated not only by the fact that Zapponi and Fellini had discovered parallels between contemporary culture and Roman civilization, the latter serving as "a powerful and evocative allegory" and "a satire of the world we live in today," but, more important, by the fact that this was a text that had survived only in fragments and that stood for an indefinable reality, allowing for greater invention and play.[44] With *Satyricon*, as Zapponi recalled, the objective was to emphasize the picaresque nature of the story and its narrative gaps, rather than ordering or resolving them: "Petronius's text is badly corrupted, crumbling like a wall, composed of bits and pieces recovered by archeology ... Sudden silences, sentences reeled off by nobodies, people who emerge from obscurity and say their little piece, like the damned speaking from their burning pits in hell. A definite direction for the style: we had to widen the gaps in the text, not bridge them."[45]

It is not surprising, therefore, that critics have equated *Satyricon* to an excavation or a dreaming up of Petronius's text, behaviours that are motivated by the artists' deliberate choices of source text and adaptation strategy. For instance, Alberto Moravia has explained the film as a dream-like, open novel in which the presence of antiquity (and of Petronius's text) is felt but is still not completely intelligible.[46] Along these lines, the critic Bernard F. Dick has written about *Satyricon*'s attempts "to uncover the images beneath the novel, images so historically and archetypically charged that they are more apt to appear in the subtext than in the text."[47] This attitude towards the source text as a subtext is what preserved the capacity to personalize the adaptation, generating an amalgamated product that invites postmodernist interpretations. Owing to Fellini's and Zapponi's adaptation strategies, films such as *Toby Dammit*, *Satyricon*, and *Il Casanova* have often been explained by the scholarly literature as deconstructing traditional representation and narrative formula as well as enacting a patchwork of classical and pop culture.[48]

The "twin neurosis" strategy that Fellini and Zapponi devised together also allowed for the necessary distance from a character such as Casanova, whom Fellini perceived as an unpleasant, verbose, and egocentric exploiter.[49] With his already strong interest in the analysis of the psychology of the abnormal, Zapponi, who demonstrated his deep involvement in this project by going as far as writing a novel inspired by the film, was a significant help to Fellini in approaching and conceptualizing Casanova.[50] According to Zapponi, it was he who advised Fellini to develop the film according to a symbolic interpretative key, namely the idea of a Casanova as a Don Giovanni, a man who is affected by a psychological complex that makes him unable to have mature relationships with women. Zapponi retold the negotiation around the character of Casanova as follows: "I used to propose to him a symbolic loophole: to transform Casanova into a Don Juan, that is, into the allegory of impotence, of the inability to love, of the desire to escape woman ... Federico would object that Casanova, being a real man, a historic persona, could not give himself to emblematic solutions. He was too concrete, too cumbersome. In the end, he chose a compromise: a real Casanova, but one who is the victim of a maternal complex."[51]

Zapponi's suggestions enabled him to identify a thread across the many volumes of Casanova's *Memoirs* to which he and Fellini (and only tangentially with Tonino Guerra) had struggled to relate all along: the monotonous self-legitimizing discourse of a neurotic and fundamentally lonely man. At that point they began to draw freely from the text, but especially creating new scenes that could plastically enact Casanova's psychosis: his awe for mother-like female figures (for example, the giant, the whale, Casanova's mother); and his insane relationship with all other women, swinging from cold and mechanical behaviours to excessively dramatic and unsustainable infatuations. Zapponi was therefore an invaluable consultant to Fellini in clarifying the psychological nature of the protagonists, an influence that may have even extended to La città delle donne – their last and less synergistic partnership – where Snàporaz, not unlike Casanova, is struggling with his complexes within the sphere of the feminine. In fact, it was likely that, during his scouting of a community centre occupied by feminists, Zapponi identified the important sense of "awkwardness" characterizing Snàporaz's relationship to women.[52]

Fellini and Zapponi's partnership ended when the director decided to invest again in Tonino Guerra, with whom he had written Amarcord, a project that Zapponi had tried to discourage, considering it a dead end and a danger to Fellini's artistic development.[53] After their last film together, La città delle donne, Fellini briefly jotted down a dream he had about Zapponi in the spring of 1981, which documents the director's need to replace his screenwriter. In this dream entry Fellini draws a caricature of the writer sweating worriedly and notes: "Leaving Cinecittà (but it was as if I was leaving Via del Babuino), I run into B. Z. [Bernardino Zapponi]. He's overwrought, whimpering, crying, trembling as if he'd been struck by something way beyond his capabilities to handle."[54] In 1983, E la nave va signals the beginning of the last phase of Fellini's career, characterized by a growing sense of marginalization from the contemporary world and a mourning at the gradual death of the poetry and magic of cinema, both on a personal and on a societal level. While in the following years Bernardino Zapponi focused his activity as screenwriter primarily on erotic comedies, Fellini returned to the collaborators who had been connected to some of his best films during the 1970s and earlier, working again with Tonino Guerra and Tullio Pinelli; at the same time, he was exploring new literary exchanges.

Chapter Four

The Poets

Italy's transition from a rural society to a primarily industrial one in the 1950s, and the growing importation of cultural models and values from North America, dramatically transformed the country and its people. The weight of this phenomenon cannot be understated, and historians have described it as nothing less than "the end of the seven or eight millennia of human history that began with the invention of agriculture in the stone age," the end of "the long era when the overwhelming majority of the human race lived by growing food and herding animals."[1] Fellini's generation traversed this period of change in the 1950s, and for many it was a traumatic mixture of an uneasiness and alienation towards the present and a longing for the more familiar world they had experienced during childhood. Not only did such feelings imbue most of Fellini's films from *La dolce vita* on, but also virtually all the writers whom Fellini attracted into his orbit were actively voicing their concerns and nostalgia for the disappearance of a rural world and the appearance of a new, disconcerting one on the horizon. In particular, Fellini's collaborations with poets such as Brunello Rondi, Pier Paolo Pasolini, Tonino Guerra, and Andrea Zanzotto were based for the most part on a common reaction to these sweeping societal changes. Their intersecting perspectives are traceable, however, in different forms of expression including the poetic deployment of music, the presence of animal and feminine images, and the use of pre-grammatical lyrics. With varying weight and continuity, these poets crafted dialogues that could provide linguistic effect, and they served as counsellors in the conceptualization of Fellini's films.

While Pasolini was initially hired as an expert on Roman street slang for *Le notti di Cabiria*, Zanzotto contributed lyrics and dialogues crafted in a pseudo eighteenth-century Venetian language for *Il Casa-nova di Federico Fellini*. Even Guerra, who first joined Fellini for *Amarcord* as a principal screenwriter, enriched this film with several dialogues and lyrics written in the Romagnol dialect. These collaborations were not limited to the linguistic domain; rather these poets – including also Brunello Rondi, who was artistic consultant and collaborator to many screenplays from *La strada* on, contributed, in more or less explicit ways, to the very subject matter of Fellini's cinema.

To enable a better understanding of the fluid nature and the intertex-tual breadth of the artistic relationship between Fellini and these poets and the function of their collaborative partnerships, the practices as-sociated with this type of unconventional screenwriting role need to be explained. Rondi's monograph *Il cinema di Fellini*, an enthusiastic tribute to the director's opus until 1965, remains a precious first-hand account of the modus operandi of this director, besides clarifying what Rondi found valuable in Fellini's films. This volume is also an interesting case of scholarship caught between the canon of auteurist criticism and the desire to account for the experience and knowledge born of the creative exchange. Rondi's book at times negotiates between the celebration of the single author's vision and the description of the endeavours of the other working minds to fully explain the meaning of certain sequences. Rondi used the image of the "filter" to define the role of the collabora-tors on the set, seeing them as passive instruments through which the director's vision could flow and be refined; yet, when speaking of the screenwriters, and especially of himself, Rondi preferred to use words such as "affinity" and "telepathic dialogue."[2] Along these lines, dur-ing an interview, Rondi spoke of a "mysterious" "creative transference" that unconsciously guided him to meet the director's expectations.[3] In the mid-1960s, with the tension growing between Fellini, Flaiano, and Pinelli, the director's relationship with Rondi grew in importance. This is confirmed both privately by letters in which Fellini shares with Rondi his notes about his new films, hoping to receive from him "a dazzling illumination," and publicly by praise for Rondi's "invaluable listening skills" and, in particular, his "overflowing enthusiasm" upon hearing Fellini's first idea for *8½*, which the other screenwriters had received with scepticism.[4]

In his monograph, when describing Fellini's work with the screen-writers, Rondi explains the director's habit of working separately with them, often keeping each in the dark about the work of the others and especially alternating his meetings, with Rondi alone and then with

Flaiano and Pinelli. This practice was likely necessary to avoid the friction existing between two very different writers such as Flaiano and Rondi. Also, it suggests that Fellini would often move forward in his inventive process by comparing his collaborators' differing points of view and testing possible solutions of his own. By having such different personalities on his team of writers and by secretly playing the role of mediator between them, Fellini was evidently able to capitalize on their diverse sensibilities and backgrounds, thus enriching and strengthening his central idea and the overall philosophic and aesthetic texture of his films.

The function of Rondi in Fellini's team was clearly different from that of Pinelli and Flaiano, as it was for the other poetic consultants addressed in this chapter. When it came to defining the role of the artistic consultant or collaborator to the screenplay, Rondi underscored the importance of his activity during the brainstorming phase of Fellini's new films. This phase took place through letters or preferably during drives in the car around Rome, when Rondi could cater best to Fellini's legendary openness and curiosity, acting as an intellectual support and a necessary sounding board, a thinker even before being a writer. Even when Rondi was hired as screenwriter for *La dolce vita* and *8½*, he served, unlike Pinelli and Flaiano and as reported by Kezich, like a *sceneggiatore da campo* (set screenwriter), simultaneously merging together the functions of artistic consultant and writer: "In the troupe many do not understand the true function of Fellini's intellectual support, [Brunello] Rondi, who remains at the edge of the set and occasionally hands the director sheets of foolscap containing nervous and frenzied calligraphy. Besides editing the changes that Fellini's subversive improvisation progressively brings to the dialogue, Brunello hands him suggestions, notes, reflections. He is a sort of interlocutor to whom Fellini speaks during the shooting pauses when he wants to debrief what he has been shooting and what there is left to do."[5]

A similar role was played by Tonino Guerra, whose unconventional approach to screenwriting has become known in the context of his numerous and important collaborations with directors such as Michelangelo Antonioni, Francesco Rosi (1922–), Vittorio and Paolo Taviani (1929– and 1931–), and Andrei Tarkovsky (1932–86). Tonino Guerra's work with Antonioni, beginning with *L'avventura* (1959) and continuing with every one of Antonioni's major accomplishments except *Professione: Reporter* (*The Passenger*), was as equally deep and long lasting as the one shared with Fellini. A screenwriter such as Guerra actively participated in the constant shifting process of creative invention before and during shooting, acting as a sort of "psychoanalyst or confessor" for the director, as Riikka Pelo has put it, "to relieve and challenge buried, unconscious images." In her study of Guerra's collaboration with Tarkovsky, Pelo states that the work of a screenwriter such as Guerra was to elaborate the material "into meaningful constellations, structural and syntactic units and a moving image narrative, into a 'language' of cinema, without shattering the often very abstract and fragile core ideas and the mystery involved in their creation."[6] Such subtle organic dynamics of inspiration find confirmation in gender-centred perspectives on collaborations, such as those proposed by Rebecca West. In her defence of Tonino Guerra's authorial importance as a screenwriter, West has used familial analogies in which the screenwriter occupies, in opposition to the "traditionally empowered 'paternal' figure," a "more invisible, nurturing, and supportive 'maternal' figure." For West, Guerra was the quintessential representative of this type of maternal writer, who, with his decision to be both a dialect poet and a screenwriter, remained marginalized in cultural and authorial spheres and refused to enter the struggle for power.[7] At the same time, though, Guerra was a frugal but penetrating storyteller, as Vittorio Taviani recalled in connection with their collaboration on the film *Kaos*: "Tonino entered into the film with small things – small for narrative quantity but that are actually deep – he has unravelled many knots. Guerra is also a great builder. At the level of the structure he has ideas that are very simple and clear."[8] When Guerra was working with Fellini, his activity also unfolded at a very deep level of conceptualization, as shown by the subtle contributions described in this chapter.

Even the collaborative exchanges with Pasolini and Zanzotto privileged the screenwriter as a poetic consultant able to participate in a fluid dialogue, clarifying philosophic nodes and generating new images. Fellini's work with Pasolini, subtle yet crucially instrumental, began as they explored together the impoverished outskirts of Rome during the late 1950s, and their many conversations continued for several years later in private and public spheres. In the instance of Zanzotto, his collaborative contributions during the planning and making of *Il Casanova* came mostly through letters (owing to the poet's reclusive lifestyle). Both Pasolini and Zanzotto aided Fellini with rational precision and intellectual coherence, which he likely needed in order to contain his magmatic inspiration, especially when it came to manifesting the archetypical weight of maternal symbols. During an interview

Fellini remembered the intellectual rigour that he pursued in his con-versations with Pasolini: "There was eagerness, attentiveness, and a vivid and inexhaustible curiosity in his eyes. There was a quality that I have always appreciated in him, namely his availability to absorb, to assimilate, to transform, but at the same time to maintain in his mind a very precise and attentive laboratory in which the artist's creation was screened and judged (generally with approval). He was at once a creator and a very acute and implacable critic of his own work. This quality of inexhaustible critical presence is one that I lack completely."[9] Conversely, Pasolini once emphasized Fellini's chaotic and shifting imagination: "Fellini's human form is constantly shaky, always rear-ranging itself. It is like a large blob that might resemble a polyp, an amoeba enlarged under the microscope, an Aztec ruin, or a drowned cat, according to fancy. Only a soft blow of west wind or a veering of the car is sufficient to transform the shapeless blob into a man. He is an extremely tender, intelligent, cunning, and frightened man."[10]

Along these lines, in one of his letters to Fellini, Zanzotto acknowl-edged having the sensation of being "overly rational" in comparison to "the unpredictable and rich visual creativity" of the director.[11] As did Rondi and Pasolini, Zanzotto spoke of Fellini's extraordinary curiosity and capacity for observing human nature and, in a poem dedicated to him, described the director as an "eager alien spy," "lying in wait at the point where the target is crowded with the human being's de-sires."[12] In considering the details of Fellini's collaborations with Paso-lini and Zanzotto, and also with the other poet screenwriters, one must therefore remember that the multifarious and chaotic wealth of Fellini's genius was the other side of the coin of his extraordinary receptivity. The latter is indeed a quality celebrated by most of his collaborators, friends, and biographers and stands ultimately as the human and artis-tic trademark of Fellini, a characteristic that made the unstructured col-laborations with the poet-screenwriters especially productive for him.

An Organic Mind: Brunello Rondi from *La dolce vita* to *Prova d'orchestra*

Federico Fellini and Brunello Rondi met for the first time when they were working side by side as screenwriters on two of Roberto Ros-sellini's most religiously minded films, *Francesco giullare di Dio* and *Europa 51*.[13] Their role was mainly that of screenwriters; however, Ros-sellini's loose and flexible directorial style allowed them to occasionally help as assistant directors. Rondi first joined Fellini's team in 1954 as an "artistic collaborator" on *La strada*, a role that he continued for *Il bidone* and *Le notti di Cabiria*; from 1959 to 1965 Rondi was listed as the screenwriter of *La dolce vita*, *8½*, and *Giulietta degli spiriti*, not without discontent from Flaiano, who had an instinctive aversion for the artsy and prophetic pose that he observed in Rondi. The dislike coming from Flaiano might also have been caused by Rondi's close affiliation with Pier Paolo Pasolini, who had encouraged Rondi's poetry and whom Rondi used as a role model, for both his eclecticism and his poetic exploration of eroticism.

In the early 1940s Brunello Rondi was influenced by his brother Gian Luigi Rondi (1921–), who had been a prominent film critic since the end of the war and had been an active member of the Christian Left.[14] As a result, Brunello became associated with the Catholic Communist Movement, an anti-fascist and anti-Nazi group that embraced Marxism as a path to freedom and to the construction of a new historical reality and socialist state. During the occupation of Rome the movement, led by Adriano Ossicini (1920–), Antonio Tatò (1921–92), and Franco Rodano (1920–83), organized partisan groups and clandestine publications such as *Voce operaia* (The worker's voice) and the booklet *Il comunismo e i cattolici* (Communism and Catholics).[15] In Brunello Rondi's thinking, Marxism and Christianity were fused together and consequently he gave a spiritual meaning to Marxist ideas.

Across his extremely eclectic activity as a scholar, poet, screenwriter, playwright, and film director, Brunello Rondi expressed, at times with redundancy, his syncretic philosophy, which early on he labelled "organic," reinterpreting the Gramscian notion of the "organic intellectual" in a more spiritual sense. As was the case with Antonio Gramsci (1891–1937), Rondi believed that the new proletarian "intellectual" must know the real struggles of his class and party and therefore become an expression of collective conscience and a cultural force of change.[16] Rondi took from Gramsci the value of human artistry as an agent for social change; however, in his writings Rondi – in contrast to Gramsci – assessed the social benefit of art for its capacity to respond to spiritual needs, and the word *organic* became for Rondi not an idea for political activity, as it was originally, but a metaphysical ideal.

In the wave of the enthusiasm spurred by his early work in cinema, Brunello Rondi wrote *Il neorealismo italiano* (1956, Italian neo-realism), with a preface by Roberto Rossellini, and *Cinema e realtà* (1957, Cinema and reality), with a preface by Federico Fellini. In these long essays Rondi understood neo-realism's call for the moral regeneration of the collective consciousness as a way out of the general existential crisis of modernity. For example, he reinterpreted the Marxist concept of *coralità* (chorality) from the point of view of his study of music history, seeing it more as the harmonic fulfilment of an individual's vital impulses in relationship with other human beings as well as with nature, than as the expression of a collective political agency. In introducing one of his poetry collections, Rondi expresses his credo with prophetic fervour: "I perceive reality as an organism of relationships that entangle us from every side, and fuse us within a concrete chorality, which is History and Nature ... I am interested in searching for and saying through poetry that which today, and especially tomorrow, will be the 'land of man,' which is his most extreme organic prospect ... This is my 'Happy Land': the new world of organic, humanistic, and natural relationships."[17]

The organization of his ideas went hand in hand with his poetic med-itations on the overarching theme of human relationships and erotic love, as shown in his poems from volumes such as *La giovane Italia* (1957, Young Italy), *Amore fedele* (1958, Faithful love), and *La terra felice* (1961, Merry land) and developed within the philosophic framework of treatises such as *Esistenza e relazione* (1958, Existence and relationship) and *Esistenza ed essere* (1960, Existence and being). However, it is in his treatises on the evolution of Western classical music – *Il ritmo moderno* (1949, Modern rhythm), *La musica contemporanea* (1952, Contemporary music), *Il cammino della musica d'oggi e l'esperienza elettronica* (1959, The journey of today's music and the electronic experience) – that Rondi best merged philosophy and art. Music and musical analogies return as heuristic principles in all areas of his versatile endeavours, including his work with Fellini. Taken as a whole, the objective of Rondi's 1965 monograph on Fellini, already quoted above, weaves together a for-midable and overwhelming eulogy of Fellini's creative talent. Rondi's enthusiasm was certainly sincere, but the glorification of Fellini goes hand in hand with the ennoblement of Rondi's own ideas. Rondi's de-sire was to turn Fellini into a monument of his own organic philosophy, thus reflecting splendour on Rondi's work, as can be inferred from the following passage:

I have seen few men capable, as Fellini is, of instinctually and joyously blending ... with the crowd of the 'others,' with the people of the streets, even in the noisiest and most violent occasions ... Fellini likes humanity with its dense and colourful entanglements, its power and subtle flux; and he likes it in its most blissful (and distressing) vital aspect ... as an obscure, generous mystery of presences ... The energy with which Fellini almost violently searches and builds himself is almost moving. With this energy he yearns for an authentic life, which is the exact and harmonious development of the human person towards the richest authenticity, found and recognized in the context of a harmonious and renewed society and, I would say, on the side of a new chorality.[18]

As it happened, a consultant such as Brunello Rondi became especially essential to Fellini during the time of heated political and moral debate surrounding *La strada*, and especially when, in 1955, Massimo Mida (aka Massimo Mida Puccini) published a public letter to Fellini in the Communist magazine *Il contemporaneo*, accusing *La strada* of lacking social significance and of dangerously departing from the ethical path of neorealism. Interestingly, the content of Fellini's letter of reply reiterates the relational existentialism that Rondi had begun theorizing, following in the footsteps of thinkers such as Enzo Paci (1911–76) and Ugo Spirito (1896–1979), and is filled with the erudite references (for example, Aragon, Doniol-Valcroze, Sadoul, Mounier, Engels) that Rondi would likely be aware of and use.[19] Furthermore, this letter presented elements that reoccur in Rondi's heterogeneous writings: the emphasis placed on solitude and incommunicability as the main cause of man's modern crisis, the conception of realism as being the most beneficial form of art, and the prophetic anticipation of a new and better humanity. Rondi's interest in the philosophic implications of human relationships especially between man and woman must have proved valuable to Fellini during the making of *La strada*, which is entirely based on the deepening of the spiritual significance of Gelsomina and Zampanò's relationship. Moreover, at that time and thanks to Brunello Rondi, Fellini became acquainted with the Jesuit father Angelo Arpa, another lifelong intellectual consultant and invaluable support to the director, especially at delicate times in his relationship with the Church.[20]

For an intimate glimpse into the impact of Rondi's intellectual strength and support on Fellini, *Il libro dei sogni* also becomes relevant. Rondi appeared in Fellini's entry dated 12 November 1961 as the top student of his class, easily and quickly passing an exam, which is likely associated to the questioning that Fellini endured in that period during the religious and political polemics triggered by his films (see figure 6):

Figure 6. Fellini's rendition of a dream with reference to Brunello Rondi, 12 November 1961

A written exam! Stuck at a school desk at night in a piazza in Florence, dawdling, hoping that things will get better on their own because the difficulty of the first essay topic that has been assigned is too much for me. Brunello Rondi has already finished; he gets up, turns in his exam notebook, and takes off. The second subject is extremely difficult for me as well. The truth is that I don't know a thing; not only that, but I don't care either. This was often my attitude even when I was a young boy and really went to school. The professor walks away, and I beg the girl at the desk near mine to help me ... The girl is really nice and she immediately reads to me what she's written.[21]

Peter Bondanella discusses this dream in his monograph and identifies it as one in which Fellini harbours doubts about his creative powers.[22] The dream entry, however, is the director's affirmation of the autonomy of his imaginative inventiveness, and his uncertainty, if any, lies not in his creativity but in his intellectual faculties, especially in comparison to those of Rondi. Occurring after *La dolce vita*, this dream likely encapsulates Fellini's frustration at being examined and forced to articulate in countless interviews the meaning and position behind his work. It is not surprising, therefore, that Brunello Rondi was first considered as an actor to play the role of the critic in *8½* (though it was eventually played by the French writer Jean Rougeoul).[23] As the drawing accompanying the text shows, the examination takes place in the centre of a square, specifically the Piazza del Duomo of Florence. The dominating presence of the basilica, set at the teacher's place in front of the students' desks, suggests the interrogating and judging eye of the Vatican, by which Fellini was indeed being severely evaluated after *La dolce vita*. In Fellini's class (and, in a sense, his artistic team) Rondi was the one who could answer all the posed questions. In the dream's narrative Fellini appears to doubt his intellectual capacities or has little interest in grappling with problems that are solved through rationality and logic. But he does not doubt his creative muse, the girl smiling next to him: with her, he has a special rapport, and that is all he cares about.

The character of Steiner in *La dolce vita* presents the ideal opportunity to trace the intersections of differing authorial influences. As mentioned in chapter 1, Pinelli had prepared the scene of the evening party at Steiner's house as a fresco of perfect familial serenity, which was supposed to end abruptly with Steiner's infanticide and suicide, thus raising the ghost of desperation and emptiness that had been lurking beneath an overly rationalized and self-absorbed life. This plan was thwarted by Fellini's insertion of a collection of questionable artists and intellectuals orbiting around Steiner, which for Pinelli had the unwanted effect of assuaging the tragic actions that led Steiner to murder his children and kill himself. This change by Fellini, however, was functional to Brunello Rondi's idea of Steiner and bears the mark of the collaborator's particular vision for the character. The words that Rondi once used in explaining his interpretation of the Steiner episode provide a number of informative and palpable clues to the way he intended to develop his own philosophic discourse through this character:

> Fellini well understood the idea that Steiner is a character who has intuited a new and original harmony of relationships, almost as the glimmerings of a new world ... Steiner's fate is that of all disarmed prophets ... perhaps he is the only character that endures beyond *la dolce vita* ... Therefore, it quickly seemed necessary to Fellini, and to us, to build in Steiner's home and in his friendships the quality of a positive solitude, one rich in intuition and with a happiness that goes beyond worn-out and conventional terms. We imagined an ambiance of tranquil intelligence, of subtle but not cerebral intimacy, and one not of pretentious culture. Steiner has his guests listen to electronic music and then to the sounds of nature from his record player, evoking around this almost initiatory gathering the strong and sweet face of nature as it manifests itself through its voices, through its presence that can either disperse or elevate man ... In this way we built the 'evening at Steiner's home' as a sort of anxious vigil and like the eve of a new world, intuited by individuals who, however, lack the weapons and the concrete instruments necessary to build it; individuals who also reflect, at least halfway, the pale face of decadence ... It was in this twofold sense that we imagined that 'rediscovery' of the sounds of nature: as Steiner's act of love for all things and for reality and as his guests' moment of profound awe, as if they had lost, from time immemorial, their capacity to see and listen to the voice and to the concrete and intimate face of nature.[24]

In contrast to the idea that Pinelli conceived for the character of Steiner, Rondi envisioned him – using the image of the "disarmed prophet" that Niccolò Machiavelli (1469–1527) had coined for Girolamo Savonarola (1452–98) – as the only one who seems to have found the secret to serenity, a martyr, a positive yet tragic character, whose solitude and approaching demise are rendered visible during his attempts to reawaken the party's guests with his poetry about the simple things of life.[25] Well before the scathing remarks made by the writer Alberto Arbasino (1930–) targeting this sequence of the film, Rondi was aware of the helplessness of the intellectual and artistic figures assembled in Steiner's presence, who are overtaken by the desire for a more harmonious life and world but are miserably incapable of creating it.[26] The idea of Steiner as the martyr of Rondi's organic credo, who was supposed to stand out from the mediocre world of *La dolce vita* by pursuing an ideal of fulfilment through relationships, is further clarified during one of Steiner's monologues in the film: "It would be necessary to live outside passions, beyond sentiments, beyond the feeling of harmony and the enchanted world that exists within a successful work of art. It would be necessary to be able to love each other so much, to live outside of time, detached, detached."

The authorial interplay behind Steiner explains the complex and, at times, contradictory nature of this character, who was presented on the one hand as a lost soul, in line with Pinelli, and on the other hand as a martyr, in line with Rondi. In addition, Fellini's comical directorial hand finally portrayed the community of helpless and somewhat squalid artists around Steiner in his usual caricaturist manner. Fellini inserted Rondi's artistic community and ideals but with a touch of ridicule not envisioned by Rondi, shifting instead, much to Pinelli's dislike, the cause of the suicide away from Steiner and to the superficiality of his social world. In fact, in choosing the cast for this scene, the director selected artists like Anna Salvatori (1923–78) and Leonida Rèpaci (1898–1985) who had been fixtures of the mundane life of post-war Italy and whose talent, especially in the case of the latter, had been put into question.[27] At the same time, Fellini kept Pinelli's tragic ending, thus questioning and undermining, to Rondi's dislike, the prophetic stance of Steiner's credo.[28] In conclusion, the party at Steiner's house was modified by Fellini to neutralize the unwanted influence of both writers: at once softening the inexplicable tragedy instilled by Pinelli and lowering with ridicule the heroic intellectual figure conceived by Rondi. This case is a good example of the way in which Fellini cunningly employed differing contributions, thus offsetting the qualities that he appreciated less in his writers.

The musical discourse that Rondi develops through the character of Steiner follows the specific coordinates of his treatises on the evolution of Western classical music, culminating in the praise of electronic music. Rondi interpreted contemporary classical music through an existentialist lens, praising the courage of composers such as Igor

Stravinsky (1882–1971), who had faced and voiced the fragmentation, isolation, and disillusionment inherent in modern life.[29] To him, as to many others, Schoenberg's dodecaphonic language and the new forms of orchestral music that disrupt the laws of tonality expressed the utter scattering of the human being's transcendental possibilities and were therefore the highest representation of the crisis of modern man. As early as 1949, Rondi wrote that contemporary classical music "was the echo of a disjoined society, of a metaphysics that has been consumed and corrupted, of an individuality inscribed within an elevated nucleus of crisis."[30] Rondi declared his optimistic view that the times were ready and that it was now possible to find a solution to such crisis. Together with Italian existentialist philosophers such as Nicola Abbagnano (1901–90), Rondi believed that existentialism was now outdated and limiting to the mind, and he applied this idea to the history of music, indicating what, in his opinion, might be the route to the achievement of a new metaphysical harmony. Even though Rondi knew that "Bach's music represents the total victory over time" and that "modern music represents the total defeat under time," he did not propose a nostalgic resurrection of the immaculate height of tonal harmony but instead praised the human and cultural potentials of electronic music.[31]

Rondi often described the instrument of the organ as a symbol of the polyphony of the past, the emblem of a bygone harmonious relationship with the cosmos. In the film *La dolce vita*, Steiner meets Marcello in a church and introduces the organ with these words: "We are no longer used to listening to these sounds. What a mysterious voice, it seems to arise from the bowels of the earth." After the playful and painful contrast between the church's sacred space and the chaotic jazz piece that Steiner improvises for a moment, he then dives into Bach's celebrated beginning of the "Toccata and Fugue in D minor." The music is like "the gold from a mine: very deep, subterranean, blinding" and annihilates Marcello with the sound of "a very ancient bell," as Rondi wrote, bringing to light his distance from the solemnity of such holy fullness and at the same time ominously prefiguring his spiritual perdition.[32] The final version of the script reads: "Marcello is engrossed, as if oppressed by that wave of sound, which is precise and evocative of a mystery that he is not prepared to solve and which fills him with anxiety."[33] Both Steiner and Marcello know that the sacredness that music embodies, arising from the depth of time, does not belong to their world and cannot be sustained for long.

Rondi considered electronic music to be the future of the European classical music tradition and saw it as a possible way to overcome dodecaphonic fragmentation and incommunicability and embody a more vital rapport with life. For the same reason that made electronic music a means to reconstruct a new modern "duration," a new foundation from which to regain harmonious relationships, Rondi saw electronic music as a new instrument for research into reality. In his essay on electronic music he states that "the opening of the musical soul unto the spaces of electronic sound" consists of "a plunge into pure matter, into the still uncategorized infinitely coloured and variegated myriad of noises and pure sounds, where sonority has the objective and foreign richness of an unexplored mine."[34] Moreover, "the music that is constructed with already known material places the listener into contact with references of reality, with something alive and familiar, while the music built upon new material throws one into a totally unknown and unfamiliar state."[35] The novel and uncoded sound structures of electronic music were to him an ideal probe into the unknown, certainly more so than the sentimental and comfortable scores written by Nino Rota.

Unlike Brunello Rondi's electronic selections, the rarefied simplicity of the music that Nino Rota created for Fellini's films did not point to or try to contend with the fragmentation of the crisis of modern man. Rota's isolation within the learned musical scene of his time, as well as the marginalization of his music by critics, was due to the apparent backwardness of his compositional style. Rota's music did not reject tonality, and his sensibility did not share the sense of existential disorientation expressed by most of the composers of his time. Nino Rota was part of a late and still tonal Puccinian and realist tradition, which he was able to integrate within a vast array of popular and modern forms. Since Rota's early studies, his interest had been geared towards the origin of symphonic music, and his dissertation examined Gioseffo Zarlino's *Delle istituzioni armoniche*, the 1585 text that summarized and codified the aspects of music that Renaissance composers considered beautiful and ugly and that provided the basis of the European musical culture after that time. Indeed, one can conclude that Rota's apparent backwardness did not contrast with Fellini's sensibility, because the nostalgic immediacy of harmonic tonal music evoked the anti-modernist candour that was so dear to this director, his longing for a nucleus of metaphysical coherence, for a "primordial mechanism" springing "from sources so distant in time as to be historically unidentifiable ... from the mysterious places where all keys are still scrambled," as Andrea Zanzotto once put it.[36] The universal and timeless virtues of Rota's music also depend on the composer's affinity for early sacred music, in turn linked to his fervent interest in esotericism. Rondi's influence on the musical discourse of Fellini's films was likewise oriented towards a quest for a harmonious relationship with the world – not through a nostalgic adherence to the harmonic tradition but by embracing the experimental developments of contemporary Western music and going beyond the realm of tonal harmony and traditional sounds.

During the scene at the party at his house in *La dolce vita*, Steiner shyly discloses his secret experiments with music to recapture the perfection of Bach's cosmic harmony through the recordings he has made of the sounds of nature – thunder, rain, birds, wind – reorganized in a new man-made electronic order. The entire scene of Steiner's experiment with sound is absent from the shooting script, a fact that further testifies to the major changes that this part underwent during filming with Rondi working as screenwriter on set. In his description of Steiner (quoted earlier in this chapter) and of this scene Rondi explicitly spoke of an "electronic music" using sounds from nature.[37] Steiner's sound experiments recall the aesthetic play with sound recording and tape manipulation by Pierre Schaeffer (1910–95). Pierre Schaeffer is the inventor of the movement referred to as Musique Concrète, which became known in France and the rest of Europe in the 1950s and influenced electronic composers such as Tod Dockstader (1932–), whose creations were also employed in the soundtrack of *Satyricon*. Steiner, with his own tape manipulations, is enacting Rondi's programme and attempting to find a new synthesis between man and nature: "Far from being an intellectual trick, it is a moment of obscurely religious emotion. The noises and the sounds of pure objectivity (almost as manifestations of the pure Being of which Heidegger speaks) pass – as if through astral distances – on the faces of these creatures lost in their abstract and personal mythologies."[38]

Rondi pursued this philosophic discourse, often through music, in the films that he directed as well. *Velluto nero* (1976, Emmanuelle in Egypt) is an example of Rondi's search for a hybrid form of electronic and natural music and a first example of his artistic struggle within the erotic genre. *Velluto nero* contains a revisiting of the community at Steiner's house in the 1970s. Here a group of women and men, moved by a desire for a fuller and freer life experience, find themselves in Egypt, seeking more vital mystical and sexual bonds through the re-enactment of pharaonic myths. A sequence from this film stages an initiatory ritual in which a group of aspiring artists and intellectuals is attempting to generate a sense of harmony among themselves and with the world through music and nature but also, and much more explicitly than in *La dolce vita*, through sex. For *Velluto nero* Rondi likely had the composer (Alberto Baldan Bembo) incorporate in the banal ambiance music that was typical of the erotic genre a mélange of electronic sounds, voices, and folk songs that could suggest the mixture of past and present, man and nature.

After several years of absence from Fellini's team, Brunello Rondi was called to assist with the screenplay of *Prova d'orchestra*. The musical discourse that Rondi relates to the expression and realization of his organic philosophy, as it has been traced throughout this section, clarifies the link existing in this film between a broader philosophic discourse about human nature and an apology for a humble dedication to absolute artistic values. In fact, the presence of Rondi within this film unites apparently opposed scholarly interpretations of this film, such as that by Peter Bondanella, who finds there the drama of a failed attempt to harmonize "the forces of reason and the demands of the instincts" and to manifest the "redemptive power of art"; and more recently that of Andrea Minuz, who, viewing *Prova d'orchestra* as a "public dream" with numerous political ramifications, finds in the film a portrait of the chaos of late 1970s Italy and the deterioration of the Platonic ideal of social order.[39] Speaking about his participation in this film, Rondi hinted at his musicological expertise as one of the main reasons for his role: "I am a technical expert of music; therefore, one can intuit how passionate I was about the discourse relating to the orchestra."[40] Among the many statements that could be extracted from Rondi's earlier musicological essays, the one below offers a good example of the way in which he used musical production to explain social and cultural well-being:

> Contemporary music is rich with rhythm because it is music in crisis, because it knows the crisis of man. The man in peace, the civil man, gave up all his rhythm, which is no longer present as strength; the new strength consists of towers of melodies. In this harmonious music all numbers of the universe are directed and resolved in such a way that they appear to be a singular number. All music in crisis is made of rhythm: it is explorative music, and it brings what is hidden out into the sun. A rhythm exudes from all accents and fibres of the discourse, and this rhythm no longer leads them; it is a great protest that looks like a great dynamic.[41]

A perspective that situates the musical expression of the crises of modern times within the predominance of rhythm over harmony is especially relevant to *Prova d'orchestra*, in which the contrast between the towering force of harmony and the disjointed explosion of rhythm is a central musical and narrative dynamic.

In the final part of the film, the contrast between rhythm and harmony surfaces strongly, as the protest of the musicians finds its musical analogy in an entanglement of beats, at least until a "dark, abstract, metaphysical" demolition ball hits the oratorio, re-establishing a sense of order, which in turn quickly degenerates into a new atmosphere of dictatorship as the film comes to a close.[42] However, this contrast was to be revealed from the very beginning of the film; a working draft of the script indicates that opening titles were to appear against a soundscape made of "a chaotic and disjointed collection of extremely violent sounds, music, and events taken from the news of today," expressing the "nightmarish mixture of the delirious dimension of an absurd universe."[43] The inability to sustain musical harmony is the inability to follow universal and ex parte codes where "we are at once conductors and the conducted" and where "the orchestra finally expresses all of its happiness" and one can hear "its unmistakable sonorous explosion."[44] The communicative and interpersonal success represented by this view of harmony coalesces fully with Rondi's philosophic and aesthetic ambitions.

The film ends on the brink of a greater catastrophe, and Rondi's vision for the establishment of new harmonic relationships ushered in by a new type of organic music and art is no longer in sight. The body of the harp player found among the ruins is clearly symbolic of such loss. After ten years of failing to express his vision as art film director, culminating in the questionable results of his erotic cinema, Brunello Rondi had lost much of his confidence in the possible existence of a new art for a new organic society. In line with the pessimist streak running throughout his volume of theatre criticism, *Il nuovo teatro* (1979, The new theatre), which was published the same year and emphasized the crisis of human relationships in modern society and theatre's possible therapeutic role, *Prova d'orchestra* is also an expression of Rondi's disappointed philosophic and artistic idealism. In spite of this, Rondi's presence continued to aid Fellini's cinema, especially in his next film, *La città delle donne*, also bringing to it, as will be shown later, a wiser and less euphoric understanding born from the revision of his positions and from his unfortunate experiments with erotic cinema.

You Are My Labyrinth: The Poetic Brotherhood
with Pier Paolo Pasolini

In 1956 Pier Paolo Pasolini was invited by Fellini to collaborate on his new film *Le notti di Cabiria*.[45] At first it seemed that his responsibility would be limited to that of linguistic consultant for the dialogues in Roman slang. Pasolini's eagerness to contribute, however, surpassed the director's expectations. As Fellini's remembered, "I invited him to collaborate on the dialogue for *Le notti di Cabiria* because nobody who was writing for the cinema at the time had his same ear for the dialect of the Roman slum. I had asked him for a contribution of about ten pages, and he sent me forty pages."[46] Besides editing the dialogues, Pasolini went on to become a close consultant to the director, a sort of personal guide through the *borgate* of Rome, as Fellini once recalled:

> I travelled with him [Pasolini] through neighbourhoods immersed in a disturbing silence. These hellish parts of town had suggestive names reminiscent of medieval China: Infernetto, Tiburtino III, Cessati Spiriti. He led me there as if he were Virgil and Charon fused; he had the appearance of both; but he also resembled a sheriff, a little sheriff who was checking out localities familiar to him. He enjoyed observing my distress; he stood there with the smile of one who has already seen much more, much worse, and who wished that even worse events had unfolded before us to satisfy his tourist-guest friend. Regardless of what could have happened, he was there to explain and to defend you – the mysterious sheriff. Once in a while – out of certain windows, doors, or dark corners – surprising presences would appear: fellows that he was pleased to introduce to me as if we had been in the Amazon among fantastic, wild, and ancient beings.[47]

In this curious western-like re-enactment of a Dantesque Hell, Pasolini is both protective and sadistic, both tainted and at the same time somehow above the foreign and potentially hostile environment.[48] With an eye for similar fantastic possibilities, Fellini had enjoyed reading Pasolini's controversial novel on the youth of the Roman slums, *Ragazzi di vita* (1955, *The Ragazzi*), which was the reason for their initial contact. In this novel Pasolini explores the meanderings of his young protagonists in order to voice their fragility as well as their vitality in the midst of the changes that Italy underwent after the Second World War. Pasolini's capacity to recreate in a realistic and lyrical fashion the life of a group of Roman boys impressed Fellini, inspiring him with the prospect of exploring a little-known realm ripe with universal significance, in which desperation and grace coexisted: "Naturally I fell in love with the book [*Ragazzi di vita*], for its clear expressive style, for its courageous descriptions of Roman street urchins. I liked it to the point that I invented a story about a band of homeless boys who occupied an entire building in the outskirts of Rome. I wanted to focus on the strange and virtually telepathic means of communication that existed among them. It was a film project influenced by Pasolini's novel and by Buñuel's *Los olvidados*, and it is one of thousands of projects that I have set aside."[49]

The mention of Luis Buñuel's 1950 film about the children living in the streets of Mexico City, a special case of the cinematic blending of social realism and surrealism, foreshadows an interest in researching a totally new world that was kept alive in the secret dimension of youth, a theme so dear to Fellini. The examples in Fellini's films where children receive the full attention of the camera and are regarded as special beings to be watched and observed closely, beings who are abundant with revelations, are too many to enumerate, but it suffices here to bring to mind a few characters, such as the young station worker in *I vitelloni*, Osvaldo in *La strada*, the schoolboy playing the flute at the end of *8½*, and adventure with the circus in *I clowns*. In another interview Fellini further explained his interest in the project involving children that was inspired in part by *Ragazzi di vita*:

The film that I regret the most not having made – but which is practically impossible to make – is a story about thirty children, two or three years of age, who live in a large building in the outskirts of the city. I am attracted by the mysterious telepathic communications among children, the looks that they exchange when they bump into each other in the stairways or on the landings of the tenement, when they are behind a door or inside a cradle, or when they are held in someone's hand like bundles of fresh salad. The film would represent the life of a community seen and conceived entirely through the eyes of children, with stories of all-consuming love, of hatred and unhappiness, spent on staircases, access ways, yards. The peace of the community would last only until the children are eventually caught like hares and brought to school, and there, from the very first day, they are stripped of their freedom. Among all of my stalled projects, this one, together with *Mastorna*, stares at me with reprobation. It could be a very moving and comical film. These little guys are to me repositories of great riches; they have a small and immense safe-box inside their heads, hearts, bellies, filled with secrets that will gradually vanish.[50]

In the end, however, little of this will transpire in *Le notti di Cabiria*, except a fleeting but eloquent image of a group of children playing, high up on a gigantic metallic grid near Cabiria's shackles, far from the city's centre, symbolically expressing the "telepathic" network among them.

When he met Fellini, Pasolini was relatively new to the Roman art scene. He arrived with his first critically recognized collection of poetry, *La meglio gioventù* (1954, *The Best of Youth*), most of which was written in the Friulan dialect of Casarsa, his hometown in the northeastern part of Italy, where he was forced to leave his teaching job because of the scandal caused by his discovered homosexuality. In 1950 he moved to Rome, and until 1954 he taught and lived in Ponte Mammolo, one of the poorest areas on the outskirts of the city, near the prison of Rebibbia. The novel *Ragazzi di vita* was an attempt to bring awareness to the human reality of the lower classes who were living in the pauperized districts of Rome and to reflect on the people who were excluded from the economic miracle that was so celebrated at the time by the Italian middle class. In this novel, as in most of Pasolini's works, a political and social concern is combined with a lyrical feeling that celebrates the spontaneity and innocence of such marginalized individuals. In spite of their derogatory language, violent behaviour, and association with prostitution, theft, and other criminal activities, the destitute of Rome became tragic heroes in Pasolini's writing, which, however, led to accusations of obscenity and censorship of his work.

Franco Zabagli's careful philological reconstruction of Pasolini's work for *Le notti di Cabiria* has already led to the revelation of a number of significant collaborative dynamics; in the subsequent pages, the already sizeable literature on a number of elements of their minor collaboration serves as the basis for a broader comparison of the two artists, which is especially heuristic in understanding the fundamentals of their respective thought and work and, more importantly, the creative function of their exchange.[51]

Pasolini received a completed first draft of *Le notti di Cabiria* and provided his sociological and linguistic expertise to identify any inconsistencies in the behaviours, appearances, and speech of the story's prostitutes, pimps, and common people. During the revision process of the screenplay Pasolini did not restrain himself from proposing narrative and poetic solutions for the story as a whole and even single-handedly wrote a few scenes, most of which were excluded from the final screenplay and film product. Pasolini's adjustments for the opening sequence of "Alla passeggiata archeologica" (The promenade at the archaeological site) were geared to give a sense of the verbal and physical aggression of the prostitutes, emphasizing the peer pressure towards the violence that governed the world of the *borgate*. Pasolini's primary concern during the collaboration with the level of environmental realism has been emphasized by previous scholarship, in particular by Victoria Tillson, who has drawn a link to Auerbach's *Mimesis* (which was a central source for Pasolini's work at the time) and also proposed a number of hypothetical Dantean correlations among Pasolini's novels and *Le notti di Cabiria*.[52] To be sure, in his revisions Pasolini not only gave realistic coherence to the characters linguistically by adding several morphological and lexical corrections throughout the screenplay, but also tried to show sociologically how the bestial state of the characters resulted from the harsh world that surrounded them. For example, the resentment between Cabiria and her competitor Matilde leads to a fight that is instigated by youth walking by. Referring to the violent struggle between two male lions over a lioness that occurred at a circus in Rome in 1956, one young man says, "They look like Tarzan and Tobruk, the two lions of the Togni circus!"[53] A similar pattern is also expressed by the episode of "La corsa pazza" (The crazy race), which, according to Zabagli, Pasolini independently wrote in order to bridge the sequence at the actor's house with that of the visit to the sanctuary.[54] In this scene two young hustlers pick up Cabiria and Matilde in a truck and progressively become drunker and more aggressive towards them. After being forced to assist them in unloading stolen goods, the women are then driven to a squalid country road outside the city, taken advantage of sexually, and abandoned. This sequence would certainly have been the grimmest part of the film, conveying intensely the dangers of the life of a streetwalker, yet certainly clashing with Fellini's sensibility. Moreover, Pasolini's suggestions were also cut from the final screenplay owing to Flaiano's dislike of Pasolini's representations of the Romans. Alluding to the section "Alla passeggiata archeologica" edited by Pasolini, Flaiano criticized the type of realism that he promoted: "The temptation of 'setting the ambiance' with its jargon, its superficial realism, is always very strong in Rome, but it is necessary to ask ourselves whether this tendency has actually had the effect of distancing the 'Roman' public from cinema."[55] Pasolini included in the manuscript a note defending the insertion of his newly proposed scene (which he compares below to another less fortunate variation that involves a rendezvous with two soldiers):

> Yes, it truly seems that the soldiers' episode is a tangent that leads to a dead end, with both plot and characters. The other idea of the crazy race is also somewhat tangential, but is much more violent, and places Cabiria in a new and more dramatic situation; and, above all, it opens into the episode of the Man with the Sack. The Man with the Sack episode must in turn have a greater weight on the structure of the film. For example, the Man with the Sack – besides forcing Cabiria to be honest with herself and with her past – must also help her to intuit the possibility of a new life (maybe through the address of a nuns' institute or something of the like, where she could work for a while and live honestly). All this could be useful in the end and provide a moral and personal narrative line, saving Cabiria from a gratuitous poetic divertissement.[56]

This note testifies to the depth of Pasolini's involvement at the level of the overall narrative development of *Le notti di Cabiria* and to his contribution to the protagonist's inner travail, which he intended to further underscore by contrasting her with the violent and corrupt world in which she lived. In both Fellini's and Pasolini's work, femininity is the stronghold of a purity that has been lost in the modern world. This type of polarization between an angelic character and a sinful world was well suited to the sensibility of Pasolini, who, through the contrast between an angelic feminine figure and a violent world, would convey in his films what has been identified by Colleen Ryan-Scheutz as "humility-based innocence," a poetic element that is part of a more complex make-up wherein "purity derives from their suffering and subordination, their miserable homes and oppressive settings, and their constant subjection to the demands of others."[57] Most interestingly though, Pasolini's sneering final words in the above-quoted note are symptoms of the writer's initial difficulty in accepting Fellini's level of poetic stylization, especially in the cartoon-like representation of Cabiria. In another note on the script Pasolini laments Cabiria's Scottish overcoat, rubber rain-boots, and umbrella, which did not match the clothing of a real Roman prostitute but were rather "non-human and purely chromatic," part of a "curious, amused, and strange point of view" that risked transforming the prostitutes' lives into a "joke."[58] Although Pasolini and Fellini each strove for a poetic cinema, their visions were rooted in two different stylistic sensibilities. In essence, while Pasolini's art reaches poetic heights by locating the human soul in its passion through the stark scenario of extreme historical and existential marginalization, Fellini's lyricism is based on empathy with the soul that is caricatured in the moment of its confrontation with spiritual awakening.

With links to the innocent character already crafted by Giulietta Masina for *La strada*, the character of Cabiria was for Fellini more symbolically connected to a childlike figure than representative of the Roman prostitute. Fellini once said that in his films with Giulietta there is always "a little creature who wants to give love and who lives for love," hinting both at her childlike nature and at the conflict that such a nature experiences within a selfish and loveless world.[59] Pasolini's contribution moved, as he put it, to improving the "amalgamation" of realism and symbolism and "lifting the environment a little towards Cabiria, and significantly lowering Cabiria towards the environment."[60] Nonetheless, Pasolini's chief concern for the level of social realism in this film should not lead one to disregard what Pasolini absorbed from Fellini's more abstract artistry. In point of fact, Pasolini would eventually develop a similar and recurring poetic child figure in his own cinema, striving for a middle ground at the level of stylization, first in *Uccellacci e uccellini* (1966, *Hawks and Sparrows*) with the character personified by Ninetto Davoli and second with an attempt to reach the comic-book-like characters typical of Fellini in the short film *La terra vista dalla luna* (1967, *The Earth Seen from the Moon*).

For Pasolini, the experience of *Le notti di Cabiria* was influential in terms of his pursuit of a cinema of poetry, which for him entailed integrating lyricism with social realism or "passion and ideology" (the title he gave to a 1960 collection of critical essays) – one of the many contradictions that have been at the heart of much of the scholarship on Pasolini.[61] This revelation is made explicit in his reflections on the film, where he identifies a genealogical line between Roberto Rossellini and Fellini, hailing such heritage, and thus embracing it, as the chief force responsible for the creation of a new level of lyrical dynamism in Italian cinema and of an expansion of the aesthetic potentials of the media itself:

> The real world of the films of Rossellini and Fellini is transfigured by their excess of love for their reality. Both Rossellini and Fellini place such an intensity of affection in their cinematographic representation of the world – which

is brought into focus by the brutal and obsessive hyper-eye of the camera – that their films often magically create a tridimensional sense of space ... where the air itself is photographed ... [Fellini] has taken everything from neo-realism: virtues and vices, freshness and decrepitude, enchantment and rubbish, and has made all of this explode together thanks to a love for reality that is not only pre-realistic but also prehistoric.[62]

Fellini is represented here as the genius of what is romantic and expressionistic in neo-realism. For these reasons, in February of 1960, defending the accusations against *La dolce vita*, Pasolini elaborated on the lyrical understanding of neo-realism that is characterized by "an excess of love for reality." He identified the existence of an unwittingly Catholic ideology underpinning Fellini's cinematic world, ruled by the principle of Grace. His essay on *La dolce vita* flows into an emotionally charged eulogy on the value and power of Fellini's art cinema, which for Pasolini was a monumental expression of an "undifferentiated and undifferentiating love" that was able to find its vital and sacred force even within the mass of the Roman *piccola borghesia*.[63] Given such understanding and admiration, it is not surprising that Fellini became a point of reference and even a model for Pasolini, especially in his first years as a director.

Unfortunately their relationship was disrupted by a misunderstanding tied to the financing of Pasolini's debut film, *Accattone* (1961). The misunderstanding, sometimes referred to as "the Federiz incident," climaxed during October of 1960 when Fellini apparently denied financial backing for Pasolini's film, provoking a bitter reaction from him. Federiz was a production company formed at the time by the producer Angelo Rizzoli and Federico Fellini. Pasolini's shooting tests of what was eventually to become *Accattone* were initially rejected. In the emotive diary piece that Pasolini published in the newspaper *Il Giorno* on 16 October he places the confrontation with Federiz's corporate and self-referential artistic vision within his own broader struggle to defend the human rationale behind *Accattone*, complaining that Fellini did not seem to appreciate "the poverty, the carelessness, the crudeness, the clumsy and almost anonymous scholasticism" in his filming, characteristics that were in part caused by Pasolini's lack of experience but that were also elements of his own style. Actually the decision to reject Pasolini's film stemmed from administrative problems within the production company and from the unfortunate role played there by producer Clemente Fracassi. In fact, Pasolini was not the only film director to be affected by the decision; Vittorio De Seta's *Banditi a Orgosolo* (1961, *Bandits of Orgosolo*) and Ermanno Olmi's *Il posto* (1961) – two other very significant films – were also rejected. Pier Paolo Pasolini persisted without the help of Fellini and went on to complete *Accattone* with the support of producer Alfredo Bini.[64]

Even though reciprocal trust was diminished by the production incident, the affinity that Fellini and Pasolini felt for one another continued to leave traces in public and private spheres. In the winter of 1961 Fellini recorded a dream with Pasolini that was pervaded by a strong sense of affection, which appears to sublimate his anxieties about the stigma of deviancy surrounding Pasolini's reputation as a homosexual, into a platonic brotherly tie: "I am in bed with Pasolini in the little room in Rimini where I studied as a young boy (thirty years ago). We slept together all night long like two little brothers, or perhaps as husband and wife because now that he's getting up wearing a T-shirt and underpants, heading for the bathroom, I realize that I am looking at him with strong feelings of tender affection."[65]

Fellini's anxiety about accusations of homosexuality seems to date from the years of *Il miracolo*, when Roberto Rossellini forced him to dye his hair blond for the character of the vagabond / Saint Joseph, an event that, as Pinelli recalls, attracted the ridicule of friends and probably exacerbated Fellini's already present complex that was tied to his high-pitched voice. It is likely that Fellini, having decided to spend time with Pasolini, was not completely immune from the fears of being stigmatized by social opinion. He probably had to confront resistance from Giulietta, who deplored Pasolini "as a corruptor of innocent young souls."[66] Perhaps this context clarifies certain choices made by Fellini, such as the previously mentioned rejection of Zapponi's scripts on the subject, and the representation of homosexuality in the scene from *I vitelloni* in which the young playwright (Leopoldo Trieste) is invited by the old actor into the darkness of the beach; Leopoldo's feelings, which are described in the script as "an infinite bitterness and disgust clutching his throat and freezing his heart," are embodied in the film by a frightening close-up of the old actor.[67] The dream entry quoted above, which is part of a cluster of dreams that are tinted by a sense of anxiety towards otherness, stages Fellini's rediscovery of affection for Pasolini – a feeling that, as we shall see, will return in other dreams with this collaborator. Here, Fellini seems to be placing homosexuality within the scope of a more socially accepted bond, which blurs marital and brotherly ties. This need to normalize the potentially compromising situation might be motivated by Fellini's desire to avoid the social humiliation and punishment associated with homosexuality and sexual diversity, a fear that dominates other dreams and especially the dreams grouped under this same date. Within this group, the dream with Pasolini – pervaded by a peaceful emotional tone and set at dawn rather than at night – has the effect of resolving homosexuality into a serene experience of kinship that forms the backdrop of their creative understanding.

At it happens, a subtle intertextual dialogue can be traced among their films at this time. The evolution of the protagonist of *Accattone* is strikingly similar to that of the swindler of Fellini's *Il bidone*. Both Augusto's and Accattone's deaths are tragic and sublime. Both characters are repentant in extremis, elaborating on Dante's image of Buonconte da Montefeltro from *Purgatorio* V. As Brunello Rondi reported, Pasolini agreed with Rossellini in considering *Il bidone* to be one of Fellini's masterpieces, and, more specifically, Pasolini appreciated the swindler's terrible and glorifying death.[68] The inspiration went both ways, as the sequence in which Accattone dreams of his death, with its stillness, blinding light, and enigmatic presences, prefigures Guido's dream at the cemetery in *8½*.

Fellini's defence of Pasolini in the aftermath of the scandal generated by the first showing of *Accattone* in late summer of 1961 – reciprocating therefore Pasolini's sympathetic aid in the upheaval caused by *La dolce vita* – significantly warmed their relationship again. On 16 October 1961, following the decision by the censorship committee to block *Accattone*, which was accused of presenting thieves as heroes, the producer Alfredo Bini and the magazine *Europa letteraria* organized a round table in Rome to protest the committee's decision. Fellini, Pasolini, and others were present. During the RAI radio broadcasting of the round table Fellini stated that *Accattone* was "a deeply human and deeply Christian film" and called for the writing of "a letter that might express the opinion of all of us" and in which "the positive effect of this film can be clarified." On 28 October, thanks to Minister Alberto Folchi, the censorship committee gave permission for the film to be distributed.[69] The mutual support in managing the scandals around their films and personas was indicative of Pasolini's and Fellini's shared sensibility at being objects of the media and having roles on the public stage. After all, in their films they both express a strong awareness of being characters in the collective imagination, as is shown by films such as *Il Decameron* (1971, *The Decameron*), in which Pasolini plays a medieval painter, and *Roma* or *Intervista*, in which Fellini plays himself as the director.

In a nightmarish dream recorded about eight months before Pasolini's murder (2 November 1975), Fellini's imagination senses a looming danger around Pasolini concerning not only his association with unsavoury individuals from Roman low life but also his public attacks against the political leadership of Italy at the time (see figure 7).[70]

In this dream the two artists, in the company of one of Pasolini's "*amichetti*" (young and reprehensible friends), are walking down a muddy dirt road on the far edges of the city where the countryside begins. The atmosphere is gloomy and sinister; a storm has left the road filled with puddles, the sky is murky with "large, ragged and ugly clouds," and a phantasmagorical yellow moonlight is spreading through the clouds and reflecting its ill glow on the surroundings. Around Pasolini and Fellini are a number of monstrous bat-rats sneering and looming as if preparing to attack, and behind the scene stands the unsettling eye of a camera spying on the men's every move. Furthermore, the actions and words of the men are described as artificial in the dream, "as part of a script," in connection with their mutual experience of the pressure placed on them by the media.

In February 1963, shortly before the release of Fellini's *8½*, Pasolini made the meta-cinematographic short *La ricotta*. Here a film director, played by Orson Welles, is working on a cinematographic interpretation of the Deposition. At a certain point the director is interviewed and asked, "What is your opinion about our great director Federico Fellini?" The director, after a pause for reflection, cannot say anything other than, "Egli danza" (He dances).[71] This deferential statement (note the use of *egli* instead of *lui*) summarizes Pasolini's admiration for Fellini's creative freedom. Perhaps it was also because of this homage that Fellini felt obliged to be present at the ceremony for the Grolla D'Oro (in Saint Vincent on 4 July 1964) and personally hand Pasolini the prize for *La ricotta*. Pasolini's admiration becomes even weightier when one considers a subterranean fact regarding the script of *La ricotta*. The script presents a few variants of the scene, the most relevant of which is that the journalist's question originally was, "What is your opinion ... about the writer-director P.P. Pasolini?" This intriguing variant reveals Pasolini's identity and artistic struggle around the figure of Fellini. By substituting his name with Fellini's, Pasolini secretly admits that the artist who dances, namely he who expresses visual poetry purely and without restraint, is not he but is instead Fellini.

Figure 7. Fellini's rendition of a dream with reference to Pier Paolo Pasolini, 28 March 1975

During the late 1960s Fellini did his part to follow Pasolini's burgeoning critical and artistic presence in the world of Italian cinema, which consisted of a number of avant-garde films such as *Mamma Roma* (1962), *Il vangelo secondo Matteo* (1964, *The Gospel According to St Matthew*), *Uccellacci e uccellini*, *Il Decameron*, and *Salò o le 120 giornate di Sodoma* (1975, *Salò or the 120 Days of Sodom*), as well as influential articles on the semiotics of the cinema of poetry. Pasolini's name is explicitly mentioned in *Toby Dammit* when the character of the critic-priest tries to instruct the dazed British actor that the film in which he is going to star is in a style somewhere between that of Carl Theodor Dreyer (1889–1968), Pasolini, and John Ford (1894–1973). Coincidentally, in a dream dated 1968, Fellini, entangled in the frustrating task of properly framing the mount of a mysterious portrait with the camera, seeks help from his faithful collaborators Giuseppe Rotunno, Otello Martelli, and Pasolini, but none is able or disposed to assist him (Pasolini is busy "laughing with his sinister lovers").[72] It is possible that this framing of the frame in Fellini's dream is a result of the pollination of the theories that Pasolini was proposing at the time, trying to analyse the nature of the shot, which for him was the equivalent of the morpheme in literature, and therefore the film's minimal and pre-rational linguistic element.[73]

Pasolini's critical stance also instigated a need to label his fellow artists and their work. In 1960 Pasolini had categorized Fellini as "neo-decadent," insisting that his use of the term was only historical and not moral, and defining the term as a romantic type of classicism.[74] Yet, the way he had labelled the Romagnol poet Giovanni Pascoli "a decadent" already implied an ethical limit, representing Pascoli as an artist enclosed within the privileged horizon of a small bourgeois class. With the passing of the years Pasolini continued to argue this point, much to Fellini's dismay, and added to it an allusion to the lack of anti-fascist fervour, when reviewing the published story of *Amarcord* that Fellini wrote together with Tonino Guerra. In that instance Pasolini lamented their false rendition of Rimini's pre-industrial *borgo*, which was portrayed as a "native town that is not very wild at all" and has "horrid sediment of small-bourgeoisie."[75] Revealingly, in his review Pasolini destroys what he once considered to be Fellini's ethical saving grace – the capacity to love (and therefore to know) even the most despicable of his characters – now explaining away this trait as the final proof of Fellini's sinful nature. With a peremptory tone and an aggressiveness that has not been evident before, Pasolini describes the sterility of Fellini's approach to art: the story subjugates the readers to a falsely universal point of view, one that ultimately views reality as pure enigma and is nothing but a dead end. Pasolini accuses Fellini of hiding such ideological weaknesses under the mystification of a sense of void and under nervous comedic distance. Although the perception of the nervous quality in Fellini's comicality is sensible, it is not linked to an underlining insecurity in the film's aesthetic mechanisms, but is more likely an expression of Fellini's perception of the instability of the ontological reality itself resulting from his "ambiguous adherence" to matters of esotericism discussed in the introduction of this book. At any rate, the inflamed and jumbled accusations alluded to in the essay express Pasolini's anger and his uneasiness, almost as an attempt to eradicate conclusively Fellini's figure from his mind.

Clearly Pasolini's position towards Fellini's work was highly volatile and riddled with contrasting emotions. In his vitriolic review of *Amarcord*'s story Pasolini imagines how Fellini would film it, which would involve taking a clichéd domain of life and making it extraordinary by means of expressionistic dilatation. However, only three months later, after having seen the actual film *Amarcord*, Pasolini published a new review in which he retracted his pessimistic previsions. Fellini's cinematic poetry again seduced Pasolini, who returned once more to describe Fellini's style in a positive light. Even though he still felt that the film was entrapped in a decadent style, Fellini was able to avoid the risks that such a position entails. Pasolini expressed his awe at the coherence and the degree to which the film maintained the coexistence of realism and stylization, an objective that he also strived to achieve.[76] Pasolini concluded his review by finding in *Amarcord* an original and theatrical revival of neo-realism, where the characters and objects exist both in their vital physicality and as elements of style.

In 1960, Pasolini was already aware of the irony in calling attention to the decadent roots of Fellini's art, since he also shared them. The very core of the romantic anthropologic view of peasants, proletarians, and the Third World is at the base of Pasolini's art and is linked to the myth of the "good savage" that has been traditionally held by aristocratic elites. Naturally, Pasolini was at the same time a revolutionary Marxist and a decadent bourgeois. In the end, his conflicted relationship with Fellini's art is not dissimilar to the relationship he had with Giovanni Pascoli's poetics. In the poem "L'umile Italia," contained in his acclaimed 1957 collection, *Le ceneri di Gramsci* (*The Ashes of Gramsci*), Pasolini enters into a dialogue with Pascoli by mourning the absence of swallows – one of Pascoli's chief symbols for the unfathomable – from the skies of the Roman suburbs. In comparing a youth of Rome with the youth of a small Padanian town such as San Mauro, where Pascoli lived at the turn of the century, Pasolini realizes that the swallows' ancient voices and graceful airplay cannot bring solace to the world of the south that carries "the weight of obsessive resignation."[77] Indeed, Pasolini expresses his longing for a Pascolian world view and at the same time his sorrow at the impossibility of singing it amidst the social reality of his present time.

It must be noted that Pasolini's description of Fellini's Pascolianism is not an austere literary acknowledgment but is a joyful and sentimental discovery, memorably recorded in his observation on Fellini's manner of speech. On more than one occasion Pasolini described Fellini's voice as one "spreading around the most curious phonemes ever produced by a crossbreed of Romagnol-Roman, shrills, exclamations, interjections, diminutives, the entire arsenal of Pascolian pre-grammaticality."[78] On another occasion, describing a dinner he attended with Fellini, Pasolini also wrote: "Fellini ordered the dishes with the precision of a magician. The supper – in that *Dolce vita*–like restaurant – was a real production. Fellini used his regional technique – like Pascoli. I could have hugged him, with those big black-ringed eyes of his, those big flabby cheeks."[79] The parallel between Pascoli and Fellini that colours this portrait of Fellini is rooted especially in the idea of *fanciullino* and is a well-known and important ingredient of Fellini's ideology. *Il fanciullino* is the title of Giovanni Pascoli's poetic manifesto, first published in the literary magazine *Il Marzocco* in 1897, in which the entity of Fanciullino represents man's child-self, a purer and more authentic portion of the self that is in closer contact with life and with the ability to express it. In this universal and yet subjective Child, who eternally marvels at the infinite mystery of life and spontaneously expresses it through songs, Pascoli identifies the source of the purest poetry. According to Pasolini, Fellini's cinema is dominated by a similar principle, which is also one of the causes behind Fellini's baroque style: "the 'fanciullino' that is inside Fellini and to whom Fellini gladly – and with diabolic cunningness – gives permission to speak is primitive, and therefore its function is that of adding rather than connecting; it does not know how to coordinate and subordinate; it only knows how to complicate."[80] Much scholarship has emphasized Fellini's connection to Pascoli, even showing how Pascoli's poetics of the *fanciullino* was integrated in quite a deliberate way at the lexical, symbolic, and thematic levels in Fellini's screenplays.[81] Curiously, the insistence at pointing out

Pascolian characteristics in Fellini's cinema was parodied by the director himself in the sequence in the waiting room of the television studios of *Ginger e Fred*, in which the playfully obscene rhymes invented
by Fred (Marcello Mastroianni) are ridiculously qualified as having a
touch of Pascoli.

Within the long meditation about the nature of his love for reality and
for humanity, which is contained in *La religione del mio tempo*, Pasolini
contrasts himself with Fellini as a way to confront his inner dilemma
between "passion and ideology." As he recounts a nocturnal excur-
sion in a Cadillac driven nonchalantly by the pensive and enthusiastic
director around the area behind Torvaianica outside of Rome, likely
during their work on *Le notti di Cabiria*, Pasolini expresses his empathy
towards Fellini as well as his desire to differ from him. In Pasolini's
verses, Fellini is presented as "one of the best" who, as a *fanciullino*,
abandons himself to a faith in the divine law "of an ambiguous, desperate destiny"; he is endowed with an "amused and sacrilegious pity"
and with the confidence of being able to love humanity "case by case,
creature by creature," finding everywhere a "shining fragment of the
divine." While he recognizes that he shares Fellini's enthusiastic love
for existence, Pasolini becomes aware of a critical distance in his own
passion, rendering it a form of nostalgia. Rather than being supported
by a faith in a direct and divine capacity to understand and include
the other, Pasolini experiences a sense of loss for the facets of human
existence that he knows he will never be able to fully comprehend.
The poem continues with Pasolini and Fellini cherishing their shared
passion for life, which even seems to conjure up the violent appearance of the divine itself, illusorily reified by a cloud of mist from the
Tyrrhenian sea.[82]

An adequate reply to Pasolini's above-discussed fervidly ambivalent celebration of the force of Fellini's vision and work is to be found
in Fellini's oneiric re-enactment of his kinship with Pasolini after the
poet's death. In *Il libro dei sogni* Fellini summons Pasolini's presence in
order to evoke intuition and solutions for his own work in progress,
including what concerns him ethically and aesthetically.

In June 1977, Fellini dreams of being on set, shooting the last sequence
of a film, which he eventually identified as being *Mastorna*. However,
Pasolini, who in the dream is working as an actor ("kind, pleasant, and
full of good will") for Fellini, begins to leave the set before the director
is able to shoot an important close-up of him. The director then reaches
Pasolini's car and takes off with him and Fellini's childhood friend

Luigi "Titta" Benzi (1920–). Again, what might be considered socially as an act of homosexuality is sublimated into innocent and playful brotherly affection as their hands "sought each other and linked up jokingly with tenderness." As the car moves on, Fellini describes the events that follow in this way: "Pier Paolo Pasolini watched the ancient Roman walls pass by on the left, which appeared framed by modern marble. 'How will anyone ever describe those marvellous ruins!' sighed Pier Paolo, smiling and melancholic. 'It's life and also death ...' I can still hear that song, that night, and the mysterious yet crystal clear meaning of that verse. Was that the end of the film?"[83]

The dream contains the emotional core of *Mastorna* and points to Pasolini's propitious presence in it, as further evidenced by a note that Fellini later included in the folder with the screenplay. Here, in listing

Figure 8. Fellini's rendition of a dream with reference to Pier Paolo Pasolini, 6 June 1977

the reasons that still made the project appealing to him, Fellini wrote: "the idea at its base, namely, *è la vita anche la morte*, as it was sung by the choir in that dream with Pasolini."[84] The only words that form the lyrics of the festive song that Fellini says he heard during the entire dream and even after waking are saturated with meaning but are also very enigmatic and hardly translatable. In the two-faced logic of the line "È <u>la vita</u> anche <u>la morte</u>" (life is also death), which does not allow for univocal readings, lies the metaphysical expressionism of the words that unites life and death in an inseparable and continuous Möbius strip. As was clarified early on in this book, *Mastorna* was in fact meant to be a film showing the falsity of institutional depictions and understandings of the afterlife, revealing it as the individual projection of one's desires and fears, a hell reflecting the obsessions of the human mind, but also a therapeutic journey to free oneself from them. Through the death experience, as Fellini envisioned it and explained it to the first unfortunate producer of this project, one will "deserve once again life's humble learning."[85]

In recording his dream, Fellini also notes that the mysterious song was supposed to come from Verdi's *Il Trovatore*. Even though such lyrics are not to be found in the opera's libretto, the enigmatic and reiterated verse would easily fit within the aura of Verdian music, where unfathomable mysteries are constantly looming over human existence. Instead, the persistence of this song imbued with a quality that Pasolini would have probably described as "desperate vitality" (as goes the title of one of his poems), and the fact that it dominates a dream about the potential finale of *Mastorna*, shares deep connections with the remarkable ending of Pasolini's short film *Cosa sono le nuvole?* (1967, *What Are the Clouds?*), thus pointing to an intriguing case of intertextuality.

At the end of Pasolini's short, which is a reduction of Shakespeare's *Othello*, two marionettes face their death as puppets and are loaded onto a garbage truck. The garbage man, L'Immondezzaro (Domenico Modugno), begins to sing an intensely poignant song, and as the marionettes are discarded into a dump, they are taken by the beauty of the clouds floating freely above them. In Pasolini's original plan, *Cosa sono le nuvole?* should have been combined with his earlier short film *La terra vista dalla luna* and with a third never-realized short into an episodic film titled *Che cos'è il cinema?* (What is cinema?), a project that remained unrealized owing to the death of the actor Totò, who was playing an essential role in the film.[86] It must be noted that both of Pasolini's short films seek to manifest a detached perspective on human existence, which is forcefully achieved through heightened stylization and grotesque comicality, two qualities that Pasolini had observed in Fellini's work, hence further explaining Fellini's interest in this unique phase of Pasolini's cinema. Moreover, the almost superhuman or extra-terrestrial point of view at the foundation of Pasolini's shorts grants a broader view of existence, where life and death are not separate but are parts of a whole, tied together by reciprocal relationships: while *La terra vista dalla luna* explicitly concludes with the teaching "essere vivi o essere morti è la stessa cosa" (to be alive or to be dead is the same thing), in *Cosa sono le nuvole?* one of the puppets declares that "siamo in un sogno dentro un sogno" (we are in a dream inside a dream).

The meaning of the lyrics "è la vita anche la morte" that Fellini heard in his dream with Pasolini about *Mastorna* is therefore to be found in Pasolini's own incomplete and stylized project about life and death.[87] Fellini's dream suggests that the sense of kinship that he felt with Pasolini became clearer or more powerful in later years, pointing to the coming together of their artistic trajectories around the topic of death. This dream also testifies to the depth and the long-lasting influence of his creative partnership with Pasolini, which Fellini successfully re-enacted even on an oneiric level, continuing to borrow themes and ideas from Pasolini's persona and opus.

A few months later, in a dream dated 26 September 1977, Fellini emphasized a different node of his relationship with Pasolini, the one relating to ideology and direct political involvement, apparently seeking resolution to his differences with the departed poet on this point (see figure 9).[88]

In this last dream with Pasolini, Fellini visits the tiny modest home where his collaborator is awaiting his execution. While in a previously mentioned dream Pasolini was the object of the watchful eye of a television camera, here the innocent Pasolini has been condemned to death by an invisible system of powers against which Fellini is helpless. Pasolini is represented in a saintly posture, imperturbably serene in spite of the tragic circumstances and manifesting a Franciscan respect for his dog, which is granted a chair. The dog recalls here emblematically the qualities of resigned poverty and innocence that are typical of Pasolini's street characters and, more explicitly, Pasolini's animal character of the stranded Roman dog Grigio, from the short script that he wrote for Ermanno Olmi's documentary in the same year as he wrote *Cabiria*.[89]

Without feeling humiliated, Fellini takes his seat on the floor, finding a place opposite the dignified dog; on the other side is Pasolini who is

Figure 9. Fellini's rendition of a dream with reference to Pier Paolo Pasolini, 26 September 1977

seducing them both with his aura of moral strength. At this point in the dream Fellini confesses to Pasolini that he is feeling energetic and eager to begin a new project, and Pasolini proposes that he employ such energies by taking on a story entitled *Agnese*, which he had written with the explicit hope that Fellini would make it into one of his films. In reality, Pasolini never wrote a story with such a title; this is instead a reference to *L'Agnese va a morire*, the novel that Renata Viganò wrote in 1949 and that the director Giuliano Montaldo had adapted for the screen and released in 1976, a year before this dream, stirring much emotional resonance in the public at the time. Coincidentally, Montaldo's adaptation represents at some level an intersection of Fellini's and Pasolini's cinema since its cast included actors such as Bruno Zanin (*Amarcord*'s protagonist, who played Fellini's childhood friend Titta) and Ninetto Davoli (Pasolini's most employed and emblematic actor).

The reference to the story of Agnese, hinging on the uncomfortable and controversial distinction between heroes and traitors during the chaotic last years of the Italian resistance, suggests in this dream an opportunity for Fellini to prove to Pasolini which side he is on. The sense of rare affinity with which the dream is imbued as the artists stare at one another in silence, both filled with mutual concern and affection, indicates Fellini's desire to relate to Pasolini's political engagement. While Fellini's films follow closely the developments of the Italians' collective history and identity, the director's activism had been predominantly triggered in defence of artistic expression, as it had been in rejecting *Accattone*'s censorship and later in criticizing Silvio Berlusconi's invasive advertisement policies that caused the disruption of the unity of artistic films broadcast on television. In his last years Fellini's films certainly expressed a growing polemical stance on modern consumerist Italy as well as a concern for the decay of traditional cultures; in this sense, the admiration for Pasolini's political commitment and strength, which is contained in the dream, points to yet another way in which the writer's significance continued to grow in Fellini's eyes after his tragic death.[90]

Coming from two rather different but equally eclectic backgrounds, Fellini and Pasolini met at a time when they were both searching for their individual approaches to film-making, and they recognized in one another a common pursuit of a cinema operating from a lyrical gravitational centre. Throughout the 1960s and 1970s, their respective authorial journeys took sharp turns and changes of direction. As they pursued new expressive territories, they continuously pondered on each other's work and personalities. Their dialogue over the years carried on publicly and privately, and their relationship, manifested through a variety of intertextual cases, influenced and sustained them in clarifying the fundamental elements of their individual work. Among Fellini's poetic relationships, Pasolini's was one of the most intense and complex, and yet the least visible from an examination of his scripts and films, precisely because it unfolded at a very deep and abstract level. Throughout the years, their views crossed and diverged, at times anticipating and at other times trailing one another, the dance of a poetic brotherhood.

Eroticism as Dream and Nightmare:
A Dialogue with Brunello Rondi

Rondi's organic philosophy and its emphasis on the idea of reality as a network of multiple relationships found its core in eroticism and led him to explore the possibility of an erotic-religious aesthetics where the feminine rises to a symbol of transcendental Otherness with whom man yearns to merge in organic unity. In his poetry the woman's body comes to represent the distillation of nature's forces; it becomes a landscape where men recognize a sense of brotherhood in their common drives and where sexuality is equated to a form of intelligence: "My road is marked – step by step / by the force that I find in myself in the morning, / arch of sex and of the forehead ... / the love belonging to every man, to the comrades / alive with me through the years."[91] In his vision, eroticism was to be idealistically transfigured and interpreted as a beneficial force leading towards a greater organicity of relationships with the natural world and with humanity. Femininity originates from nature as a vital form, and the woman's body illuminates the mystery of the world; it also awakens the poet's communion with the physical reality.[92] This broader aim is made explicit by Rondi's introduction to the poetry collection *La terra felice*: "The woman is poetically realized ... in her holistic participation with Nature and with History. Her being is the main frontier with the heart of the earth, thanks to her pure maturity (that is also the medium of a powerful terrestrial sense of belonging); the woman is also expressed in these books [Rondi's poetry] as the companion and aide of History, and thus she rises to a symbol of active civilization."[93]

The presence of a person such as Brunello Rondi, who was so entranced with the creation of a philosophically sustainable erotic art, within the team of Fellini's collaborators is not surprising given the nature of Fellini's cinema. Fellini is a hallmark figure of the sexual revolution in Italy and abroad. As early as 1948 the story of Rossellini's film *Il miracolo*, written by Fellini and Pinelli, attracted censorship for placing sexuality and sanctity side by side.[94] In the United States the supreme court would eventually reject a government ban against *Il miracolo* and continue with the historical decision to grant movies the right to freedom of speech.[95] A conspicuous example of the controversial juxtaposition of holiness and sensuality in this film is found in the scene in which the shepherdess Nanni (Anna Magnani) abandons herself to the vagabond (Federico Fellini), whom she believes to be Saint Joseph. As she twists her body in anticipation of the saint's attention, she invokes his beauty and glory, creating a scene that is reminiscent of a boorish and peasant version of Bernini's Ecstasy of Saint Teresa.[96] This coexistence of sexuality and religion is more than a Boccacian element of satire of Catholicism; it is also a subtle underscoring of the interdependency of sexual and mystical impulses. A theme within Fellini's early work as a screenwriter for Rossellini, this conjunction returns in *Roma, città aperta*; here, Fellini inserted the irreverently humorous gag in which Don Pellegrini, played by Aldo Fabrizi (1905–90), is irritated by the proximity of a statuette of a saint to that of a naked woman.[97] A similar pattern is also present in Rossellini's *Francesco, giullare di Dio*, for which Fellini was also a screenwriter, in the scene during the visit of St Clair and her sisters; great excitement is generated in the community of friars, and, in the script, the friar known as Frate Ginepro retells a dream in which he was carnally tempted by the devil. Behind this passage of the script, which seems to have been purposefully assembled to interject a subtle sexual theme into the episode of the sisters' visit, Tomaso Subini finds the shadow of "Fellini's ironic hand."[98] The connection between religious quests and sexual experiences remains a focal point in Fellini's own cinema and appears in several instances, such as the rendezvous in the darkness surrounding the villa during the séance sequence of *La dolce vita*; the clergyman's refusal to accept his sexual nature, leading to madness, in *Le tentazioni del Dottor Antonio*; the erotic education that is imparted by the guru in *Giulietta degli spiriti*; and the esoteric rituals of love making in *Il Casanova*.

With *La dolce vita*, Fellini's films continued to challenge the sexual taboos of the time, and here, too, the Church forbade any good Christian to see the film. The accusations of obscenity endowed *La dolce vita* with the aura of erotic cinema, greatly helping with ticket sales but also reducing the expectations of a good portion of its audience to sexual titillation. Pietro Germi's *Divorzio all'italiana* (1961, *Divorce Italian Style*) includes a portrait of the erotic frenzy spurred by *La dolce vita*; in a memorable sequence, a movie theatre in a small Sicilian town is invaded by a largely male crowd that is lured by the rumour that the film contains striptease and orgy scenes. Of course, as previously discussed in connection with Flaiano's contribution to the scene at the Trevi Fountain, Anita Ekberg's seductive curves also exist in the film to convey archetypical and poetic ideas, and Germi, whose comedy underscored the gap between the mindset of the Italian population and the reforms that were being proposed regarding the divorce law in the 1960s, understood that any attempts to manifest a poetic, philosophic, or socially concerned discourse through the representations of nudes, sexuality, or erotic appeal entailed grave artistic limitations in terms of reception from both the public and critics. Even in the case when the director was freer to express himself outside of the production systems of popular genres – as was the case with Fellini, Pasolini, and, before them, Giuseppe De Santis (1917–97) – the presence of attractive bodies tended to be received as commercial ingredients of *divismo*, as part of a strategy of capitalizing on the iconographic expectations of the erotic industry and stardom.[99]

Brunello Rondi, who was deeply involved in the making of *La dolce vita*, stated that he left his "personal mark" in sequences such as the miracle of the Madonna, but even more so in the aristocratic party at the castle, as well as the orgiastic night at the end of the film during which Marcello finally abandons himself to artistic and spiritual ambitions.[100] Indeed, this sequence contains a central idea that seems to come directly from the wisdom contained in the work of the famous ethnographer Ernesto De Martino (1908–65), whose study on magical practices in southern Italy called *Sud e magia* (1959, South and magic) likely resonated with Rondi for its existential treatment of magic as a cultural element satisfying the "sense of void" that Rondi saw widespread in modern times.[101] At the beginning of this sequence a lady speaks of Italy as a land rich in ancient cults and places endowed with natural and supernatural power, a country where the divine takes on many forms and names, therefore suggesting that whether the miracle is being performed by the Madonna or not is actually irrelevant – an ethnographically sound statement that De Martino himself commended during a round table on *La dolce vita*.[102]

Moreover, the noble family's party and the final sequence – which Rondi claimed to have rewritten entirely – are representative of the dark eroticism and the disturbed female characters that were increasingly becoming the centre of Rondi's art. As Fellini also observed in his preface to Rondi's play *Rosa dei venti* (1960, Rose of the winds), the experience of writing *La dolce vita* significantly galvanized his collaborator's subsequent work that hinged on female figures lost amidst the many currents and influences of society.[103]

In the early 1960s, after Rondi's philosophy had matured through numerous and varied publications and after his long apprenticeship with Fellini, he undertook his own work as a film director. In the programmatic nature of his work, as well as in his eclecticism, Rondi followed the model of Pier Paolo Pasolini. Moving parallel to Pasolini, whom he had often consulted regarding his poetic work, Rondi sought to transfer his identity from poet and essayist to film-maker. As a homage to Pasolini's work, his first attempt was a co-direction with Paolo Heusch of Pasolini's novel *Una vita violenta* (1962, *Violent Life*). His first solo film was *Il demonio* (1963, *The Demon*), narrating the life and passion of a young woman living in a village in southern Italy who was believed to be a witch. For this film Rondi consulted De Martino's *Sud e magia*, even drawing from the photographs included in this publication and recreating them in the sets. Rondi's experience with this film certainly intrigued and possibly influenced Fellini's similar research into the world of magic and the paranormal for *Giulietta degli spiriti*, which was begun shortly after *Il demonio*. In the 1970s, likely encouraged by the critical and financial success of Pasolini's *Decameron*, Rondi similarly mingled erotic and literary tones in his films, moving away from the comedic and fable-like to the more sadistic. While Pasolini began working on *Salò o le 120 giornate di Sodoma*, Rondi was turning to his own dark tales of abuse: *Prigione di donne* (1974, *Riot in a Women's Prison*) and *Prosseneti* (1976, The procurers).

Rondi's work as film-maker, which was supposed to represent the culmination of his philosophic and poetic research, and centred largely on society's misunderstanding of the transformative power of Eros, unfortunately coincided with some of the bleakest years of Italian cinema. In the 1970s, owing to a dire financial crisis, badly thought-out laws, increasingly aggressive competition from the United States, and most of all the growing dominion of television, ticket sales dropped vertiginously, production companies closed, and the entire Italian film industry almost came to a halt. Red-light theatres gradually became the only sustainable ones in many Italian city centres. It was not long before erotic cinema dominated, and from the second half of the 1970s onwards it quickly spiralled into the ranks of hard-core pornography.[104] The impelling commercial needs required to produce a film in those years, coupled with the sexual revolution that had begun to furiously attack taboos in Western countries, allowed for a nightmarish array of all sorts of sexual perversions to take place on the screen.[105]

Rondi, like the majority of emerging film-makers at the time, was striving to attract greater audiences and therefore chose to work within the erotic genre, which offered greater financial security. Eroticism helped Rondi in the financing of his film projects during a time of economic crisis in the Italian film industry; however, his philosophic ambitions and aesthetic unity were largely misplaced and contradicted by the weighty requirements of the erotic and soft-porn genres within which he worked.[106] In the hands of producers who had very little interest in his intellectual and poetic refinement, Rondi's ambitions were partially wasted and nullified. Rondi's collaborator Roberto Leoni narrates that the director would abandon the set when the producer Oscar Brazzi insisted on having more scenes with explicit sexuality, at which point the producer would often take over and direct the scenes himself.[107] The changes made to the titles of Rondi's films speak volumes; for instance, the lyrical title of *Quest'amore così tenero, così violento, così fragile* (This tender, violent, frail love) becomes the more indecent *Le tue mani sul mio corpo* (Your hands on my body), while *Maestro d'amore* (Master of love), which evokes visions of Dolce Stil Novo, turns into the humorously obscene *Racconti proibiti ... di niente vestiti* (Forbidden tales ... having nothing on). Rondi's case is a particularly instructive parable in understanding the hardships endured by the film-makers who stubbornly continued to believe in the value of the art film at this difficult juncture in the Italian economy.

In spite of the general artistic failure of his cinema Rondi persisted in directing films until the end of the 1970s, proving true to Cesare Zavattini's observation a few decades earlier about the streak of obstinacy and fanaticism in Rondi's character that made him blind to his limits; he came to resemble "a child trying to preserve the order of his game of cards in spite of the wind blowing on it and destroying its very structure."[108] As a director, Rondi was capable at times of generating intriguingly stylized frames, and the depth of his philosophy was occasionally expressed in fascinating sequences, as for example in *I prosseneti*, starring Alain Cuny (who had also played Steiner in *La dolce vita*) in the role of a high-class, philosophizing procurer who arranges for different types of men to meet the women of their dreams. In a sequence from this film, a politician meets a prostitute and wants her to assume the role of a woman who was once his greatest love. To make his memory of her more concrete, the politician has the prostitute stand in front of a curtain and projects over her a film of his previous love. The ritual that plays out in this sequence poignantly expresses the obsession of memory and nostalgia and is even a satire of the politician's alienation from reality.

Furthermore, Rondi attempted to cultivate the discourse begun in his poetry with the image of the "arch" and employed it in his films at climatic moments. In *Il demonio* the protagonist, a possessed girl (Daliah Lavi), poses, arching her back during the long and dramatic sequence of exorcism inside the church, thereby expressing an uncontainable sexual force. During a session of erotic poses in the already discussed *Velluto nero*, the character of the arrogant and womanizing photographer – who in this film stands for the aggressive eroticism of the pornography industry – angrily shouts at the model to arch her body to the utmost limit; in another scene, the body of the same model in a trance will again arch her back as she unconsciously expresses her anguish at being a sacrificed victim. However, Rondi's attempt to successfully create a cinema of poetry failed because he could not sustain lyrical tension in his films; the results often felt coldly programmed and frequently led to a schizophrenic quality, owing to the struggle between a lofty intellectual subtext and the less subtle and intrusive requirements of the erotic production.

Fellini, who remained a close friend of Rondi until his death in 1989, was aware of the problems inherent in Rondi's cinema. In a dream entry from *Il libro dei sogni*, dated 6 January 1977, Fellini recorded a telling vision of his collaborator. As revealed by a note below the date, the dream relates to Fellini's intention to resume his work on *Il viaggio di Mastorna* with Rondi and therefore represents his qualms about weaknesses perceived in his collaborator (see figure 10).[109]

Perched on the tree of his abstractions, Rondi is attempting to reanimate and reorganize the integrity of his movements. Within the context of Rondi's peaking artistic crisis, the image of a malfunctioning and awkward marionette-like body is Fellini's representation of the blaring inelegance and disjointedness of Rondi's work. Curiously, the dream also contains an element of rivalry for the attention of Roberto Rossellini, for whom they both worked as screenwriters for *Francesco, giullare di Dio*. It seems that here Fellini is drawing a mental comparison between the fate of Rossellini's two apprentices, suggesting

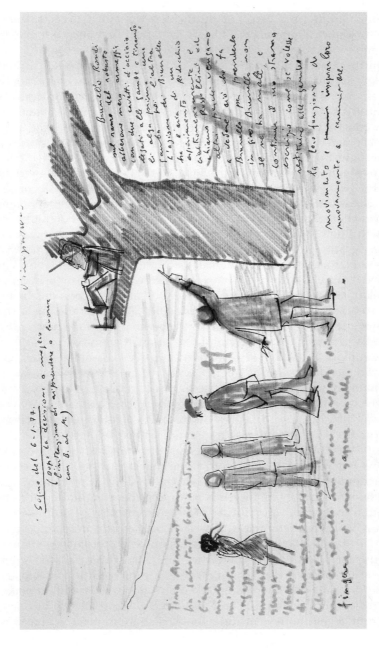

Figure 10. Fellini's rendition of a dream with reference to Brunello Rondi, 6 January 1977

that he is questioning who among them is the most successful heir of the "ancient cinematic progenitor," as Rondi had once referred to Rossellini.[110]

From the time of his contributions to the design of the debauched parties of *La dolce vita*, with its plethora of female characters caught between their desire for an authentic love relationship and the destructive nature of the roles assigned to them by society, to his first and arguably most accomplished film, *Il demonio*, Rondi explored the ways in which man's repressed sexual desires transform a woman into a monster and eventually destroy her. Rondi's interest in gender roles and the psychological turmoil of women was likely inspired by both his participation in the making of Rossellini's *Europa 51*, which retold the passion of the Umbrian saint in a modern feminine version, and his existentialist investigation into love relationships. Even in his plays Rondi explored the female character in extreme situations, as it was for Rosa in the already mentioned *Rosa dei venti* and for Julia, the American woman in *Gli amanti* (1963, Lovers, later adapted for the screen by Vittorio De Sica) who lures the Italian engineer Valerio into a consuming love relationship while knowing that she is ill and will soon die. In another of Rondi's films, *Ingrid sulla strada* (1973, Ingrid on the road), the male's objectification of the woman leads her to prostitution and tragic suicide. Again in *I prosseneti*, a couple of criminally minded and sophisticated ruffians deal with a series of maniacs and mentally disturbed men who are seeking out women to satisfy their bizarre sexual fantasies. Owing to such experience in the realm of sexuality, Rondi was an ideal collaborator for Fellini's exploration of male sexual fantasies in *La città delle donne*, which in fact presents instances of intertextual dialogue with Rondi's films, though also transcending their limitations.

La città delle donne centres on the male's fascination and obsession with the female. Rondi's imprint can be detected in various parts of the film, especially during the feminist's slide show of natural images that resemble female genitals, thus glorifying them as did Rondi's poetry, but also directly reproducing another almost identical slide show that was in *I prosseneti*, made two years before. The most important and interesting authorial interplay is presented by the intertextual relationship between *La città delle donne* and Rondi's *Ingrid sulla strada* (made seven years before). At the beginning of both films a sensual woman, who represents the object of man's desire, is applying makeup in the restroom of a train, and without any reservations she opens the door to a libidinous man and offers herself to his ravaging passion.

This particular scene in the train's restroom is not present in the early notes and the treatment for *La città delle donne* drafted by Fellini and Zapponi alone.

In spite of the focus on sexuality in his films Rondi rarely succeeded in reaching deep into the psychological nature of man's relationship to the feminine universe. This was mostly caused by the already mentioned limitations of the production system in which he was working, a system that thrived on the spectator's abandonment to a shared myth or erotic fantasy and did not welcome attempts to raise the spectator's level of awareness. In Fellini's *La città delle donne*, women are also represented as embodying a man's erotic fantasy; however, while Rondi's *Ingrid sulla strada* does not concretize the awareness of such a dynamic, Fellini's film strongly does. In Fellini's cinema the unconscious realm of the psyche becomes the object itself, rather than a "trick" to engage the viewer (as tends to happen in the popular erotic films and subliminal television spots). If one is to speak about an ethical ambition behind Fellini's cinema, it is to be found in Fellini's objective of stimulating viewers to the realization of the power of myths and therefore helping his viewers to live more comfortably and conscientiously in them. In this way Fellini's later cinema appears faithful to Jungian psychoanalysis in terms of its therapeutic ambitions, aspiring to achieve the "self-realization" of the spectator, which may in turn be reasonably seen as Fellini's attempt to satisfy neo-realist ambitions for social and moral change.

Consequentially, what Fellini tried to accomplish in the domain of eroticism, in *La città delle donne* as well as in many other films, was to challenge and enlighten the male spectator and therefore to debunk the unconscious spell of the myths that empower the popular erotic film genre. On the day of the Roman premier of *La città delle donne* Fellini described his intention to show cinema as the space in which men's fantasies about women are played out.[111] Rightly so, feminist critics have recognized the way in which Fellini's cinema "explores masculine projections" and "subverts masculine notions of male subjectivity."[112] However, this discussion invalidates a position such as that of Marie Lederman, who accuses Fellini of perpetrating myths that alienate the reality of woman; on the contrary, a film such as *La città delle donne* is clearly not about "real women" but about the male fantasy of the woman. Differently from what happens in most erotic genre films, Fellini's films feature fantasies critically and subversively, thus deconstructing the process of the objectification of woman.[113]

It is therefore fitting that *La città delle donne*, which was the last collaboration between Fellini and Rondi, would open with the sequence echoing Rondi's *Ingrid sulla strada* and the erotic film genre as a whole. Fellini's film unfolds entirely within a man's dream, and the protagonist gradually grows in his awareness of the ways in which he has constructed his fantasy about the woman. Within this perspective, the film's initial sequence indicates the male's maximum unawareness, coinciding with Rondi's film and the erotic cinema of the time. *La città delle donne* was a pivotal learning experience for Rondi as well, and from that time on he abandoned his authorial struggle within the erotic genre and concluded his career as film-maker with the film *La voce* (1982, *The Voice*), narrating with the assistance of Tullio Pinelli a biographical reconstruction of the development of Mother Teresa of Calcutta's vocation.

Remembering Corporality: Tonino Guerra in *Amarcord* and *E la nave va*

In 1973, Fellini returned to the world of his boyhood to make *Amarcord*, a film set in a Romagnol *borgo* during the years of the fascist regime. As noted in a previous chapter, this was a project that his main screenwriter at the time, Bernardino Zapponi, opposed because he felt it was going to fossilize Fellini in a private and redundant exhumation of childhood. Fellini then found another writer, the poet Antonio (Tonino) Guerra, who was originally from the town of Santarcangelo di Romagna, a few miles inland from Fellini's hometown of Rimini. Besides having an intimate knowledge of Romagna, Guerra was truly fascinated by the theme of childhood, which he considered to be an Eden-like state where the artist should make his permanent dwelling. In a recollection of how they came to work together on *Amarcord*, Fellini attested to this auspicious commonality between him and Guerra: "He had stories that were similar to my own to tell, characters who had the same craziness in common, the same ingenuousness, the same ignorance of children badly raised, rebellious and subjugated, pathetic and ridiculed, arrogant and humble."[114] In terms of writing the film's scenario, the transition from working with Zapponi to working with Guerra on *Amarcord* was not drastically different, because the storytelling style of Guerra – in whose novels the apparently disconnected chapters gradually clarify their narrative ties in a lyrical whole – allowed for the fragmented exploration

that was supported by Zapponi's collage-like play around psychoanalytical nodes.

During all phases of film-making, Guerra's intervention as writer
and counsellor manifested through his clarification of the deeper meaning of visual and narrative elements. Guerra's bitterness over modern
Italy and his lyric discourse about recovering a pre-modern sense of
wonderment and a dimension of corporeality, which is often expressed
through the use of animal images, are evident in Fellini's films. After
more than twenty years, spent mostly in Rome where he developed
his career as a screenwriter, Guerra returned to his provincial roots,
relocating first to Santarcangelo and then to the more isolated town
of Pennabilli set in the rustic hills of the Montefeltro Apennines.[115] In
this cloistered world rich with vistas of the surrounding valley, Guerra,
who was also a visual artist, installed several structures, statues, and
inscriptions attesting to the vital connection between his region and his
inspiration. This interdependence is only one of the signs of the deep
relationship that Guerra established with the peasant world of this region, manifested more fully by his poetry written in dialect. Since the
years of his detention in the German concentration camp of Troisdorf,
Guerra had sought refuge in dialect, and from his book *I scarabocc* (1946,
Scribbles) onward it was the primary language of his verses. Guerra
became one of the most important figures of Italian poetry, beginning
with *I bu* (1972, Oxen), a publication that coincided with the start of his
collaboration on *Amarcord* and that sought to portray the essence of his
childhood and, poetically speaking, of Italy's childhood.

Fellini, who greatly enjoyed Guerra's lyrics in dialect and used to recite
them when they visited each other in Rome as early as the years of *I vitelloni*, chose one of Guerra's poems for the title of *Amarcord*.[116] The poem
was "A m'arcord," meaning "I remember" in Romagnol dialect, but the
film's title is compressed into one word, thus further estranging the language and shaping it into the suggestion of "bitter heartache" (*amar +
cor*). This poem includes an attempt to restore the independence and force
of a more authentic self by establishing a link with the interconnected
spheres of dialect, childhood, and nature, and it opens the film's scenario:
"I know, I know, I know, / That a man at fifty / Always has clean hands /
I wash them two, three times a day. / But it is only when I see my hands
dirty / That I remember / When I was a boy."[117] The poem indicates a need
to find a way back to the psychological frame of mind of the *burdèll*, the
child, bringing back memories of childhood games and muddied hands.

The idea of something precious being hidden in what is considered lowly, such as mud, is forcefully represented by a part of the scenario that is not included in the film, in which an aristocratic family calls upon the man in charge of cleaning the town's drains to ask him to find a ring that has been lost in the sewer.[118] At the root of the amalgam of comical realism and lyricism characterizing the work shared by Fellini and Guerra rest unfettered instincts that are expressed in the anarchic behaviours of youth and in creative freedom. The dream entry dated 14 December 1974, a year after the release of *Amarcord*, suggests the resonance and pervasiveness of this idea. Here Fellini sees himself on a balcony, drawing sets that have the same theatrical quality as those of *Amarcord* and depict ancient steps and gardens marked by the passage of time. Fellini feels both happy and guilty at letting himself enjoy such pleasurable reveries of the past; his guilt finds a comical parallel as he attempts to urinate into one of the balcony's vases and is seen by a woman at one of the nearby windows, while Tonino Guerra observes him, laughing at the entire situation (see figure 11).[119]

The inherent self-indulgence and anarchic stance typical of adolescence, as well as the peasant perspective, all of which are so central to the fabric of *Amarcord*, are best expressed through dialect, which in the film delineates the geopolitical conflicts of authority and the peasant's practical logic that powerfully unmasks and derides oppression.[120] Cosetta Gaudenzi underlines the political ramifications of the many dialects present in this film and how they set the stage for the conflict between the locals and the foreign authority figures coming from other parts of Italy, especially the teachers and fascists who speak with accents typical of Naples, Florence, Rome, and Turin. Furthermore, the subversive power of dialect is clearly understood in connection with the integration of Guerra's poem "I madéun" (The bricks), in which a bricklayer abandons himself to a moment of marvelling at a paradox: even though his grandfather, his father, and he are bricklayers and have built most of the town's houses, his family does not possess a home of its own.[121] The poem was slightly changed for the film, generating a carnivalesque sequence at a construction site by the sea.

However, the socio-political discourse arising from the employment of dialect in a film such as *Amarcord* is also associated with the recovery of a state of marvel. The poem "Cantèda Quéng" (Fifteenth song) from Guerra's collection *E' mel* (1982, Honey) exemplifies this world view, which is typical of Guerra's poetics. Here a black cloud hovers above valleys and mountains, taking on various forms, and when it occasionally

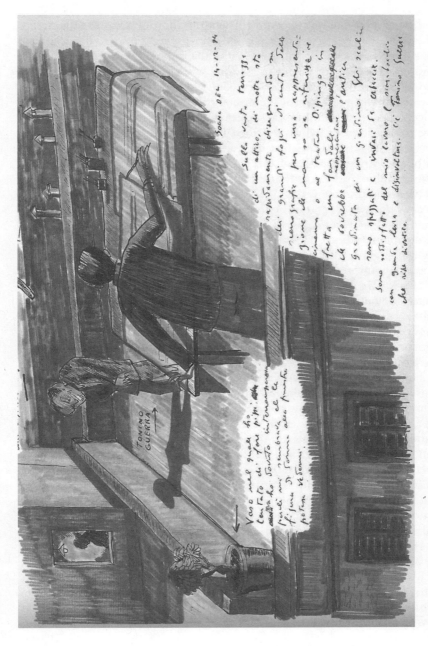

Figure 11. Fellini's rendition of a dream with reference to Tonino Guerra, 14 December 1974

touches the land, it leaves behind clear spots that are similar to the circles of ashes left by bonfires; gradually an entire green valley turns pale white. One day the black cloud jumps beyond the last mountain on the horizon and disappears. The poem concludes with the childlike questioning, "I wonder if they were locusts."[122] The poet pretends not to know that the cloud was a swarm of locusts, and he wants the reader to experience for the short duration of the poem a state of wonderment, witnessing something not yet demystified by reason. Guerra aligns with this sense of astonishment, attracted by what Natalia Ginzburg (1916–91), in her acute description of the poet's character, called his devotion to the "humble and minimal particulars" that are found on "the tracks of an incomparable image."[123] Likewise, the peasants of *Amarcord* are overwhelmed by natural phenomena, be they the flight of fluffy seeds or the flakes of snow. When Titta's family spends the day in the countryside, the father, Armando, marvels at the perfectly rounded shape of an egg.[124] Even though this scene of pastoral ecstasy is filled with Fellini's comical distance, the caricature of the simple man's admiration shows humanity in a state of poetic wonderment in which the simple things of nature are not explained but are tasted and valued by the measure of their perceived mystery. Moreover, by showing the peasants equally overcome by the awesomeness of racing cars, motorcycles, or luxurious ocean liners, *Amarcord* manages to revoke the aura of superiority ascribed to technical innovation in the first part of the century.

The other side of the coin of the poetic inspiration that Guerra drew from his self-exile in the peasant world of Romagna was his bitter polemical stance on modern Italy. This position is certainly exemplified by the protagonist of one of Guerra's novels, *L'equilibrio* (1967, Equilibrium), a prisoner of a concentration camp and then a graphic designer, who pursues first physical liberation from the Nazi camp and then mental liberation from the consumerism of post-war Italy, seeking a life in which he might "entrust himself to his body, to his arms, to the instinct as the animals do."[125] The liberation and expression of the body's wisdom, shown through both anarchic adolescent behaviour and lyrical epiphany, and the consequent recovery of a more spontaneous rapport with nature have arguably formed the central topic of Guerra's writings and work with Fellini.

Referring to one of the tales that Guerra wrote with Luigi Malerba (1927–2008) from *Storie dell'anno Mille* (1977, Tales from the year one thousand), in which the arm of an evil character revolts against its owner and kills him, the critic Giuliano Gramigna forged the compelling notion of "cosmic corporality": a beneficial and rebellious wisdom contained in the body that can provide a way out of a modern state of alienation.[126] This entrusting of oneself to the body is fully played out in *L'uomo parallelo* (1969, The parallel man), in which a man's limbs suddenly stop obeying the pull of society and begin moving in accord with their own will. In some instances, this division comes at the expense of innocent creatures: a peaceful and curious approach by a seagull provokes a violent reaction in some part of the divided protagonist, which, in spite of his desire to pet and be with the bird, forces his hands to strangle it.[127] *L'uomo parallelo* also stages the struggle between the man's programmed, and often wicked, mental habits and the serene boundlessness of instinct. The vicissitude of the protagonist, a sculptor, stands for that of contemporary humankind as a whole, apocalyptically culminating in his experience of North American society as a place where people live in a state of inner conflict with their own nature, an ill fate that Italy seems also to have suffered.[128] Guerra maintained close ties with Russia, and in a later novel this country is identified as "a sort of *madeleine* that awakens in him dormant nostalgia, emotions gone by, impossible desires, outdated ideas that he found upon returning to his hometown."[129] Curiously, highlighting here a point of difference between them, Russia was for Guerra what America was for Fellini. America represented the motherland of modern fantasy through comic books and Hollywood. When Fellini and Guerra travelled together to New York to present *Amarcord*, Fellini drew four portraits of Guerra, all showing him in the same seated pose but with different backdrops; in one, Guerra is surrounded by the metropolis's skyscrapers and has a dissatisfied and uneasy facial expression, while in another, he is rendered serene against a background dominated by natural colours, bright greens and browns.[130]

The break with modern life and the formation of a cult of the rural world (of Romagna as well as other regions) are inextricably connected to the rediscovery of corporality and to a poetic discourse best conveyed by the use of animal images. In Guerra's poetry, animals are often silent guides that unwittingly lead men to a deeper understanding of the emotions such as compassion and love and free their imagination. In a memorable sequence of *Amarcord*, the count's peacock, one of Guerra's favourite animal symbols, lands on the town square and opens its plumage amid the white of the snow, generating a moment of awe for the onlookers.[131] The bird's shape, meant to resemble female genitals, stops the boys from chasing the sensual Gradisca through the snow and stands out as a gigantic and glorious apparition; this is underlined by the sexually connoted exclamation made by one of the boys, "Che pataca!" (in this case meaning "What a pussy!"). Another similar connection unfolds intertextually between the poem "E' gat sòura e' barcòcal" ("The Cat on the Apricot Tree") from *I bu*, in which a madman climbs up a tree and pretends to be a cat, and the sequence in the film in which Teo, the mad uncle, stubbornly clings to a tree and begins screaming his need for a woman.[132]

A dream dated 24 February 1973, when Fellini was shooting *Amacord*, reinforces the collaborative relevance of this thematic pattern; here Fellini and Guerra are attempting to recall the mysterious and important message spoken by a pregnant cat that is standing by the tobacconist shop Dante in Rimini (see figure 12).[133] In this case, the animal's presence suggests fertile and oracular possibilities, even though the cat becomes more explicitly connected to sensuality in the film as feline qualities are transferred to the performance and make-up of the nymphomaniac character of La Volpina.[134]

Guerra's poetic use of animal images to express the friction between nature's instinctual goodness and modern man's desensitization is indeed characteristic of his writings. *I bu*, which is Guerra's most famous poetry collection, is named after the Romagnol word for "ox," taken here as an emblem of the twilight and agony of peasant culture. In one of the poems Guerra invites anyone who might be brave and cruel enough, to walk up to the oxen and tell them that, after having toiled for millennia for humans, they will be substituted by tractors and sent to the slaughterhouse.[135] In this light, the unforgettable apparition of the ox in the fog sequence of *Amarcord* illuminates the scene's critical and historical significance, in addition to its oneiric tone. The animal in general represents not only the distant past but also, more importantly, the state to which man needs to return, as Pippo Botticella (Marcello Mastroianni) voices upon seeing a monkey in Fellini and Guerra's last major collaborative effort, *Ginger e Fred*: "There is no longer any doubt that we descend from monkeys; the trouble is that we are no longer able to make our way back to them ... to reclaim those gifts of instinct and natural innocence."[136] This discourse through animals, at once nostalgic and polemic, can also be traced in the films on which Guerra worked as screenwriter for other directors, for example *Stanno tutti bene* (1990, *Everybody Is Fine*); the poet's work with Giuseppe Tornatore contains a sequence in which highway traffic is interrupted by

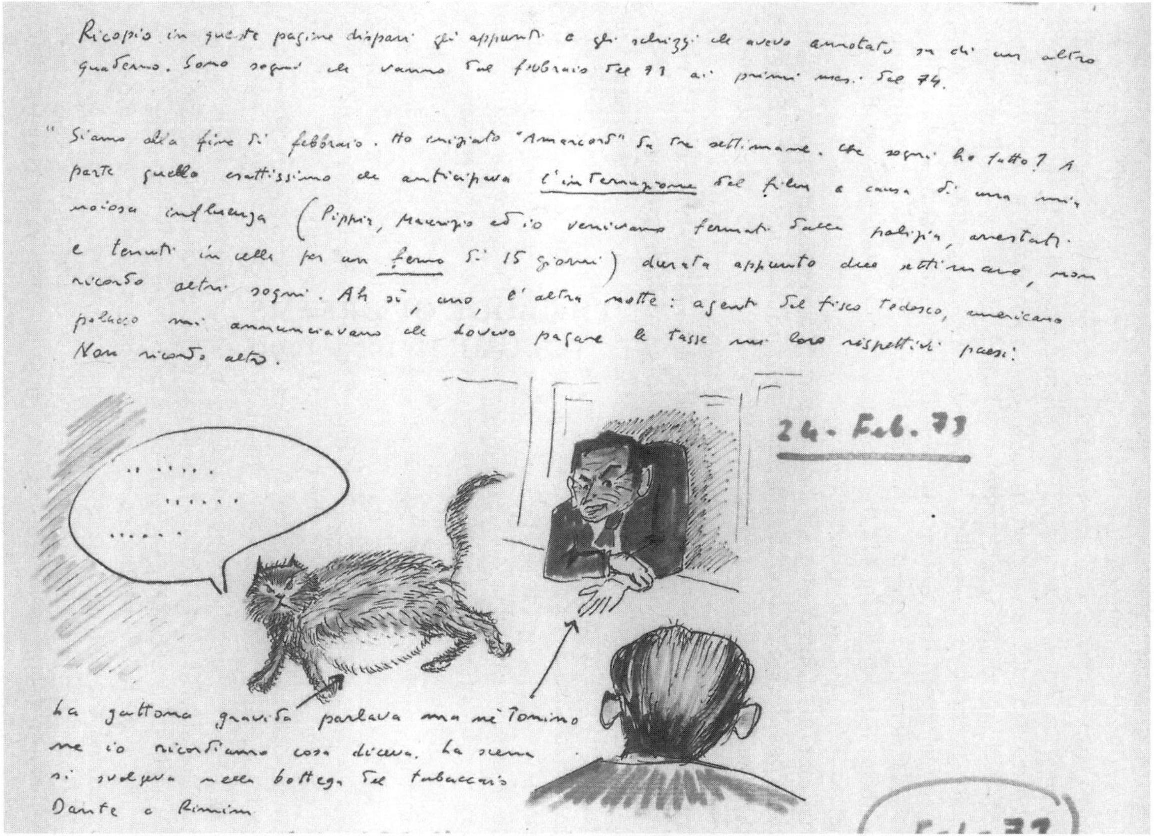

Figure 12. Fellini's rendition of a dream with reference to Tonino Guerra, 24 February 1973

an elk standing in the middle of the road as the mighty and sacral presence of nature.[137]

In addition to supporting Fellini's vision in the early 1970s for *Amarcord*, Tonino Guerra also assisted Fellini in the 1980s, beginning with *E la nave va*. On 30 December 1980 Fellini dreamed of the unsuccessful take-off by a large dirigible from Rimini's seaboard, which violently exploded and disintegrated after crashing into the low wall of an old seaside holiday camp. Fellini, depicted here as a young and frail man, runs away from the catastrophe, together with a person who reminds him of Guerra.[138] Not until two years later did Fellini seem to find clarity about the significance of this dream, which he then perceived as the inevitable end of an outdated way of flying through the skies of his imagination, limited by past landscapes and creative methods (possibly reconsidering Zapponi's objections regarding *Amarcord*).[139] Fellini's understanding was spurred by a new dream that occurred sometime in February 1982 in which he dreams of a more effective and modern alternative to the flimsy dirigible; he launches a powerful and dark warship that is capable of travelling as a submarine deep into the waters of the unconscious. In fact, the old flying machine, associated with the dream in Rimini and perhaps with the aerial perspective at the beginning of *Amarcord* – which follows the descent of the feathery seeds (*le manine*) released by the thistle trees in springtime – is substituted in the film *E la nave va* with a dark warship standing for a new and different way to continue the cinematic journey into the collective unconscious of the nation.

In the summer of 1980, they had met to discuss a story based on the news of the ceremony that had followed the death of the Greek diva Maria Callas (1923–77), in which her ashes had been scattered in the Aegean Sea; in the film she becomes the mysterious singer Edmea Tetua. After considering a few variants for representing an elaborate, grandiose, and chaotic funeral, they wrote the scenario of *E la nave va*, which was eventually filmed three years later in 1983.[140] In the script the funeral held at sea comes to represent the burial of opera, the most representative art of nineteenth-century Italy, instituting a historical parallel with the death that they believed Italian cinema was undergoing during the last decades of the twentieth century.

Even though critics have not been able to account for Guerra's artistic presence in *E la nave va*, the apocalyptical point of view generated by the funeral is certainly in tune with the writer's state of mind at the time regarding the fate of poetry and humanity. However, the animal theme already described above offers a clue to finding Guerra's thread in *E la nave va*. A failed meeting between man and animal, reminiscent of the one in *L'uomo parallelo*, returns in the sequence where a seagull enters the dining room of a luxurious passenger ship. For the aristocratic crowd assembled there, nature's encroachment on their sealed and protected space is an exceptional event, frightening for some, adventurous for others. In the film the journalist Orlando, the protagonist and narrator, ironically underscores the fate that has befallen the bird: "And the bird flew free in search of his cage." In the end the chaos generated by the crowd prevents any possible communication with the bird, which, with the aid of a sailor named Tonino (Guerra's first name), is finally liberated via a window.

Another alien animal presence on board is an ill rhinoceros, which is looked after by a beastly keeper who speaks "an almost incomprehensible dialect."[141] Andrea Zanzotto, who wrote the opera lyrics for the film, imitating the language and the style of the librettists of Verdi or Rossini, was evidently on the same wavelength as Fellini and Guerra when it came to the symbolism behind the rhinoceros; he understood it to be an "allusion to the most massive and obscure forces upon which reality and life stand."[142] According to the passengers' diagnosis of the ill rhinoceros, confirmed by its keeper, the animal is suffering from a mixture of love and nostalgia. The psychic illness of this imprisoned beast is therefore caused by the separation from the object of its love, its native environment. The painful and dissatisfied love for one's origin looms over the ship's journey in the form of the animal's pervading and persistent stench, which the captain fails to cover up. Eventually, so that its soiled body can be washed, the animal is brought into daylight, lifted by a crane high above the deck, and sprayed. The pachyderm here is a message of truth, forcefully asking to be witnessed, standing for the passengers' irreparable sense of separation from their dying past.

At the end, after the ship has been sunk by a dark and mysterious Austro-Hungarian cruiser (apparently the modern vessel that Fellini dreamed about in connection with the shedding of his artistic old self), and "an enormous cloud of black smoke hides the sea and the sky" in a "tragic silence" that signals the "end of everything," the journalist Orlando and the rhinoceros find themselves travelling together on the only lifeboat in sight.[143] In the open sea, the breeze, and the sunlight the rhinoceros is now feeling better. Orlando stands close to him "with the same trust that a peasant has for his cow" and expresses his regained solace in the discovery that, as he concludes, "the rhinoceros gives excellent milk."[144] This apocalyptical and satirical conclusion shows the human being alone and destroyed by his technology, turning now for help to the stinky beast that was previously abhorred; it is no longer the traditional, familiar cow or ox but the more intractable rhinoceros. The preposterousness of this newly established relationship is directly proportional to the chaotic destructiveness of progress that has ruined the original natural bond. Nonetheless, the return to corporality still seems to hold untold aid for the continuation of the journey on and beyond the stormy seas of modernity.

Maternal Pre-grammaticality: Pasolini, Guerra, and Zanzotto

In Fellini's cinema, language is often employed with expressionist effect to create suggestive atmospheres that pierce the rational level and contribute to the plastic and visual effect of the film. In *Le tentazioni del Dottor Antonio*, when Anita Ekberg's billboard comes alive in Dottor Antonio's epic hallucination, at first she is a kind of King Kong and then, as if to satisfy the protagonist's obsessions and his Puritan crusade, she becomes the embodiment of pagan and satanic eroticism, a hellish goddess of Eros and Thanatos, who, as she herself says, is able to arouse a "pleasure as great as death." In tune with her otherworldly nature, she chants a nonsensical spell, giving evidence of her demoniac alterity. In *8½* there is the case of the nonsensical childhood language that is extracted from Guido's memories by a prestidigitator; the spellbinding formula "Asa Nisi Masa" triggers a reverie of the dying embers in a fireplace from the world of Guido's childhood, the rural universe of Romagna. For *Satyricon*, Fellini requested the assistance of linguists and classicists to help him generate a language that would evoke the syncretic and decadent age of Nero as seen by Petronius.

Such expressionist, pre-grammatical use of languages heavily characterized Fellini's collaborations with Tonino Guerra and Andrea Zanzotto. As previously discussed, the Romagnol dialect of Guerra's poems in *Amarcord* played a role in a broader discourse about the reviving of corporality and wonderment. Andrea Zanzotto's contribution consisted mostly of experimental lyrics that were written in an archaic form of Venetian for *Il Casanova* and in a made-up Mitteleuropean language for *La città delle donne*, both being used to achieve specific poetic aims. However, the first screenwriter to apply the notion of the pre-grammatical to Fellini was Pier Paolo Pasolini when he playfully qualified the director's speech as "Pascolian pre-grammaticality."[145] This idea came to Pasolini from the work of the scholar Gianfranco Contini (1912–90), one of Pasolini's mentors, who played a key role in promoting the collections of dialect poetry written by Guerra and Pasolini. As Pasolini's description of Fellini's speech suggests, pre-grammaticality was a characteristic of Pascoli's poetry, as theorized by Contini in his incisive essay "Il linguaggio di Pascoli" (The language of Pascoli). Here, Contini saw in Pascoli's style an attempt to create a space before the onset of rationality and before the poetic discourse itself, through the employment of lyrical artifices such as onomatopoeias, suspension, dead languages like Latin and Greek, and virtually unknown and very circumscribed dialects.[146] This idea of pre-grammaticality was especially useful to Pasolini, who, while reflecting on the experience of writing poems in Friulan dialect throughout the 1940s, explained that he had related to dialect as a new language, as the language of the mother, which was nostalgically rediscovered in its graphic transcription with the promise of a virgin perspective on the world.[147]

Somewhat different was Pasolini's use of the slang of the Roman *borgate* in his novels *Ragazzi di vita* and *Una vita violenta*, in which he emphasized (with the aid of his Roman friend and collaborator Sergio Citti) violent expressions to heighten the tragic tone of the characters' vicissitudes. In fact, even in his linguistic notes and revisions to the dialogues of *Le notti di Cabiria*, Pasolini laboured at bringing to the foreground the harshness of the prostitutes' lives through popular and realistic linguistic choices, which the director eventually deemed inappropriate for the film and also potentially dangerous in terms of censorship. Confirming his fears in this regard, Fellini once remembered: "I used only a handful of the dialectal expressions, worried that this street language, smart, sordid, and highly eroticized, would have stirred the Catholic censors. The film, in addition, would have had a much darker and sinister look than the tragicomic look it took on."[148]

Zanzotto, who in certain ways occupied a role similar to that of Pasolini in his creative relationship with Fellini, likewise understood the director's peculiar aesthetic concern with language. According to Zanzotto, Fellini sought a parallel between the visual and phonetic elements of a film, between "luminous plasma" and "gut-voices," as Zanzotto once put it.[149] Films such as *Amarcord* and *Il Casanova* employ dialect for its alterity – that is, as a language of opposition to modernity and utopian thought. Besides, both being severe critics of a simplistic and euphoric idea of progress, Zanzotto and Pasolini admired each other's work and often engaged in debates. By comparison with Guerra's verse, however, Zanzotto's poetry was far less nostalgic and anecdotal and was engaged in a coherent excavation of the layers of history, both ancient and contemporary, found in the human and natural landscape (that of Pieve di Soligo, in the north of Veneto). His poetry, which during the 1950s represented a hermetic investigation of elegiac forms, becomes increasingly interested in the structures of subjectivity and language. Zanzotto was one of the leading experimental Italian poets of the twentieth century, with extremely innovative volumes such as *Dietro il paesaggio* (1951, *Behind the Landscape*), *La Beltà* (1968, *Beauty*), *Il Galateo in Bosco* (1978, The book of etiquette of the forest), *Fosfeni* (1983, Phosphenes), and *Idioma* (1986, Idioma).

Fellini's initial invitation to Zanzotto to collaborate on *Il Casanova* was motivated by the poet's expertise in moulding languages and especially in employing the archaic linguistic resources of the Veneto area. Fellini met Zanzotto in 1970 during the premiere of *I clowns* in Venice. Pier Paolo Pasolini's cousin and biographer, Nico Naldini, who was also a poet and was then working as publicist for *Il Casanova*, encouraged Fellini to contact Zanzotto as a possible collaborator for the film.[150] Fellini was impressed by the way in which Zanzotto had used the material of the "baby talk language" that was peculiar to the poet's hometown to construct his "Elegia in petèl" ("The Elegy in Petèl") in *La Beltà*. In his letter to Zanzotto in July 1976, Fellini quotes a passage from Zanzotto's poem that exemplifies the type of nursery-rhyme language in which he was interested: "Bono ti, ca, co nona. Béi bumba bona."[151] Then Fellini continues by articulating the reason that this experimental poem could be a beneficial model for the aesthetics of his film: "It seems to me that the liquid sonority, the confused gurgling, the sounds, the syllables that melt in the mouth, that sweet broken baby's singsong in a mixture of milk and dissolved solids, a sleep-inducing sound re-proposes once again and efficaciously suggests the kind of subaqueous iconography that characterizes the film, the placental, amniotic image of a decomposed and shifting Venice of algae, mossiness, and musty dank darkness."[152]

After having given an indication of the linguistic perimeters for the film – somewhere between the theatrical and vulgar Paduan dialect of Angelo Beolco (1502–42), also known as Ruzante, and the more refined and filtered Venetian of the playwright Carlo Goldoni (1907–93) – Fellini admitted that the film's language could be fashioned partially by "rediscovering archaic forms" and partially by "inventing phonetic and linguistic combinations," so that "the verbal endeavor also reflects the reverberation of the confused visionariness" that he had in mind for *Il Casanova*.[153] As it happens, the made-up, eighteenth-century Venetian language that was employed in the film was chiefly a lyrical enterprise, in which Fellini asked Zanzotto to focus on the plastic potential of the language, perhaps even more than on its literal meaning, where the dialogue's function moved from being narrative to having a type of sound effect, thus forming an evocative soundscape that went hand in hand with the film's visual poetry and archetypical imagery.

In one of his essays on linguistics, Zanzotto, in line with the previously mentioned reflections by Pasolini on the poetic potential of dialect, explains that dialect offers itself as a type of "'first mystery' that escapes every possible contemplation as well as every objectifying detachment" for its very quality of marginality and otherness in relationship to the standard language.[154] In Zanzotto's words, dialect "is capable of framing, even if in encrypted terms, the most dazzling opening into the forms of the future, of alterity, and of active dissolving."[155] For its otherness and vitality, dialect resides in an infantile space before writing, where the reality can be expressed in its most fluidic state. The evocation of nostalgia for a state of psychic origin was therefore at the forefront of both the writer's and the director's mind in making *Il Casanova*; however, Zanzotto's lyrics are not simply inserted into the film but, as Victoria Surliuga noted, are hidden and repressed by the film, because they are often barely audible, are muttered, or are overpowered by other sounds, an editing choice that further highlights the sense of loss of origin in the cinematographic experience.[156]

Zanzotto had only recently begun experimenting with dialect, and the successful lyrics he wrote for *Il Casanova* inspired him to write his longer poem "Filò" ("Peasants Wake") all in dialect. Interestingly, for Zanzotto the collaboration was also an opportunity to clarify his position towards cinema, which was in many ways typical of that taken by other literary poets before him but which, in his case, flowed into a more sophisticated and experimental search for a pre-logical verbal expression. In the first part of "Filò," Zanzotto manifests the commixture of repulsion and attraction that poets such as Guido Gozzano (1883–1916) had also felt towards the seventh art at the beginning of the twentieth century. Like Gozzano, who thought of cinema as a parasitical fly that had descended onto Italy to steal the elegance and grace of Latin artistry, Zanzotto wrote of film stealing and confusing humanity's dreams.[157] However, cinema is also a spectacle with the capability at times to "blaze, burn, and give light," leading mankind to new and strange paths, which agrees with Gozzano's earlier and more positive description of film as a vertiginous experience capable of conveying the magnitude of sacred events (as in the case of Saint Francis's miraculous life, about which Gozzano wrote a remarkable screenplay).[158] Early literary writers such as Gozzano – but also Luigi Pirandello, Gabriele D'Annunzio, Giovanni Verga (1840–1922), and many others – though intrigued by cinema's philosophic ramifications, its capacity to transfigure reality, and its attraction to the masses, generally did not acknowledge film as an art form, cautiously relegating it instead to a form of entertainment that was ruled by industrial requirements rather than by artistic genius.[159] Zanzotto, too, expressed his need to justify his involvement in cinema when he described Fellini as a rare and unique case, an individual born out of "the poor, great beyond of light and plastic," either a supernatural or a mutant being, who is at one with cinema and therefore able to transcend its limitations, to make poetry of it.[160] Zanzotto acknowledged the enigmatic power of Fellini's cinema, which led the writer into new lyrical territories "to bring up from who knows where" and "to dredge up" the old dialect of what he termed "head land."[161]

Consequentially, "Filò" also elaborates on Zanzotto's intention to equate his lyrics in dialect with *Il Casanova*'s opening ritual of the aquatic exhumation of the head of the "Great Mediterranean Mother, the mysterious female who lives inside each of us" (as Fellini wrote in a letter to the poet); in Zanzotto's long poem "Recitativo veneziano" (Venetian recitative) she becomes the archaic Venetian goddess Rèitia. Interestingly, even at the level of rhetoric structure and rhythm, Joseph Luzzi noted that Zanzotto's writing seems at times here to be moulded on the technique of montage, thus confirming his willingness to fully metabolize the aesthetics of cinema.[162] The visual and literary nature of the film's opening attempts to find a way back to the idea of the "head land," a principle of origin that is at the same time poetic, geographic, and historic.[163] Throughout the film, Venice, as an extension of the figure of the Mother, stands for the locus of Casanova's psychic origin.[164] Zanzotto also wrote "Cantilena londinese" (London lullaby), which was then modified and adapted by Nino Rota to merge with a primordial lullaby that was eventually titled "Canzone della buranella" (Song of the Venetian); it is sung by the giantess in the London amusement park to the two Neapolitan midgets who are attending her.

The giantess is yet another representation of the feminine deity-like figure who entrances Casanova. "Canzone della buranella," sung in the
imaginary dialect of Casanova's childhood, accentuates, as Zanzotto
put it, the protagonist's "desired regression" and the "nostalgia he at-
taches to the loss of innocence and youth."[165]

It becomes clear why Zanzotto's contribution orbits around both
dialect and the image of the Mother, as the poetic roles of these elements coincide. In *Il Casanova* this focus is also aided by Guerra's small
but memorable contribution (he was supposed to participate fully as
screenwriter but could not, owing to a sudden health crisis). For this
film, Guerra provided a poem dedicated to the vulva, based on the
Romagnol lyric "Cantèda Ventiquàtar" (Twenty-fourth song) from *E'
mel*, which was modified by Zanzotto.[166] The lyrics are chanted in the
film by a proto-clown figure, who invites the passersby to enter into
the stomach of a life-size model of a whale at the London amusement
park. Inside, men watch fantastic and eerie images of vaginas projected
through a magic lamp. The poem stresses the frightening and wondrous mystery of woman, who is compared in Guerra's text to "a spider web," "a door that leads who knows where," "a wall to destroy,"
"a mountain of sugar," "a forest where wolves run and a coach is led
by horses," and "an empty whale full of dark air and fireflies."[167] More
than anything else, the female organ is praised in song as a cosmogoni-
cal mystery, being the source of everything, including herself.

The voluptuous feminine bodies that populate the world of Fellini's
art are linked to the archetype of the Great Mother, which, as Fellini's
analyst Ernst Bernhard maintained, dwell deep within the Mediterranean and especially the Italian mind.[168] The mother archetype, like dialect, is a thread that is common to Fellini's work with both Guerra and
Zanzotto and also to his previous collaboration with Pasolini. While
Pasolini's tragic and violent narrative and linguistic solutions did not
merge with Fellini's sensibility, the two artists did see eye to eye when
it came to the meaning of the already mentioned prostitute character in
Le notti di Cabiria who is ironically nicknamed La Bomba (The Bomb,
after Rita Hayworth). In this figure they both found a representation of
primeval energies and archaic humanity. Together Fellini and Pasolini
spent several nights surveying Roman nightlife and looking for this
mysterious and enormous prostitute. As Pasolini recalled, La Bomba
had reached an "almost symbolic significance" to the point that they
"did not want to find her," because "truth had to remain hidden, in-
ternal, and ideal."[169] This majestic and terrifying woman, dispensing

primitive vital energy, appears in the original and uncensored filmed sequence of "L'uomo col sacco" in *Le notti di Cabiria* only as a simulacrum of herself, old and emaciated; instead her vital and awesome nature can be found in a few abandoned scenes of the screenplay that received Pasolini's attention.

In a sequence that was cut from the screenplay of *Le notti di Cabiria*, Cabiria, returning from the sanctuary with her friends, spots La Bomba's powerful silhouette emblematically displayed among ruins. With an aggressiveness born of desperation, she begins to verbally attack La Bomba, who readily reveals her primeval and animalistic connotations: "A confused grumbling noise comes from the ruins; then, between two large stones, the enormous figure of a huge woman slowly appears. She is ancient but not old. Her thick hair falls over the heavy and worn-out characteristics of her face. With a weighty and rancorous voice she grumbles insults at the girls. But the presence of the young men makes her peer out from the shadows, as if waiting ... She seems a fantastic animal surprised in its den."[170]

When Cabiria throws her a firecracker, La Bomba "jumps and makes a kind of growl." As the company leaves with their motorbikes, La Bomba catches Cabiria before she has time to escape: "towering with all her beastly mass ... her eyes whitish and immobile like those of a lioness ... the large woman pants heavily."[171] As a Great Mother figure, she is both destructive and compassionate, and after having almost suffocated Cabiria, she slowly lets go of her without a word, as if overcome by a caring instinct. It is a theme that returns in other moments of the exchange between Fellini and Pasolini. Pasolini also worked on the script of *Viaggio con Anita*, a film that was supposed to follow *Le notti di Cabiria*. The plot has the director Guido travelling with his mistress, Anita (who was going to be played by Sophia Loren), to Fano, a provincial town on the Adriatic coast, to see his dying father. In his analysis of the script Andrea Bigini detects certain traces of Pasolini's contributions, especially in connection with mother and feminine figures, such as in the scene of the visit to Piero della Francesca's painting *La Madonna del Parto*, and in the unbridled pagan celebration of femininity in the town of San Giovanni.[172] A note contained in the folder of *Viaggio con Anita* confirms Pasolini's frame of mind about this project; he understood Guido's story as a journey to the pre-modern world of childhood: "It is a going back to the old world of tradition, of the province, of nature, of simple souls, of an inferior culture."[173] Later, when collaborating on *La dolce vita*, Pasolini wrote the sequence in which Maddalena and Marcello pick up a prostitute and drive to her shabby apartment in the outskirts of the city. Even here, the prostitute is described in an archetypal tone; as Maddalena and Marcello enter her dark and exciting world, she appears as "a large, dark, pale motherly beast," and later, when interacting with her pimp, she reveals that "her corruption is as ancient as her innocence."[174]

The character of La Bomba is an early example of the archetype of the Great Mother, one on which Fellini elaborated artistically through his dialogue with Pasolini and that he then perfected through his consultation with Zanzotto. La Bomba is the blueprint for the Saraghina of *8½* and the many other prostitute figures of Fellini's world, such as those in *Block-notes di un regista, Roma, Amarcord*, and *Intervista*. The maternal symbols scattered throughout the films of Fellini unfold according to the psychoanalytic parameters specific to this archetype, combining both frightening and caring qualities. In Jungian psychology, as Erich Neumann theorized, the central figure of the Great Mother contains, in an undifferentiated whole, characteristics considered good and bad, or caring and destructive, as well as feminine and masculine (unlike other more polarized figures such as the Terrifying Mother and the Caring Mother).[175] Aesthetically, this duality suggests the auspicious influence and yet fatal dangers implied in abandoning oneself to such a myth. In a previous chapter, related considerations were made about Sylvia in *La dolce vita*, whose transformative potential was curbed by Flaiano's disillusioned perspective. The examples are several, but the development of this archetype finds its most explicit appearance in connection with Zanzotto's lyrics in *Il Casanova*, such as the "Recitativo veneziano" in the ritualistic opening of the film, where the goddess Rèitia is worshipped as the embodiment of the forces of life and death and of every feminine role – friend, spouse, mother, and queen.

While the analysis of Brunello Rondi's contribution to *La città delle donne* is especially relevant in understanding Fellini's critical relationship to eroticism as a genre, and Bernardino Zapponi's role here suggests the origin of certain funereal atmospheres and visual variants of male obsessions and fears (which acquired political nuances with the concomitant explosion of feminism), the minor presence of the poet Andrea Zanzotto in this film confirms his role as linguistic consultant, as well as his previously described understanding of the mother archetype.[176] With regard to the linguistic domain, Zanzotto, aided by the scholar and writer Claudio Magris (1939–), created the monologues in a hybrid form of Venetian and German for the sequence of the peasant woman biker.[177] His intellectual involvement with the film was significant, though, as attested by his essay "Ipotesi intorno alla *Città delle donne*" (Hypothesis about *The City of Women*), which represents the poet's most significant cinematographic analysis. Here, Zanzotto declares his affinity for Fellini's spiralling quest for a truth of the psyche and continues to trace the spectacle of the "intermittence" of the Mother archetype, in its constructive and destructive influences, a theme that in *La città delle donne* explodes into a vast pageant of all its psychic representations.[178] The nostalgic pursuit of a mythical origin that intersects the poetic sensibilities of Fellini and poet screenwriters such as Pasolini, Guerra, and Zanzotto is reflected in dialect and in the image of the mother figure, where pre-grammaticality is a quality functioning at both the linguistic and the visual level.

Conclusion

In his correspondence with Tullio Kezich, Ennio Flaiano once confessed, with his usual sarcasm, to "admire Fellini's capacity to select his nourishment, and his capacity to steal it whenever necessary wherever he finds it ... as a way to give order to chaos."[1] The most precious aspect of a director's talent might very well be his flair for choosing the right collaborators at the right time, and Fellini was certainly not lacking in this vital skill, which was coupled with a remarkable openness to ideas and suggestions. It is indeed astounding to consider the voracity and effectiveness with which Fellini's cinema absorbed and metabolized some of the finest Italian writers of the twentieth century.

The cultural implications of Fellini's screenwriting collaborations that are traced throughout the chapters of this book have significantly remapped the literary context for several of his films, though the analysis of the numerous cultural domains herein is in no way exhaustive and merits further research. This context was drawn from the intersection of the writers' independently produced (and often lesser-known) works, their contributions to the conceptualization of films, and the unfolding of their conversations with Fellini in public and private sources, including the recently published *Il libro dei sogni*. In this process Fellini's oneiric journal was employed to clarify concrete aspects of the director's work, as relevant dreams revealed their historical significance when placed alongside the director's documented creative exchanges.

Specifically, the contrastive analyses of the artistic and philosophic concerns of Fellini and those of his writers have clarified and contextualized the centrality and functionality of Fellini's ambivalent position towards the miraculous and the supernatural. His unique perspective on mystic and esoteric matters, at the same time self-indulgent and critical in nature, appeared to be central in motivating and shaping several of his long-term artistic partnerships, and it enabled the director to blend both spiritually inclined and disenchanted points of view from widely differing authors such as Pinelli, Flaiano, and Rondi, as well as other equally varied literary sources.

It was Pinelli who laid down the narrative foundation for the expression of the supernatural and spiritual themes that later became dear to Fellini, even though the playwright's traditionally Christian narrative was modified by Fellini's significantly more existentialist and ecumenical form of spirituality. The genesis of *La strada* is probably the best case study to demonstrate such a dynamic, though their spiritual interests continued to manifest themselves in films such as *Giulietta degli spiriti* and in several unrealized projects dealing with mediums, ancient mysteries of the Middle East, and shamanic cultures of Latin America. Interestingly, the assessment of the collaboration with Flaiano revealed that his resistance to Fellini's and Pinelli's metaphysical bent did much to heighten the self-ironic component of Fellini's ambivalent spirituality. While Fellini and Flaiano inspired one another in pursuing a compassionate Pirandellian form of satire, their perspectives differed, as the variants of the finale of *8½* emblematically encapsulate, especially regarding the outcomes of epiphany and the validity of magical and psychoanalytical routes to self-realization.

The principal common denominator in the creative partnership between Fellini and one of his next major screenwriters, Zapponi, was the artistic exploration of the liminal space between the conscious and the subconscious, the known and the unknown. For example, this common dynamic was discovered by the unveiling of the textual history of *Toby Dammit*, which integrates stories where Zapponi plays on the ambiguity between hallucination and paranormal events. Moreover, in theorizing a "twin neurosis" approach to adaptation, which was in line with strategies practised by Pier Paolo Pasolini and Carmelo Bene, Zapponi played a crucial role in supporting Fellini's personal recreations of literary classics in the 1960s and 1970s. Fellini's experimental documentaries in these years were also facilitated by Zapponi's experience with collage-like publications and psychoanalytic issues.

Fellini's work with his poet screenwriters often rested on the common desire to express the friction between a mental space of individual and collective childhood and the advance of modernity. Brunello Rondi's eclectic artistic pursuit for renewed harmony in human relationships, originating in a metaphysical interpretation of the Gramscian notion of the organic, was shown to be subtly expressed by musical references and eroticism in *La dolce vita*, *Prova d'orchestra*, and *La città delle donne*. While the quest for the expression of a mythical origin through the mother archetype was found to be a common thread in Fellini's exchanges with Pier Paolo Pasolini, Tonino Guerra, and Andrea Zanzotto, the contribution of the latter two came also through a strategic pre-logic use of dialect. Furthermore, animal images in *Amarcord* and *E la nave va* were seen as instruments for an ecologically minded discourse that idealized the peasant perspective and critiqued modernity, a discourse that was traced to Guerra's poetry and prose.

It seems appropriate to close by underscoring the fact that the differentiating elements (or, to use a phrase suggested by Pinelli, some degree of "complementary diversity") were often responsible for enriching the quality of Fellini's creative work.[2] The cases of the collaborations with Pinelli and Flaiano are good examples of this, since much of the poignancy of *La strada* was revealed to originate from the clash between Pinelli's tragic and traditional dramaturgic approach to the script and Fellini's pull towards comic gags and visual improvisation (a similar dynamic was also found in *Le notti di Cabiria* and *La dolce vita*); likewise, it was through the blending of Flaiano's existential pessimism and Fellini's thirst for epiphany that the unforgettable apocalyptical and melancholic tone of a film like *La dolce vita* came into being. More indirectly, the challenging relationships that Fellini sustained with Pasolini and Rondi encouraged and enriched a mutual quest for a poetic, yet socially concerned, cinema. Private and public testimonies revealed that both of these relationships provided instrumental stimuli for Fellini to evolve the philosophic, social, and lyrical quality of his work. In all such cases, it became clear that Fellini's authorial vision developed through and thanks to conflicting collaborations, and that differences in sensibilities and interests, even though at times painful and hard to endure, were factors that lent an extraordinary complexity and completeness to many of Fellini's more acclaimed films.

Artistic activity cannot be reduced to the simplistic narrative of individualism, especially in the case of the art film and of Fellini's cinema; rather it needs to be understood within its own network of social and collaborative exchanges. To trace the ways in which Fellini inspired and was in turned inspired, to auscultate the life of these exchanges even in their less public and historically celebrated conjunctures, allows us not only to partake indirectly in some measure of the human wealth that gave life to these marvellous films but also to detect the little known elements that may open to new vistas on the films' cultural and artistic meaning found behind the scenes.

Notes

Throughout this book, translated quotations belong to the author unless otherwise indicated. All translations for Fellini's *Il libro dei sogni* are by Aaron Maines from the English edition. When a linguistic comparison is useful, as is often the case with literary texts, or in the case of particularly dense or memorable statements, the original Italian is provided in a note. Translations of film titles are the author's unless they are in italics, signifying an English version of the film.

Introduction

1 As Robert Gordon notes in his review of the new edition of Bondanella's history, adjustments in response to the new scholarly orientations are visible from the choice of a new title, which changed from *Italian Cinema: From Neorealism to the Present* to *A History of Italian Cinema*, as well as from the inclusion of lengthy chapters on the silent era and modern commercial genres and subgenres ("Film History Recut," 28).
2 See especially the debate waged by Alan O'Leary and Catherine O'Rawe against the critical institutions of realism and auteurism as tendencies preventing a scientific understanding of popular cinema (O'Leary and O'Rawe, "A 'Certain Tendency' in Italian Film Criticism"; O'Rawe, "The Condition of Italian Cinema Studies: Gender, Genres, Auteurs, and Absences"; and O'Leary, "After Brunetta: Italian Cinema Studies in Italy, 2000 to 2007").
3 Wood, *Italian Cinema*, 111.
4 The year 1954 is significant both for the release of *La strada* and for the publication by François Truffaut of "Une certaine tendance du cinéma français" ("A Certain Tendency in French Cinema"), widely considered to be the manifesto of *la politique des auteur* that was later imported as "the auteur theory" into the United States by Andrew Sarris, who rigidly

defined the attributes that rendered a director an author. For a synthesis of the history of auteurism in cinema as it pertains to screenwriting collaborations, see the introduction of Steven DeRosa's *Writing with Hitchcock* (i–xvi). For a more in-depth assessment of the movement's evolution, the reader can explore the results of a decade-long debate on auteurism exemplified by articles such as Andrew Sarris, "Notes on the *Auteur* Theory in 1962" (*Film Culture* 27, Winter 1962–3: 1–18), and "The *Auteur* Theory and the Perils of Pauline" (*Film Quarterly* 16.4, Summer 1963: 26–33); Pauline Kael, *I Lost It at the Movies* (New York: Bantam Books, 1966), 264–88; Graham Petrie, "Alternative to Auteurs" (*Film Quarterly* 26.3, Spring 1973: 27–35); and John Hess, "Auteurism and After: A Reply to Graham Petrie" (*Film Quarterly* 27.2, Winter 1973–4: 28–37).

5 The following film-makers, ranging in styles, periods, and nationality, have all expressed more or less straightforwardly Fellini's influence on their cinema: Pier Paolo Pasolini, Lina Wertmüller (1926–), Woody Allen (1935–), Terry Gilliam (1940–), David Lynch (1946–), Nanni Moretti (1953–), Giuseppe Tornatore (1956–), Lars Von Trier (1956–), Spike Jonze (1969–), and Paolo Sorrentino (1970–).

6 For a detailed taxonomy of the pitfalls of single-authorship in film criticism and a convincing argument in favour of a multiple-authorship approach see Berys Gaut, "Film Authorship and Collaboration." Throughout this book non-English titles are given with the English title and the release or publication date in parentheses the first time they are mentioned, and subsequently only in the original language.

7 Micciché, "Un cinema senza sceneggiatori?" 33.

8 Orson Welles's words are reported by Robert Carringer in *The Making of Citizen Kane*, 134.

9 Ibid., 134.

10 It is important to distinguish the present book from a militant book such as David Kipen's *The Schreiber Theory*, which contains a forceful rejection of a director-centred perspective on the history of cinema. Kipen's cause is "to explode the director-centric farrago of good intentions, bad faith, and tortured logic that goes by the name of auteurism, and to replace it with a screenwriter-centered way of thinking about film" (38). Kipen's invitation to rewrite the history of cinema by "shelving" films by writers rather than by directors appears to be a proposition that is just as unbalanced as traditional director-centred auteurism.

11 Carringer, "Collaboration and Concepts of Authorship," 377.

12 Pasolini, "La sceneggiatura come 'struttura che vuole essere altra struttura'" (The screenplay as a structure that wants to be another structure).

13 Luciani, *Verso una nuova arte*, 79–84.
14 Luciani, *L'antiteatro*, 29–30 (emphasis in the original).
15 For example, Brunetta writes of the "Zavattini effect," where he identifies Cesare Zavattini (1902–89) as the most prominent screenwriter. Indeed, Zavattini was the perfect example of the screenwriter who was better able to impose a personal plan on the films, a vision that Brunetta describes as characterized by a minimalist enquiry into language and behaviours, a preference for paradoxical and uncommon elements, and the recurring theme that interlaces travel and identity. See Brunetta, *Storia del cinema italiano*, vol 3, 264–76.
16 Muscio, *Scrivere il film*, 10.
17 Wood, *Italian cinema*, 111.
18 See Pinelli's recollections on the making of *La dolce vita* in Faldini and Fofi, *L'avventurosa storia del cinema italiano*, 4.
19 See Rondi, *Il cinema di Fellini*, 24–5.
20 The emphasis on this early step in screenwriting is also shared by Ian McDonald, who grounds the study of any screenplay in its initial core idea or essence as a way to trace its multi-authorial development (see for example his "Disentangling the Screen Idea" and "The Silent Screenwriter: The Re-discovered Scripts of Eliot Stannard").
21 The literature on the collaboration between Fellini and Nino Rota is quite vast and mature. See Fabrizio Borin's *La filmografia di Nino Rota*; the collection of essays edited by Giovanni Morelli, *Storia del candore*; and Pier Marco De Santi's "L'amico magico" (in his *La musica di Nino Rota*, v–vii). A precious technical study of creative negotiation is Van Order's *Listening to Fellini*, which unveils the narrative and poetic function of Rota's music when it is edited by Fellini. John Stubbs has effectively explored in his volume *Federico Fellini as Auteur: Seven Aspects of His Films* the multifaceted artistic partnership between Fellini and Giulietta Masina (136–70). Another creative collaboration that has received significant scholarly attention is the one Fellini shared with the comic book artist Milo Manara (1945). On this case see Antonio Tripodi and Marco Dalla Gassa, *Approdo a Tulum: Le Neverland a fumetti di Fellini e Manara*. On a minor note, Vittorio Boarini published a booklet titled *L'arte di Fellini nella collezione Gèleng e nei costumi di Danilo Donati* about Fellini's costume designer Danilo Donati and the painter Rinaldo Gèleng, who created many of the paintings and scenes that used to decorate Fellini's sets. Another publication, *Fellini & Rossi: Il sesto vitelloni*, by Moraldo Rossi and Tatti Sanguineti, offers insight into the role played by Fellini's assistant Moraldo Rossi.

22 The most significant contributions to the study of Fellini's screening collaborations are, in chronological order, Rebecca West's article "Tonino
Guerra and the Space of the Screenwriter," which appeared in 1988;
Goffredo Fofi's 1993 essay "Flaiano: O dell'ironia come forma intima di
sopravvivenza oltre la tragedia"; Franco Zabagli's 1995 study "Pasolini per
'Le notti di Cabiria'"; Dana Renga's 1999 article "Irony and the Aesthetics
of Nostalgia: Fellini, Zanzotto, and Casanova's Redemption"; and more
recently, Lorenzo Pellizzari's 2004 survey "Un filo rosso per il cinema
italiano," covering Tonino Guerra's cinematographic collaborations. In
addition, Stefania Parigi and Alberto Pezzotta have published the volume
Il lungo respiro di Brunello Rondi (2010), containing some discussion about
Rondi's collaborations with Fellini, Rossellini, and Pasolini. Luciano De
Giusti's commentary introducing his edited anthology of Zanzotto's essays
on cinema, *Il cinema brucia e illumina* (2011), includes various documents
pertaining to his collaboration with Federico Fellini.

23 Similarly, the approach of this book differs from recent production studies
such as Andrew Spicer's "The Author as Author: Restoring the Screenwriter to British Film History" and Steven DeRosa's study of Alfred
Hitchcock's collaboration with the screenwriter John Michael Hayes
(1919–2008), *Writing with Hitchcock.*

24 As Jack Stillinger has amply clarified in his work *Multiple Authorship and
the Myth of Solitary Genius*, biographically oriented sources are necessary
for a study of collaborative dynamics that wishes to integrate knowledge of the medium with knowledge of the author (see especially pages
163–81).

25 The only study that systematically integrates *Il libro dei sogni* is the 2008
article "*Il mare e il treno: I segni e i sogni dell'espressionismo di Federico Fellini*"
by Ennio Bispuri, in which the author analyses how the elements of the
train and the sea return both in Fellini's dreams and in his films, thus
unpacking their overall symbolic significance and aesthetic function. The
recordings of Fellini's dreams, which before the publication of *Il libro dei
sogni* were available only as they appeared sporadically, have been occasionally integrated by Peter Bondanella and Gianfranco Angelucci as
sources of the imagery and themes in Fellini's films, and in particular in
the television spots that he directed in the last years of his work (Bondanella, *The Cinema*, 69–150; Angelucci, *Gli ultimi sogni di Fellini*). Tullio
Kezich sometimes makes references to dreams in his biography of Fellini
to encapsulate Fellini's psychological states in various circumstances. In
his book *Linguaggi dell'aldilà*, Maurizio De Benedictis explores some of

Fellini's dreams connected with *Mastorna* to explain the overall significance of this very important unrealized screenplay and the reasons behind
its abandonment. Nevertheless, the literature orbiting around the notion
of dream in Fellini's work is vast, examining issues such as the filmic
representation of dream, the narrative function of dream, and dream as a
founding principle of Fellini's poetics; some examples include Gianfranco
Angelucci, "Fellini 15 e ½ e la poetica dell'onirico"; Marie Jean Lederman,
"Dreams and Vision in Fellini's 'City of Women'"; Lietta Tornabuoni, "Fellini oniricon"; Hava Aldouby, "A Jungian Approach to Federico Fellini's
Visual Imagery"; Stubbs, *Federico Fellini as Auteur* (37–69); and Carolyn
Geduld, "*Juliet of the Spirits*: Guido's Anima."

26 As only a few sparse pages fill the gap between the two books, there is
speculation that a lost notebook might exist. In the last years of his life Fellini stopped recording his dreams, mainly owing to a condition of insomnia
that forced him to take drugs that impaired his ability to dream (see Lietta
Tornabuoni, *Federico Fellini*, 103).

27 Pasolini, quoted in Faldini and Fofi, *L'avventurosa storia*, 273.

28 See Christian Gaillard, "Dire et non-dit du reve," and Ferdinando Camon,
"Cosa c'è sotto le cancellature?"

29 Kezich, introduction to Fellini, *The Book of Dreams*, 11.

30 The director's own interpretative approach to his dreams does not seem to
be concerned with any specific psychoanalytic method but, as Bernardino
Zapponi once described, is "a syncretism of Jung, Zen, Artemidor, I Ching, Neapolitan satire, with a touch of Freud" and chiefly "guided by his
personal and acute psychological intuition" (Zapponi, *Il mio Fellini*, 117).

31 Collecting the dreamer's own interpretation is essential to the psychoanalyst's work, but here this information is used to enrich an understanding of
cultural and artistic dynamics rather than to reach a therapeutic goal. Jung
stated, "It is not possible, except under very special conditions, to work
out the meaning of a dream without the collaboration of the dreamer," and
praised Freud's methodological advancement in having "recognized that
no interpretation can be undertaken without the dreamer" because "the
words composing a dream-narrative have not just *one* meaning, but many
meanings." It follows that "the only justifiable [dream] interpretations are
those reached through a painstaking examination of the context"
(C.G. Jung, *Dreams*, 69–73). Since dream interpretation is not the objective
of my analysis, this process having been already concluded and recorded
by Fellini himself on the pages of *Il libro dei sogni*, the notion of "context"
here is devoid of any psychoanalytic meaning.

32 See André Bazin, "La strada" and *"Cabiria*: The Voyage to the End of Neo-realism"; Renzo Renzi, *Il primo Fellini*; and Peter Bondanella, *The Cinema of Federico Fellini*.

33 Stubbs's *Federico Fellini as Auteur*; Van Order's *Listening to Fellini*; Minuz's *Viaggio a termine dell'Italia*; and Aldouby's *Federico Fellini*.

34 Fellini, "Lettera a Dino De Laurentis," in *Il viaggio di G. Mastorna*, 205. The parenthesis is added in pen to the typescript, and the word *ambiguous* replaces an erased word, now illegible. The original typescript is archived at the Swiss publishing house Diogenes Verlag in Zurich.

35 Pinelli and Pacchioni, "Intervista a Tullio Pinelli," 317.

36 As the anthropologist Cecilia Gatto Trocchi chronicles in her *Storia esoterica d'Italia*, esoteric culture has always had a strong foothold in Italy, and similar interests, merged with a commitment to social good and the fostering of new knowledge and meaning, have characterized prominent figures such as Giuseppe Mazzini (1805–1972), Alessandro Manzoni (1785–1873), Luigi Capuana (1836–1915), and Giovanni Amendola (1882–1926).

37 Zanzotto, "Lo sciamano," 121.

38 Risset, *L'incantatore: Scritti su Fellini*, 41.

39 Additional testimonies of the relationship between Rol and Fellini can be found in: Fellini, "Io sono aperto voluttuosamente a tutto," 103–4; Fellini and Kezich, "L'intervista lunga," 35–43; Kezich, "Quella sera a Torino con il mago di Fellini," 17; Lugli, *Gustavo Rol: una vita di prodigi*, 141–3, collecting anecdotes reported by Dino Buzzati in his 1965 article on *Corriere della sera*; Giordano, *Rol e l'altra dimensione*, 166–82, which also contains details regarding Rol's involvement in *Mastorna* and the medium's portrait of the director; Allegri, *Rol: Il grande veggente*, 199–210. For an overview of this medium's life and philosophy see Rol's*"Io sono la grondaia ..." Diari, lettere, riflessioni di Gustavo Adolfo Rol.*

40 Fellini's words are reported by Dino Buzzati in *I misteri d'Italia*, 47.

41 Fellini, *Fare un film*, 89.

42 Pinelli and Pacchioni, "Intervista a Tullio Pinelli," 317.

43 Early on, Aldo Carotenuto (1933–2005), one of Italy's leading psychoanalysts, noted the importance that this meeting had for Fellini's work. To Carotenuto, Bernhard was to Fellini "the father, the guide ... to traverse the labyrinth of his soul" (121). Tullio Kezich interviewed Luciana Marinangeli, the biographer of Bernhard, who told him that Fellini's sessions took place three times per week for four years. According to Marinangeli, Bernhard, who believed that dreams were in some cases more important than waking thoughts and activities since they embodied the key elements of one life's myth and destiny, worked to help Fellini become aware of

the effects of the eternal child whom he saw at the root of Fellini's nature (Kezich, *Federico Fellini* 223–4). See also Luciana Marinangeli, *Risonanze celesti l'aiuto dell'astrologia nella cura della psiche* (Venezia: Marsilio, 2007), 254–6.

44 Fellini, *Fare un film*, 91.

45 Filmed fragments of the script of *Mastorna* have been convincingly identified in various moments of Fellini's later cinema. See A. Casanova, *Scritti e immaginati: I film mai realizzati di Federico Fellini*, 53–83; and Kezich, *Federico Fellini*, 269.

46 See Kezich, *Federico Fellini*, 265–70, and Pinelli and Pacchioni, "Intervista a Tullio Pinelli," 314. On this note, *The Book of Dreams* has two dreams about Buzzati (pp. 286 and 443), the second of which is connected to Fellini's and Buzzati's inability to continue work on *Mastorna*.

47 Rondi quoted in Zanelli, *L'inferno immaginario di Federico Fellini*, 67.

48 Guerra and Martini, "Il cinema di Tonino Guerra," 15–39. In a journal entry of 11 September 1974 where Fellini records an I Ching message regarding progress in his work, he expresses his hopes that his collaboration with Guerra may help him to realize his old project (Fellini, *The Book of Dreams*, 276).

49 De Giusti, *Il cinema brucia e illumina*, 17. Kezich. *Federico Fellini*, 393.

50 Buzzati, *I misteri d'Italia*, 39.

51 For a discussion of the fusion of writing and comics as a common trait in the work of Buzzati and Fellini, both seen as pop artists, see Gargiulo's "*Poema a fumetti* trent'anni dopo: Alcune riflessioni sui 'mondi possibili' di Buzzati e Fellini." For a cursory discussion of the connection between *Poema a fumetti* and *The Voyage of G. Mastorna* see De Benedictis, *Linguaggi* (111–16).

52 "E apertamente dedicai il cuore alla terra grave o sofferente. E promisi di amarla con fedeltà, fino alla morte, senza paura, col suo greve carico di fatalità e di non spregiare alcuno dei suoi enigmi, così m'avvinsi ad essa di un vincolo mortale" (Fellini, *Il viaggio di G. Mastorna*, 161).

53 Hölderin composed three versions of *Tod des Empedokles*, the first being the version from which this passage most likely originates (see scene IV); however, the best match for the passage in Italian used by Fellini remains the one from Camus's *L'homme révolté* (Paris: Gallimard, 1951), thereby indicating that this was the source used by the director.

54 In the dream entry dated 20 August 1984, which is dominated by the image of the director sitting beneath a shimmering night sky in the company of his production manager Clemente Fracassi (1917–93), Fellini observes: "All that we can do is try to reach the awareness that we are part of this

impenetrable mystery that is creation. We obey its unfathomable laws, its rhythms, its changes. We are mysteries among mysteries" (F. Fellini, *The Book of Dreams*, 414 and 553).

55 Fellini, "Io sono aperto voluttuosamente a tutto," 102–3.

56 For details regarding Fellini and Castaneda see Tripodi and Dalla Gassa, *Approdo a Tulum*, 119–27; and Kezich, *Federico Fellini*, 359–64. Apparently Fellini was accompanied on this trip by the writer Andrea De Carlo (1952), who had recently worked as assistant director for *E la nave va* and who translated his experience into the fictional novel *Yucatan* (Milan: Bompiani, 1986).

57 Fellini and Pinelli, "Viaggio a Tulun," 31 and 34.

58 This idea is one of the organizing principles behind the critical reflections contained in Tripodi and Dalla Gassa, *Approdo a Tulum*. The comic version of Mastorna's journey, which elects the actor Paolo Villaggio (1932–) as the protagonist, was completed only in part; the comic-book version of the journey through the Yucatan, however, differs noticeably from the original script, especially in the end where the protagonist director, here embodied by Marcello Mastroianni, is explicitly held responsible for interpreting cinematographically the ancient wisdom revealed to him by the shaman, a knowledge that is materialized through the beneficial influence of a girl's sensual beauty, which was emphasized by Manara's drawings. See Fellini and Manara, *Due viaggi con Federico Fellini*, 61–76.

59 Rota's inclination for spiritual and religious matters emerged very early in his dedication to the study of sacred classical music, which led to his masterpiece *Oratorio Mysterium*, and later in his choice to compose scores for literary works dealing with spiritual themes. Furthermore, in the company of his friend, the philosopher and student of alchemy Vincenzo Virginelli (1903–87), Rota spent much of his free time and a significant amount of his resources in seeking out and acquiring a large number of alchemical texts from the fifteenth through the eighteenth centuries, suggesting that this interest was not a collector's hobby but reflected a heartfelt spiritual practice. See Vincenzo Virginelli's critical edition and catalogue for the manuscripts, *Bibliotheca Hermetica: Catalogo alquanto ragionato della raccolta Vergnelli-Rota di atichi testi ermetici* (Florence: Nardini, 1986). Vincenzo Virginelli was a follower of the influential master of neo-Egyptian hermeticism in Italy, Ciro Formisano, aka Giuliano Kremmerz (1861–1930), who was also the founder of the Therapeutic and Magic Brotherhood of Myriam. Rota also set to music Virginelli's alchemical fable *Aladino e la lampada magica* (Aladdin and the magic lamp). The oboe of Fellini's lunatic player in *La voce della luna*, who accidentally stumbles upon an unfortunate musical interval

traditionally known as *diabulus in musica* – a sinister dissonance that in the film evokes ghosts and invisible forces – is reminiscent of the haunting clarinet with which Rota had set to music Ugo Betti's *Lo spiritismo nella casa vecchia* (Spiritualism in the old house), and could be seen as a final caricatural homage to his lifelong collaborator.

1. Tullio Pinelli

1 Sainati, *Ciò che abbiamo detto è tutto vero*, 81.
2 Pinelli and Kezich, "Il teatro del mondo," 36. A similar if less miraculous character will also return in *I vitelloni*. In the version of the screenplay archived at the Lilly Library of Rare Books (hereafter referred to as LLRB) is a passage about an engineer who is trying to build a flying machine (264). This idiosyncratic minor character who appears more than once in the screenplay is shown only briefly in the film.
3 Pinelli and Kezich, "Il teatro del mondo," 33.
4 Farassino, *Lux Film*, 11–44.
5 Barbanente, "Tullio Pinelli: Ritratto di uno scrittore cinematografico," 43.
6 Other less important films that they co-authored, often with other screenwriters, were *Il passatore* (directed by Duilio Coletti, 1947), *Il delitto di Giovanni Episcopo* (directed by Lattuada, 1947), *La città si difende* (directed by Pietro Germi, 1951), and *Cameriera bella presenza offresi ...* (directed by Giorgio Pastina, 1951). They also initially worked on *Persiane chiuse* (1951), which they then passed to another group of writers who worked with Luigi Comencini. The team of Pinelli and Fellini also produced a number of fascinating screenplays that never became movies, such as *Il processo di Maria Tarnowska* (for the direction of Luchino Visconti, 1948) and *Happy Country* (for the direction of Mario Camerini, 1950).
7 Pinelli and Pacchioni, "Intervista a Tullio Pinelli," 313.
8 At times Pinelli was called on set by Fellini to make quick adjustments to the script, as happened in the case of the unsuccessful love confession between Marcello Mastroianni and Anouk Aimée in one of the party sequences in *La dolce vita*, which integrates an interesting acoustic mechanism of a castle into the storyline. For the most part, Pinelli preferred to work from the "large white and serene room" of his home, as Fellini once recalled. See Pinelli and Kezich, "Il teatro del mondo" 39, and Fellini quoted in Sainati, *Ciò che abbiamo detto*, 9–26.
9 The play, together with *Gorgonio* and *Il giardino delle sfingi*, is contained in Tullio Pinelli, *Il giardino delle sfingi e altre commedie*.
10 See Giammusso, "The Theatre of Tullio Pinelli," 11.

11 Pinelli was also a writer of librettos and collaborated with Giorgio Federico Ghedini (1892–1965) in this capacity for adaptations of operas such as *Re Hassan* (1939), *Le Baccanti* (1941), *Villon* (1941), and *La croce deserta* (1950).

12 Kezich, *Federico Fellini*, 103.

13 Pinelli quoted in Sainati, *Ciò che abbiamo detto*, 52.

14 Pinelli quoted in Zambelli and Acone, *Campane nel pozzo*, 43.

15 The following is a complete list of Pinelli's writings for the stage: *Il venturiero* (1926), *'l sofa d'la marchesa d'mombaron* (1931–2), *I porta* (1932), *La pulce d'oro* (1934–6), *Crotta, lupo* (1938), *Pegaso* (1938), *I padri etruschi* (1940–1), *L'arcidiavolo di radicofani* (1941), *Il padre nudo* (1942), *Lotta con l'angelo* (1942), *La leggenda dell'assassino* (1947–9), *Gorgonio* (1950, 1952, 1963), *L'inferno* (1954), *Mattutino* (1954), *Il ciarlatano meraviglioso* (1960–2), *La sacra rappresentazione di Santa Marina* (1968–70), and *Il giardino delle sfingi* (1975). For general discussions of Pinelli's plays see the entry dedicated to him by Kezich in *Enciclopedia dello spettacolo*; Giammusso, "The Theatre of Tullio Pinelli," which also includes Silvio D'Amico's reviews of a few of Pinelli's most popular plays; Pinelli and Salvi, "Tullio Pinelli fra teatro e cinema"; and also Curato, *Sessant'anni di teatro in Italia*, 304–12.

16 Fiocco, *Correnti spiritualistiche nel teatro moderno*, 84–93.

17 Curato, *Sessant'anni di teatro in Italia*, 309. Further testifying to Pinelli's sensitivity to the significance imbedded in human tragedy, it should be remembered that in 1943, together with Diego Fabbri, Pinelli had issued the *Manifesto per un teatro del popolo* (Manifest for a people's theatre), in which the two writers (and other Catholic as well as Marxist writers and intellectuals including Vito Pandolfi, Gerardo Guerrieri, and Orazio Costa) expressed a commitment to address the interior traumas left behind by the recent war.

18 Fellini stated: "When I told Pinelli my then still confused idea of what the film might be, he turned red from surprise and right after told me that during his summer vacation while riding along his large property in the Tuscan countryside, he had also fantasized about a picaresque tale of gypsies and street artists. We had a lively conversation for the entire afternoon; it was as if Gelsomina and Zampanò were telling us the story of their wanderings, of their encounters and of their lives" (Fellini, *Fare un film*, 58). Pinelli said: "It was at least 1953 or 1954 ... Returning to Rome, I said to Fellini right away 'Listen Federico, as I was on the road I had an idea that I like very much.' And he said: 'I too have an idea. Tell me yours first and then I will tell you mine.' And in essence it was the same thing! ... It happened as if through telepathy. Fellini was more centred on the small travelling circuses that you could find at the time on the streets and squares. My

idea was slightly different; however, since I immediately liked his idea and he immediately liked mine, we merged them together" (Pinelli and Boggio, "Tullio Pinelli intervistato da Maricla Boggio," 13).

19 Pinelli, *La strada: Dramma*, 16–17; Sainati, *Ciò che abbiamo detto*, 18.
20 Pinelli quoted in Zambelli and Acone, *Campane nel pozzo*, 43. In another interview Pinelli also stated: "I wrote it all myself, because Fellini was always busy on the set, and I would send him scenes one at a time" (Pinelli, *La strada: Dramma*, 17).
21 Fellini, *Fare un film*, 58–60.
22 Both of these plays by Pinelli are published in *Tullio Pinelli*, along with *I padri etruschi* (1941), *La lotta con l'angelo* (1942), and *La sacra rappresentazione di Santa Marina* (1970). For other remarks by Pinelli about the world of street artists see an interview in Scolari, *L'Italia di Fellini*, 262–3 and 266–76.
23 Pinelli quoted in Sainati, *Ciò che abbiamo detto*, 15.
24 Pinelli and Boggio, "Tullio Pinelli intervistato da Maricla Boggio," 16.
25 This is the earliest available version of *La strada*, bound in a volume with a final version of the screenplay (Pinelli MS. 5, box 2, IE), and of which an edited version has been published in *Fellini-Amarcord*. This analysis contains quotes from the original copy at the Lilly Library of Rare Books. In box 3 there is a previous draft of *LS1* (Pinelli MS. 7, IIA) that presents minor changes and is less readable. Besides speaking of one of these copies present at the LLRB, Tullio Pinelli speaks of another copy, one owned by Tullio Kezich, which is possibly identical to *LS1*: "I worked on this long scenario-treatment. Tullio Kezich has my original copy; I don't know where he found the typed manuscript. Another copy was requested by an American university, and I sent it to them. It is the first version of *La strada*" (Pinelli, *La strada: Dramma*, 15). The volume Fellini, *Le notti di Cabiria*, edited by Lino Del Fra, offers a lengthy quotation from *LS1* that Del Fra likely consulted before Peter Bondanella bought it in 1987 on behalf of the LLRB or perhaps used the Tullio Kezich version. Fabrizio Natalini is currently completing a survey of a number of unpublished versions of scripts written by Fellini, Pinelli, and Flaiano that were acquired through the Del Fra family, which might reveal additional details; for news on Natalini's work see Alessandra Mammì's article "Fellini segreto."
26 This manuscript is contained in a separate folder as Pinelli ms. 7, box 3, IIA.
27 "Un lampo riga le pesanti nuvole nere, ferme tra cielo e terra. Poi arriva il tuono, uno scoppio secco che rotola lontano, oltre le ultime case della città, nella campagna silenziosa. Incomincia a cadere la grandine. Chicchi bianchi battono qua e là e rimbalzano; e d'improvviso diventano fitti, grossi,

violenti, avvolgendo in una candida sonante tempesta l'antico acquedotto
semidiroccato, le baracche che vi si appoggiano, i piccoli orti fra capanna
e capanna. Le lamiere dei tetti mandano un fragore assordante; le foglie
e i fiori hanno sussulti secchi e improvvisi, e si raddrizzano mutilati; e
la terra si copre di bianco mentre rivoli impetuosi e scroscianti d'acqua
piovana corrono dappertutto, trascinando piccole dighe di tondi ghiac-
cioli grigiastri. E d'un tratto, la tempesta, magicamente, svanisce. La stessa
mano potente che l'aveva portata, l'ha dispersa e trascinata altrove; e sotto
la luce che cade dalle nuvole rotte e fuggenti tutto è diventato scintillante,
lucido, tremulo. Qualcosa di nero emerge dall'aria trasparente, piena delle
vibrazioni dell'arcobaleno, in fondo al viottolo che costeggia l'alto mura-
glione cadente dell'acquedotto. È un uomo che avanza adagio, trascinando
un carretto chiuso da un tendone barcollante. Sembra che si sia staccato
dalla terra nera e greve per l'acqua. Cammina guardando le capanne ad-
dossate alle antiche mura; cerca di orientarsi e di ritrovarne, fra tutte, una.
Il carretto lo segue sobbalzando sulla strada ineguale; e la larga cinghia di
cuoio che gli attraversa il petto quadrato gli preme ad ogni sobbalzo sul
collo tozzo, cotto dal sole e solcato da rughe in cui la nera polvere delle
strade si annida indelebilmente da anni" (*LS1*, 1–2).

28 Pinelli, *I padri etruschi*, 47.
29 Ibid., 84.
30 Bondanella, *The Cinema of Federico Fellini*, 112–13.
31 Pinelli, *La strada: Dramma*, 18–19. In fact, the examples at which Pinelli is
    hinting in this quote come from his recent book of short stories *Innamorarsi:
    Racconti*.
32 Pinelli, *La strada: Dramma*, 14; Sainati, *Ciò che abbiamo detto*, 18.
33 "Zampanò balza, come una tigre, tra il sole e l'ombra ... Ecco, ora Gel-
    somina ha ritrovato il Matto. Lo ha ritrovato riverso nell'erba spruzzante
    di rosso, la bocca spalancata, gli occhi vitrei. Zampanò si è appena risol-
    levato e guarda il corpo immobile che gli giace ai piedi. Non si è ancora
    accorto che Gelsomina è sbucata correndo dai cespugli. E Gelsomina
    sta ferma; tutto in lei è fermo il sangue, il cuore, lo sguardo, il pensiero.
    Tutto in lei è terrore mortale, che paralizza anche la disperazione. D'un
    tratto Zampanò si volge e la vede. Il furore omicida che lo possiede e
    l'ubriacatura del sangue lo buttano come una belva contro la donna che lo
    ha scoperto. Gelsomina se lo vede piombare addosso con il coltello sporco
    di sangue in pugno; e le ginocchia le mancano. Manda un grido e cade
    a terra priva di sensi. Zampanò si ferma di netto su di lei. Allucinato e
    ansante fissa la ragazza stesa si suoi piedi, e non la colpisce" (*LS1*, 72–4).
34 Ibid., 23–7.

35 "Gelsomina scivola tra il carretto e il muro; si butta nel buio della campagna. È una corsa disperata, nella terra molle, nell'oscurità fitta, con
l'incalzare terrificante dei passi precipitosi e del fiato pesante dell'uomo,
sempre più vicino. Una corsa senza meta e senza respiro. Quando Zampanò le piomba addosso e l'afferra, a Gelsomina sembra di aver corso per
un tempo infinito. Rantola; e il grido roco che manda nel sentirsi afferrata
muore subito sotto una tempesta di colpi. Essa si dibatte senza averne
coscienza; sente soltanto le percosse violente e le mani dell'uomo che la
stringono in una morsa. Si sente cadere, con l'uomo che le preme addosso;
e questa volta essa grida per un oscuro istinto ancestrale, dibattendosi
più selvaggiamente in un terrore non mai provato. Morde e graffia. Ma è
una lotta contro una forza implacabile e brutale, che la immobilizza e la
annienta. Le sue grida, sempre più roche, si perdono nella solitudine not-
turna dei campi" (*LS1*, 17).
36 Bondanella, *The Cinema of Federico Fellini*, 112.
37 *LS3*, 33.
38 Fellini, *Fare un film*, 58.
39 Pinelli and Zapponi, *La strada: Dramma in due atti*, 40.
40 Marcus, "Fellini's *La voce della luna*: Resisting Postmodernism," 242.
41 Scolari, *L'Italia di Fellini*, 269.
42 Flaiano, *Diario notturno*, 64–9.
43 Pinelli and Zapponi, *La strada: Dramma*, 16.
44 In *LS2* Fellini strikes the following lines between Colombaioli, the circus's
owner, and Zampanò: "COLOMBAIOLI: What about the girl you had before? ZAMPANÒ (with placid carelessness): Rosa. She is dead. Gelsomina
is her sister" (119). Predictably, Pinelli brings Rosa back to the forefront of
the story when rewriting *La strada* for the theatre.
45 Pinelli and Zapponi, *La strada: Dramma*, 17–22; Scolari, *L'Italia*, p. 262.
46 In an interview contained in the Criterion DVD extras, Dino De Laurentis
tells about a phone call he received from Fellini in which the director tried
to convince him to reinsert the sequence in the film (see also Kezich, *Federico Fellini*, 187–8; Zabagli, "Pasolini per 'Le notti,'" 162–3). The sequence
was reintegrated only later, for a version of *Le notti di Cabiria* presented
by Canal + at the 2003 Cannes Film Festival (F. Fellini and G. Grazzini,
Intervista sul cinema, 104). Nonetheless, Fellini had already used it in *Block-
notes di un regista* and discussed it in Gianfranco Angelucci's documentary
Fellini nel cestino (1984), emphasizing the fabulous fascination that the character had for him.
47 Pinelli, *Le notti di Cabiria*, 92–7.
48 Ibid., 106.

49 Pasolini, "L'irrazionalismo cattolico di Fellini," 84.
50 Kezich, *Su La dolce vita*, 43.
51 Pinelli quoted in Scolari, *L'Italia di Fellini*, 272.
52 Rondi, *Il cinema di Fellini*, 28–9.
53 Ibid., 281.
54 Kezich, *Su la dolce vita*, 27–8.
55 Pasolini, *Pasolini per il cinema*, vol. 2, 2316–29 (see also the note on pages 3198–9).
56 Fellini, *The Book of Dreams*, 126 and 492.
57 Pinelli also scripted Masina's parts for the two mini-series *Eleonora* (directed by Silverio Blasi, 1973) and *Camilla* (directed by Sandro Bolchi, 1976). See Kezich, *Federico Fellini*, 103.
58 Fellini, *The Book of Dreams*, 126 and 492.
59 Both statements are contained in Pinelli's preface to his plays in *Tullio Pinelli*, 6.
60 Pinelli and Salvi, "Tullio Pinelli fra teatro e cinema," 39.
61 S. d'Amico, "D'Amico on Pinelli," 56.
62 *LS3*, 61–71.
63 Pinelli and Zapponi, *La strada: Dramma*, 63–6.
64 *LS2*, 91–3.
65 Ibid.
66 Ibid., 316–17.
67 Ibid., 317.
68 Ibid.
69 "PIETRO: (*fissa Davide in silenzio. Poi, terribile*) Così. Di me ti resti soltanto questo orrore. Ti forzerà a vincere la carne, quando sarai tentato di negargli il martirio. (*pausa*) Io l'ho respinto, e scendo al martirio eterno. DAVIDE: No. Non ancora. PIETRO: Orribilmente giusto. Ma te, dal fondo dell'abisso ti vedrò con gli angeli nostri fratelli, vicino a Lui. Mio figlio. (*pausa*) Vederlo dappresso, per tutta l'eternità. DAVIDE: (*mormorando*) Dio di misericordia. PIETRO: Gloria a Lui. DAVIDE: Spera. Salvati. PIETRO: Non è giusto. DAVIDE: Lo ami ancora? PIETRO: Farò tremare gli inferni, cantando gloria a Lui. DAVIDE: (*mormorando*) Se Lo ami, il nemico non può passare. PIETRO: (*in un mormorio*) Dio Padre! Dio Padre! DAVIDE: (*quasi parlandogli all'orecchio*) Sei salvo. Lo ami ancora? PIETRO: (*in un soffio*) Da morire. DAVIDE: Sei salvo. (*pausa. Lentamente si leva in piedi, lo sguardo fisso su Pietro Rovere che, gli occhi vitrei, sbarrati, volti al cielo, giace immobile riverso sulla poltrona*)" (T. Pinelli, *Lotta con l'angelo*, 139).
70 "Zampanò si è fermato e ascolta. Ascolta quello che non ha ascoltato mai: il silenzio. Un brivido improvviso lo scuote da capo a piedi. È un brivido

di terrore. E al terrore succede lo sgomento per questa non mai provata paura del nulla. Non la paura della fame, o della prigione, o di un altro uomo: la paura del nulla. Le ginocchia gli mancano. Zampanò si accoscia sulla sabbia. Come colto da un male sensibile e terrificante, un male non mai provato, Zampanò si dibatte contro qualcosa che faticosamente nasce nella sua anima di bruto: l'angoscia. Nell'ombra si ripete all'infinito il fruscio delle onde, e Zampanò, per la prima volta nella sua vita, piange. Una donna è nata ed è morta per questo. L'alba sul mare è come il principio del mondo. Luminosa, nuova e innocente come il principio del mondo. Zampanò dorme profondamente sulla rena. Non come sempre rannicchiato e contorto quasi in istintiva animalesca difesa: le sue membra giacciono aperte e abbandonate, con la serena fiduciosità di un sonno infantile. Il suo volto è pacato ed umano" (*LS1*, 101–2).

71 *LS2*, 70–1.
72 Bazin, "La strada," 58.
73 Nonetheless, Bondanella rightly acknowledges Fellini's attempt to render the story less literary and more visual and open ended, a behaviour that becomes more evident as Fellini's directorial style evolves (Bondanella, *The Cinema of Federico Fellini*, 112).
74 See Bazin, "La strada"; M. Marcus,"Fellini's *La strada*: Transcending Neorealism."
75 The 1986 publication *Ginger e Fred*, edited by Mino Guerrini for Longanesi, is still a rich source for understanding this film and includes the text written by Guerra and Fellini, but fails to recognize the import that Pinelli gave to this film. On the contrary, the LLRB archive contains a copy of a full-fledged screenplay authored by Pinelli and Fellini.
76 Sainati, *Ciò che abbiamo detto*, 58–9.
77 Fellini, "Io sono aperto voluttuosamente a tutto," 100–1; Kezich, *Federico Fellini*, 175.
78 Sainati, *Ciò che abbiamo detto*, 62–3.
79 Fellini and Kezich, "L'intervista lunga," 48–9.
80 Pinelli quoted in Barbanente, "Tullio Pinelli: Ritratto," 114
81 Zambelli and Acone, *Campane nel pozzo*, 39.
82 Sainati, *Ciò che abbiamo detto*, 44.
83 Fellini, *The Book of Dreams*, 342 and 536.
84 The physical resemblance to the other drawings of Pinelli that Fellini made is very strong, and Pinelli is also shown, as usual, seated on his chair as when they used to work in his home (see for instance the caricatures contained in the November 2008 issue of *Fellini-Amarcord*).
85 Fellini, *The Book of Dreams*, 387 and 546.

86 Marcus, "Fellini's *La voce della luna*," 228.

87 Sainati, *Ciò che abbiamo detto*, 25; Scolari, *L'Italia*, 23.

88 See Gianfranco Angelucci's introduction to Fellini, *Federico Fellini: La voce della luna*, p. xi. Gianfranco Angelucci met Fellini when he was writing his dissertation on him, and eventually collaborated with the director on the script of *Intervista*. For the past thirty years Angelucci has been actively promoting the work of Fellini with publications and documentaries. Angelucci's own film *Miele di donna* (1981), rich with references and homages to *La città delle donne*, seems to continue and elaborate the psychoanalytical and erotic discourse opened by Fellini. Angelucci has compiled his memories of Fellini's last days in fictional form in *Federico F.* In numerous articles regularly published in his column "Visti da Roma" in the newspaper *La Voce di Romagna* he has reported on Fellini's incursions in various esoteric areas.

89 Sainati, *Ciò che abbiamo detto*, 24; Zambelli and Acone, *Campane nel pozzo*, 38.

90 Pinelli quoted in Barbanente, "Tullio Pinelli: Ritratto," 120.

2. Ennio Flaiano

1 For a portrait of the cultural and social milieu surrounding Via Veneto in the late 1950s see Russo, *Con Flaiano e Fellini a via Veneto*.

2 Fellini's recollections about this early period are contained in an RAI interview released by the journalist Beniamino Placido and archived at the Media Museum of Pescara under the title "La Roma di Flaiano." Similar remarks by Fellini are collected in Moretti, *Flaiano e «oggi e domani»*, 150.

3 See Chicchi, "Fellini-Flaiano: La provincia d'Italia a Cinecittà," 40.

4 Flaiano quoted in Natalini, *Ennio Flaiano: Una vita nel cinema*, 61–9. Even though the novel would eventually be adapted for the screen in 1989 by Giuliano Montaldo, Jules Dassin had planned for a film adaption as early as 1950.

5 Fofi, "Flaiano: O dell'ironia come forma intima di sopravvivenza oltre la tragedia" 51–2.

6 Corti, introduction to Flaiano, *Opere*, vii.

7 Moser quoted in Rüesch's introduction to Flaiano, *Soltanto le parole*, xix.

8 Many of Flaiano's works remained incomplete and were published posthumously, as was the case with *Autobiografia del blu di Prussia*, *Il cavastivale*, *La valigia delle Indie*, *Diario degli errori*, *La solitudine del satiro*, and *L'occhiale indiscreto*.

9 Brunetta, "Flaiano ed il ritratto linguistico dell'italiano del dopoguerra," 91.
10 Flaiano, *Soltanto le parole*, 50–1. The most significant titles of his work in cinema, and those in which he likely exercised his artistic sensibility, include *Fuga in Francia* (Mario Soldati, 1948), *Roma città libera* (aka *La notte porta consiglio*, Marcello Pagliero, 1946), *Parigi è sempre Parigi* (Luciano Emmer, 1951), *Guardie e ladri* (Mario Monicelli e Steno, 1951), *Dov'è la libertà* (Roberto Rossellini, 1954), *Peccato che sia una canaglia* (A. Blasetti, 1954), *La donna del fiume* (Mario Soldati, 1954), *Totò e Carolina* (Mario Monicelli, 1955), *Calabuig* (Luis G. Berlanga, 1956), *La fortuna di essere donna* (Alessandro Blasetti, 1956), *La ragazza in vetrina* (Luciano Emmer, 1961), *Hong Kong, un addio* (Gian Luigi Polidoro, 1963), *La notte* (Michelangelo Antonioni, 1961), and *Fantasmi a Roma* (Antonio Pietrangeli, 1961). For a discussion of the evolution of Flaiano's career as a screenwriter, and his failed attempts to transition to the role of director, see Natalini, "Flaiano sceneggiatore di scrittori."
11 Flaiano's participation in *Le luce del varietà* is not clear. Even though Pinelli and Kezich spoke of Flaiano's presence, his name does not appear in the credits. This is probably because Flaiano entered the collaboration late, when the script had been almost entirely written, and was chosen to be one of the film's reviewers rather than a scriptwriter (see Natalini, *Ennio Flaiano*, 67). In 1949 Flaiano also joined Amidei, Fellini, and Rossellini on a visit to a war refugee camp to complete initial research for Rossellini's *Stromboli* (1950), a film that Flaiano would later review favourably. In an early draft of *Lo sceicco bianco*'s screenplay, which is archived at the LLRB, the name of Flaiano is indicated as a collaborator on the screenplay, and the title page reads as follows: "'Lo sceicco bianco' Sceneggiatura di Federico Fellini, Tullio Pinelli con la collaborazione di Ennio Flaiano, da un soggetto di: Fellini-Pinelli-Antonioni." For information regarding the creative negotiation with Antonioni at the inception of *Lo sceicco bianco*, see my essay "Il retro di 'Happy Country,'" 68–9.
12 Flaiano, *Soltanto le parole*, 34.
13 Flaiano, "Ho parlato male de 'La strada,'" 449.
14 Fofi, "Flaiano," 51.
15 S.C. D'Amico and M. D'Amico, *Storie di cinema*, 162.
16 Fellini and Guerrini, "Le strade di Fellini," 12.
17 Fellini quoted in Flaiano, *Soltanto le parole*, 458n3.
18 Flaiano, *Soltanto le parole*, 458n3.
19 Ibid., 53–4.

20 See the bitterly sarcastic letter that Pasolini wrote to Flaiano in 1963 (Pasolini, *Lettere*, 516). See Rondi quoted in Faldini and Fofi, *L'avventurosa storia*, 5–6. Fellini did what he could to reassure Flaiano that Pasolini was not going to take his place, extending to Flaiano the epithet of "fratellino mio" that he had also begun using with Pasolini (Flaiano, *Soltanto le parole*, 89). Fellini continued to appease Flaiano through a number of clumsily affectionate letters (Ibid., 89 and 162).

21 Bruno Rasia's sketches are archived at the Media Museum of Pescara and also appear in Flaiano, *Media Museum le arti e lo spettacolo*.

22 Pinelli, "Sono in tre a remare sulla barca di Fellini," 2.

23 "7 giugno 1964, Caro Fellini, un po' in ritardo, come vedi vengo a sapere dell'articolo di Saviane sull'*Espresso* e delle giuste proteste di Pinelli, non-ché della divertente lettera di Rondi. Mi conosci abbastanza e se ti scrivo non è per dirti che io in questa faccenda non c'entro – questo tu lo sai benissimo – ma soltanto per assicurarti di averne colto il lato comico. Bene, avrei scritto io stesso al giornale, ma non ho saputo niente fino all'altra sera; e ora, francamente, non mi sembra il caso di riaprire la questione, Rondi ha messo tutto in chiaro. Per Pinelli è un altro discorso, mi dispiace sinceramente che abbia potuto credere la cosa ispirata da me, e gli scriverò. Saviane ha detto soltanto una cosa giusta, che cioè la nostra collaborazione è finita. Se c'erano ancora dei dubbi, la lettera di Rondi li ha fugati per sempre. Mi ha divertito a leggerla, quasi quanto le sessanta pagine che scrisse per *Giulietta degli spiriti*, quelle che abbiamo buttato via. Speriamo ora che durante la lavorazione del film faccia dei bei dialoghi. È in ballo il nostro nome. Ciao, caro Fellini. Le amicizie frivole finiscono per una friv-olezza. Tuttavia, come si dice in questi casi? 'Arrivederci e buona fortuna.' Ennio Flaiano" (Flaiano, *Soltanto le parole*, 261–2).

24 "Roma, 12 giugno 1964. Caro Flaiano, non ho mai avuto dubbi sulla friv-olezza della tua amicizia, ma che vuoi farci, sei proprio fatto così e anche la lettera che mi hai scritto è frivola. Comunque, per me andava tutto bene lo stesso. Finisce la collaborazione? Mi spiace. Mi sembrava che in fondo ti divertivi a lavorare con noi e non ti facevo poi fare brutta figura come spesso ti capita con altri registi. Ennio caro, ti saluto e buona fortuna anche a te, frivolmente. Federico" (ibid., 262).

25 Kezich, *Federico Fellini*, 262–3.

26 Fellini, *The Book of Dreams*, 143 and 495.

27 Flaiano, *Soltanto le parole*, 322–3, 331; and Fellini, quoted in ibid., 347.

28 Ibid., 294–6, 390.

29 Maroni and Ricci (eds.), *I libri di casa mia*, entries 590 and 591.

30 Flaiano, *Soltanto le parole*, 365.

31 Fellini, *The Book of Dreams*, 274 and 519.
32 See S.C. D'Amico's recollections of Flaiano's bitter remarks on how Fellini had stolen even his childhood in making *8½* (*Storie di cinema*, 162). See also Jean Gili on this topic (in Flaiano, *Media Museum: Le arti e lo spettacolo*).
33 I am referring to the conclusions that can be extrapolated from Costello's "Layers of Reality: *8½* as Spiritual Autobiography;" as well as from two essays contained in *Federico Fellini: Essays in Criticism*, ed. P. Bondanella; Hyman's "*8½* as an Anatomy of Melancholy" (121–9); and Metz's "Mirror Construction in Fellini's *8½*" (130–6).
34 Fellini, *The Book of Dreams*, 298 and 525.
35 Ibid., 380 and 545.
36 Fellini quoted in Sergiacomo, *La critica e Flaiano*, 303. The second quote comes from Flaiano and Santa, "La satira, la noia e la fede," 228.
37 Flaiano, "Del varietà."
38 "Ho visto il tuo *Satyricon* e che mi ha colpito, meravigliato, tenuto sveglio e, in fondo, deliziato. Non ci manca niente. Me lo sognerò spesso e volentieri. So che si potrebbero discutere certe soluzioni, ma hai raggiungo l'essenziale: la continua drammaticità dei mostri, cioè di noi stessi. Le persone che uscivano dal cinema e dicevano "a me non è piaciuto," sembravano uscire in realtà dal film" (Flaiano, *Soltanto le parole*, 331).
39 E. Flaiano, *Ombre fatte a macchina*, 216–17.
40 Bondanella, *The Cinema of Federico Fellini*, 74; See also Gieri, *Contemporary Italian Filmmaking*.
41 "La donna, sfiorita da una vita precaria, dipinta molto e male, entra in una latteria della via Tuscolana. Il belletto, sulla sua faccia impastata di sonno, la fa sembrare un pierrot bastonato. Ha la capigliatura lustra nel tratto frontale, dietro arricciata ed opaca come una barba assira ... Pensa ad alta voce per attirare l'attenzione mia e di Fellini ... Tormenta la borsa a rete e il foulard, sospira, canterella a bocca chiusa. Ci accorgiamo che tiene al guinzaglio un cane spelato e grigio, che sembra un cane vestito da topo ... Io e Fellini prendiamo il pretesto del cane per attaccare discorso ... Infine se ne va ... mentre io e Fellini, loscamente, ridiamo. Più tardi il pensarci ci rattrista, facciamo varie ipotesi: chi sarà, come è arrivata a quel punto, come vive. E quella sua incrollabile sicurezza! È una sicurezza che la allontana dalla pazzia e dal suicidio o, forse, più semplicemente, la difende dalla solitudine. In queste donne la solitudine si ammanta di orpelli e di continui vani richiami, come quelle zattere che, andando alla deriva, inalberano le camicie dei naufraghi e sembrano, agli uccelli di mare, persino festose" (Ibid., 105–6).
42 Pirandello, *On Humor*, 113.

43 Flaiano, *Diario notturno*, 34–7.
44 Ibid., 37.
45 Flaiano, *Soltanto le parole*, 208.
46 Ibid.
47 Ibid.
48 Fofi, "Flaiano," 65.
49 See Sepa, "Flaiano scrittore per il cinema," 114.
50 Flaiano, "La notte porta consiglio," 94–5.
51 Flaiano, *Soltanto le parole*, 53–4.
52 See Mastroianni's comments in the documentary *Marcello Mastroianni: Mi ricordo, sì, io mi ricordo* (directed by Anna Maria Tatò, 1997).
53 "Ora che sta arrivando l'estate salta agli occhi che questa non è più una strada, ma una spiaggia. I café che straripano sui marciapiedi ... hanno ognuno un tipo diverso di ombrellone per i loro tavoli, come gli stabilimenti balneari di Ostia ... Le automobili scivolano come gondole a teatro, a brevi scossoni, e il pubblico prende il fresco e si muove su e giù con l'indolenza delle alghe e la falsa sicurezza dei coristi." (Flaiano, *Opere: Scritti postumi*, 575; the English translation is by Satriano in Flaiano, *The Via Veneto Papers*, 4). The entry was originally published in *Corriere della sera*, 26 June 1958.
54 "Caro Federico, ieri ho rivisto *la dolce vita* ... sono caduto nel film come se non l'avessi mai visto prima. ... Credo che resti la tua opera più viva in questo senso, proprio per la carica di pietà e di ansia per un mondo che sta uscendo dai binari e affretta il momento della disperazione. Ma anche per la grande libertà narrativa e per la forza, l'ironia del distacco che ti hanno evitato compiacimenti. Tu stavi scoprendo in quel momento una realtà che gli altri non vedevano, e la raccontavi tutta, coi suoi possibili futuri sviluppi ... Ti auguro buon lavoro e ti abbraccio. Ennio " (Flaiano, *Soltanto le parole*, 322).
55 "Il film di Fellini [*La dolce vita*] nasce da questo bisogno di raccontarci come sono andate le cose per noi della nostra generazione che abbiamo creduto di poter sistemare le nostre faccende spirituali così come andavamo sistemando quelle economiche. Vuotando il bicchiere abbiamo visto che in fondo c'era il verme. Ognuno ha reagito secondo la sua natura: chi ha ingollato anche il verme, chi ha gettato via il bicchiere, chi ha vomitato. Io continuo a vomitare. Ma senza recriminazioni. Non mi è restato che la libertà di capire e il conforto di amare il prossimo per quello che mostra di essere, senza più giudicarlo, nella certezza che la disperazione è nell'animo di tutti, come nel nostro, e che viene "da più lontano" (ibid., 213–14).
56 Fellini, *The Book of Dreams*, 190 and 504.

57 Merola, "Flaiano sceneggiatore," 209. For scholarship that argues for
    the centrality of the theme of the journey in the collaboration between
    Fellini and Flaiano see Trubiano, "Flaiano and Fellini, Fellow Travelers on
    Parallel Tracks," and Melanco, "Il motivo del viaggio nel cinema italiano
    (1945–1965)."
58 Baranski, "Antithesis in Fellini's *I Vitelloni*," 70–83.
59 Sepa, "Flaiano scrittore per il cinema," 95–101.
60 Trubiano, "Flaiano and Fellini," 83.
61 Flaiano quoted in Kezich, *Federico, la vita e i film*, 131.
62 Fellini, *Fellini on Fellini*, 153.
63 Fellini, "'I Vitelloni ...,'" 10.
64 See Maroni and Ricci, *I libri di casa mia*, entries 220 and 44.
65 The scenario was published in separate episodes in *Cinema* during 1954,
    with the names of Fellini, Flaiano, and Pinelli, in that order.
66 "Moraldo resta solo. Segue con lo sguardo la Topolino scassata che si al-
    lontana sferragliando. E si avvia verso la città. Prima adagio, poi con passo
    meno lento ... I tratti del suo volto si stanno stendendo ... Una esuberanza
    irragionevole lo guadagna a poco a poco ... Le luci, intorno, tornano a
    sembrargli gaie ... E i volti, I volti della folla che gli cammina ai fianchi, gli
    appaiono sempre meno ostili. Passa una ragazza bruna, con la chioma opu-
    lenta ondeggiante sulle spalle, e gli lascia il lampo di un sorriso ... Più in là,
    un ragazzo scamiciato pedala fischiando una canzone ... Due innamorati gli
    vengono incontro, camminando adagio, stretti uno all'altro ... Un bambino
    piange, voci di donna si incrociano ... La vita, la vita, con il suo inesauribile,
    imprevedibile tesoro di incontri, casi, persone, avventure ... Moraldo cam-
    mina rapido tra la gente, sorridendo a tutti" (Fellini, "Moraldo va in città,"
    183; the English translation is by Stubbs in Fellini, *Moraldo in the City*, 104).
67 "Così fondo è il piacere / di una città dormiente! / Ha le pose lubriche e
    severe di una donna d'Oriente. / L'uomo che scende in questo mare, / non
    torna – non torna a navigare" (Flaiano, *Un marziano a Roma e altre
    farse*, 111).
68 Trans. by Balma and Benincasa (Flaiano, "A Martian in Rome," 99–100).
    "Verso le sette ho incontrato pallido, sconvolto dall'emozione il mio amico
    Fellini. Egli si trovava al Pincio quando l'aeronave è discesa e sulle prime
    ha creduto si trattasse di un'allucinazione. Quando ha visto gente accor-
    rere urlando e ha sentito dalla aeronave gridare secchi ordini in un italiano
    un po' freddo e scolastico, Fellini ha capito. Travolto subito dalla folla,
    e calpestato, si è risvegliato senza scarpe, la giacca a pezzi. Ha girato per la
    villa come un ebete, a piedi nudi, cercando di trovare un'uscita qualsiasi.

Io ero la prima persona amica che incontrava. Ha pianto abbracciandomi, scosso da un'emozione che ben presto si è comunicata anche a me. Mi ha descritto poi l'aeronave: un disco di enormi dimensioni, giallo e lucente come un sole. E il fruscio indimenticabile, il fruscio di un foulard di seta, al momento di calarsi al suolo! E il silenzio che ha seguito quell'momento! In quel breve attimo ha sentito che un nuovo periodo stava iniziando per l'umanità. Le prospettive sono – mi dice – immense e imperscrutabili. Forse tutto: la religione e le leggi, l'arte e la nostra vita stessa, ci apparirà tra qualche tempo illogico e povero. Se il solitario viaggiatore sceso dall'aeronave è veramente – e ormai, dopo il comunicato ufficiale, sarebbe sciocco dubitarne –l'ambasciatore di un altro pianeta dove tutto si conosce del nostro, questo è il segno che altrove 'le cose son più semplici'. Il fatto che il marziano sia venuto solo dimostra che egli possiede mezzi a noi sconosciuti per difendersi; e argomenti tali da mutare radicalmente il nostro sistema di vita e la nostra concezione del mondo" (Flaiano, "Un marziano a Roma," 476).

69 "Ci sono luoghi pensava, che danno la sensazione di un intoppo, non possiamo darcene una spiegazione, ma ci sembra che stia a noi capirne qualcosa e ci torniamo col pensiero ... La verità è che niente aveva un senso, ma soltanto un'apparenza e di quella bisognava accontentarsi ... Non era una folla chiamata dalla fede, né spinta dalla speranza di nessun miracolo. Ma pure qualcosa successe, quando una donna, che insieme ad altre doveva chiedere a gran voce il miracolo, gridò che lei lo chiedeva davvero; e intanto vere lacrime le bagnavano il volto povero e informe, dove una vita di piaceri e dolori comuni aveva scavato giorno per giorno le sue rughe e che ora quel grido disperato di verità isolava nella folla. Non successe altro è poco dopo la stessa folla si ammassò nel cortile già lambito dalla luna, silenziosa e al freddo, davanti ai tavoli dove i cassieri chiamavano le comparse e le pagavano" (Flaiano, *Una e una notte*, 129–31).

70 Flaiano, *Soltanto le parole*, 227.

71 Flaiano quoted in Faldini and Fofi, *L'avventurosa storia*, 5–6.

72 Trans. by Hood (Flaiano, *A Time to Kill*, 24–5). "Lei forse conosceva tutti i segreti che io avevo rifiutato senza nemmeno approfondire, come una misera eredità, per accontentarmi di verità noiose e conclamate. Io cercavo la sapienza nei libri e lei la possedeva negli occhi, che mi guardavano da duemila anni, come la luce delle stelle che tanto impiega per essere da noi percepita" (Flaiano, *Tempo d'uccidere*, 33).

73 Fellini, *Quattro film*, 183–4.

74 The verse comes from the poem "Complainte des formalités nuptiales" ("Lament of Nuptial Formalities") contained in *Les Complaintes* (1885, *The Complaints*).

75 Ibid.
76 For a description of the function of such feminine characters in Flaiano's work see Sepa, "Flaiano scrittore per il cinema," 109.
77 Rondi's testimony is contained in Faldini and Fofi, *L'avventurosa storia*, 6 (in which can also be found Ekberg's related testimony).
78 Stoja, "Ennio Flaiano e la fontana di Trevi: Lo scrosciare ticchettante delle idee," 129–39.
79 See Fellini, *8½ di Federico Fellini*, 150–2. For the English translation see Fellini, *8½: Federico Fellini*, ed. C. Affron (220–2). Photographs of the alternate ending in the train are included in Sesti and Crozzoli, *Il viaggio di Fellini*, 132–40.
80 "Una volta, laggiù, nella pianura padana, il treno si fermò sopra un ponte di ferro. Il sole stave in quell momento scomparendo al limite di una piatta campagna e si accesero le lampade nello scompartimento di terza classe. Ero solo, il cuore mi traboccava di sentimenti mai prima provati e di una malinconia confortante: mangiando le mie provviste, cominciai a pinagere. Ero appena un ragazzo e non sopportavo, allora, quegli ammonimenti sconsolati che un paesaggio pieno di esperienza dà volentieri a chi sa guardarlo" (Flaiano, *Diario notturno*, 5–6).
81 For a study of the circular shape as the central theme and interpretative key of *Roma*, see Tassone, "From Romagna to Rome: The Voyage of a Visionary Chronicler (*Roma* and *Amarcord*)." Bonnigal wrote about circular shapes in Fellini's films in connection with a neo-baroque style, speaking of Fellini's impossibility of recreating the artistic surge he had once found in *8½* ("Il 'Casanova' Di Federico Fellini: Exorcising the Loss of the Baroque Circle").
82 Aldouby, "A Jungian Approach to Federico Fellini's Visual Imagery."
83 Flaiano, *Media Museum*.
84 Flaiano, *Il gioco e il massacro*, 170.
85 For an in-depth comparison of D'Annunzio and Flaiano see Giacomo D'Angelo's *D'Annunzio e Flaiano: L'Antitaliano e l'Arcitaliano* (Chieti, Italy: Solfanelli, 2010).
86 The comment is contained in Flaiano, *Media Museum*.
87 Cederna, "La bella confusione," 17–85.

3. Bernardino Zapponi

1 These caricatures are contained in Zapponi, *Il mio Fellini* (6 and 87).
2 Ibid., 24, 68–70, 105.
3 Zapponi and Boggio, "Bernardino Zapponi intervistato da Maricla Boggio," 31.

4 Following is a complete list of the films on which Zapponi worked as screenwriter, largely in the comedy, horror, and erotic genres: with director Mario Soldati, *È l'amor che mi rovina* (1951); with director Mauro Bolognini, *Senso civico* (1967) and *Per le antiche scale* (1975); with director Pino Zac, *Viaggio di lavoro* (1968); with director Mario Monicelli, *La bambinaia* (1968) and *Il marchese del Grillo* (1981); with director Alberto Sordi, *Polvere di stelle* (1973); with director Dario Argento, *Profondo rosso* (1975); with director Juan Luis Buñuel, *Leonor* (1975); with director Luigi Comencini, *L'ingorgo, una storia impossibile* (1979); with director Sergio Corbucci, *Questo e quello* (1983) and *Sono un fenomeno paranormale* (1985); with director Steno, *Dio li fa e poi li accoppia* (1982); with director Dino Risi, *Vedo nudo* (1969), *La moglie del prete* (1971), *Mordi e fuggi* (1973), *Telefoni bianchi* (1976), *Anima persa* (1977), *Caro papà* (1979), *Fantasma d'amore* (1981), *Sesso e volentieri* (1982), *... e la vita continua* (1984), *Teresa* (1987), *La ciociara* (1988), *Tolgo il disturbo* (1990), *Giovani e belli* (1996); with director Tinto Brass, *Paprika* (1991) and *Così fan tutte* (1992); and with director Joe D'Amato, *Paprika* (1995).
5 Fellini quoted in Faldini and Fofi, *L'avventurosa storia*, 5.
6 Zapponi quoted in Faldini and Fofi, *Il cinema italiano d'oggi*, 241–2.
7 Fellini, *The Book of Dreams*, 253, 514–15.
8 Zapponi, *Nostra signora*, 21.
9 "Lui [Fellini] mi diceva: 'Voglio fare una ripresa in elicottero: vedere, da sopra, come si formano le nuvole su Roma, riprendere queste grandi masse di ogni colore che si accumulano, si rompono, si sfilacciano ...' E ancora: 'Il Ponentino. Come nasce questo famoso venticello? Da dove parte? Ecco, mi piacerebbe coglierlo da'inizio, seguirlo nella sua via verso Roma, riprendere la gente che se lo sente passare addosso, mentre è nei più diversi ambienti: al caffè, a letto, per la strada" (Zapponi, "Roma & Fellini," 13).
10 Fellini, "Roma," archived at the LLRB.
11 McBride, "The Director as Superstar," 153–4.
12 Tassone, "From Romagna to Rome," 270.
13 The topic of Pasolini's creative and subversive strategies of adaptation has been explored in the scholarly literature on Pasolini; see for example Marcus, *Filmmaking by the Book*, 111–55.
14 Jean-Paul Manganaro quoted in Pierre Klossowski (ed.), *Carmelo Bene: Il teatro senza spettacolo* (Venice: Marsilio, 1990), 16.
15 Fellini, *The Book of Dreams*, 244, 513.
16 Zapponi and Pinelli, "Fellini au travail," 61.
17 Zapponi comments as follows: "Federico has still today the coquetry of stating that he does not need a script; he says the same thing to me, but he

knows very well that it is not true. He says that it suffices to put together six or seven wonderful sequences to make the film, but everything works because as we labour at the script, we discuss the characters so much that afterwards it is as if they come alive on their own" (ibid., 61).

18 Zapponi, *Nostra signora*, 21.
19 Zapponi, *Il mio Fellini*, 83.
20 Ibid., 241.
21 Ibid., 242.
22 Ibid., 256.
23 Ibid., 261.
24 Rondi quoted in Faldini and Fofi, *Il cinema italiano d'oggi*, 241.
25 Ibid.
26 For a detailed account of Fellini's negotiation with the producers of *Histoires extraordinaires*, see Betti, "Alla ricerca di Toby Dammit." See also Kezich, *Federico Fellini*, 281–2.
27 Zapponi, *Il mio Fellini*, 17. Zapponi quoted in Faldini and Fofi, *Il cinema italiano d'oggi*, 246.
28 Sharrett, "'Toby Dammit,' Intertext, and the End of Humanism," 125.
29 Fofi and Volpi, *L'arte della visione*, 4–7.
30 Rondi, *Il cinema di Fellini*, 19. For Fellini's cinematic references to Kafka, see Testa's "Cinecittà and America: Fellini Interviews Kafka."
31 "C'è una voce nella mia vita, / che avverto nel punto che muore; / voce stanca, voce smarrita, / col tremito del batticuore: / voce d'una accorsa anelante, / che al povero petto s'afferra / per dir tante cose e poi tante, / ma piena ha la bocca di terra." (Pascoli, *Canti di Castelvecchio*, 130–3.
32 Zapponi, *Nostra signora*, 14.
33 Zapponi, *Gobal*, 136, 155.
34 Fellini and Zapponi, "'Toby Dammit' dal racconto di Poe 'Non scommettere la testa col diavolo.'" The script archived at the LLRB offers a few interesting variants from the version published by Cappelli.
35 Ibid., 63, 69–73.
36 "La concretezza della macchina da presa, mostrando il salnitro che sgocciola dalle pareti e i teschi ammonticchiati, rischia di sostituire con immagini d'incubo più volgari, l'incubo vero dell'autore-attore, che è ovviamente imprendibile. Il lettore del racconto è situato 'dentro' Poe; l'obiettivo invece non può che essere fuori ... Trasferire Poe sullo schermo è possibile solo con un'opera d'impadronimento molto vasta, giacché non si può semplicemente sovrapporre lo schema strutturale del cinema a quello dei suoi racconti; il ritmo e le scansioni non coincidono. La suspense cinematografica fa le sue leggi; una musica quasi, che non è quella dodecàfonica di

Poe. Poe non può dare soggetti, ma stimoli; azionare nel regista un mec-
canismo che produca una gemellare nevrosi. Può influenzare con le sue
angoscie l'autore del film; suggerirgli visioni, idee, incubi, persone. Può
instaurare un processo creativo in una mente ricettiva." (Zapponi, "Edgar
Poe e il cinema," 17)

37 For related theoretical discussions, see Wagner, *The Novel and the Cinema*,
222, and Klein and Parker (eds.), *The English Novel and the Movies*, 9–10.

38 The caricature is shown on the cover of Zapponi's *Trasformazioni*.

39 Pasolini, "*La dolce vita*: Per me si tratta di un film cattolico," 2274–5.

40 Stubbs, *Federico Fellini as Auteur*, 20–36. See also Bonnigal, "Il 'Casanova'
Di Federico Fellini'"; Cro, "Fellini's Freudian Psyche between Neo-realism
and Neo-baroque"; and Degli-Esposti, "Federico Fellini's *Intervista* or the
Neo-baroque Creativity of the Analyzed on Screen."

41 "What has been repeatedly defined as Fellini's baroque mannerism
resides in his constant forcing of the photographic image from caricature
toward the visionary. In doing so, Fellini always maintains as his starting
point a specific idea that must be represented in its most communicative
and expressive form" (Calvino, "Autobiography of a Spectator," 25–30).

42 Zapponi and Curchod, "Entretien avec Bernardino Zapponi," 69.

43 Kezich, *Federico Fellini*, 297, 348.

44 Fellini, preface to *Fellini's Satyricon*, 43–6.

45 Zapponi, "The Strange Journey," 33–9.

46 Moravia, "Dreaming Up Petronius."

47 Dick, "Adaptation as Archaeology: *Fellini Satyricon* (1969) from the 'Novel'
by Petronius," 130.

48 This conclusion is drawn by several scholars, such as Marcus (*After Fellini*,
181–98), Burke (*Fellini's Films*, 223–37), and Russel ("Fellini Satyricon").

49 Zapponi and Pinelli, "Fellini au travail," 60. Even before *La dolce vita*,
Fellini had pondered the possibility of adapting Casanova's memoirs
when Tullio Pinelli originally proposed the idea.

50 See Zapponi, *Casanova: In un romanzo la storia del film di Fellini*.

51 "Gli proponevo una scappatoia simbolica: fare di Casanova un Don
Giovanni, ossia l'allegoria dell'impotenza, dell'incapacità di amare, della fuga
dalla donna ... Federico obiettava che Casanova, uomo vero, persona storica,
non si prestava a soluzioni emblematiche. Troppo concreto, ingombrante.
Infine, scelse un compromesso: un Casanova reale, ma vittima del complesso
materno" (Zapponi, *Il mio Fellini*, 88). Zapponi also helped Fellini to transform Casanova into a more pompous and ridiculous character (ibid., 90).

52 "[Fellini] entrusted me, first thing, to 'go take a look' at the community
centre in Via del Governo Vecchio, an occupied house run by aggressive

feminists ... I felt like a black person visiting the office of the Ku Klux Klan. They looked at me, frowning ... Ironic and disdainful faces stared silently at me. I myself was surprised at my awkwardness" (ibid., 107–8). Overall, Zapponi admitted that he felt rather distant from *La città delle donne* (Faldini and Fofi, *Il cinema italiano d'oggi*, 261).

53 Zapponi, *Il mio Fellini*, 80–2.
54 Felllini, *The Book of Dreams*, 371 and 543.

4. The Poets

1 Hobsbawm, *The Age of Extremes: A History of the World, 1914–1991*, 9.
2 Rondi, *Il cinema di Fellini*, 24–5.
3 Rondi quoted in Faldini and Fofi, *Il cinema italiano d'oggi*, 260.
4 Fellini, "A First Draft: A Letter from Federico Fellini to His Friend Brunello Rondi, October 1960," in Fellini, *8½ Federico Fellini, Director*, 234; and Fellini and Grazzini, *Intervista sul cinema*, 126.
5 Kezich, *Su la dolce vita*, 124.
6 Pelo, "Tonino Guerra: The Screenwriter as a Narrative Technician or as a Poet of Images?" 126–7.
7 West, "Tonino Guerra and the Space of the Screenwriter," 162.
8 Vittorio Taviani quoted in Pellizzari, "Un filo rosso," 103.
9 "Aveva qualcosa di avido negli occhi, di attentissimo, una curiosità vivida, inesausta. La sua qualità che ho sempre apprezzato era la disponibilità ad essere un artista che assorbe, assimila trasforma ma, nello stesso tempo, una parte del suo cervello sembrava un laboratorio preciso, attentissimo dove quello che l'artista aveva creato veniva vagliato, giudicato, in generale con un consenso. Era insieme creatore e critico acutissimo, implacabile, di quel che aveva inventato. Una qualità questa inesauribile presenza critica, che a me per esempio manca completamente" (Fellini and Cirio, *Il mestiere del regista*, 107).
10 "La forma di uomo che Fellini possiede è incessantemente pericolante: tende a risistemarsi e riassestarsi nella forma precedente che la suggerisce. Una enorme macchia, che a seconda della fantasia può assomigliare a un polipo, a un'ameba ingrandita dal microscopio, a un rudere azteco, a un gatto annegato. Ma basta un colpo di ponentino, uno sbandamento della macchina, per rimescolare tutto, e ritrasformare il coacervo in un uomo: un uomo tenerissimo, intelligente, furbo e spaventato, con due orecchie create nel più perfetto laboratorio di articolo acustici, e una bocca che sparge intorno i più curiosi fonemi che incrocio romagnolo-romanesco abbia mai prodotto" (Pasolini, "Nota su *Le notti*," 700).

11 Zanzotto, "In margine al copione de 'La città delle donne,'" 107.
12 Zanzotto, "Versi in onore di Federico," 65.
13 While Brunello Rondi's contribution as writer for *Europa '51* is accredited, Fellini's is not. Rondi continued to work with Rossellini also on *Era notte a Roma* (1960).
14 Gian Luigi Rondi has been the film critic of *Il Tempo* since 1946 and is currently serving as the president of *David di Donatello* and of *Festival Internazionale del Film di Roma*. From 1993 to 1997 he was also president of the *Biennale di Venezia*.
15 *Il comunismo e i cattolici* was written by Fedele d'Amico (1912–90), future spouse of the screenwriter Suso Cecchi d'Amico and son of renowned theatre critic Silvio d'Amico, who was the mentor of Gian Luigi Rondi. For a summary of the movement of the Christian Left see Adriano Ossicini, *Il cristiano e la politica* (Rome: Edizioni Studium, 1989); and G.L. Rondi, *Rondi visto da vicino* (Rieti, Italy: Edizioni Sabinae, 2008), ed. Simone Casavecchia, 20.
16 A. Gramsci, *Quaderni dal carcere*, vol. 1 (44): 40–2.
17 "Io sento la realtà come un organismo di relazioni che ci implicano da ogni lato, e ci fondono in una concreta coralità, che è Storia e Natura ... Mi interessa cercare e dire in poesia quella che oggi e soprattutto domani sarà la 'terra dell'uomo,' cioè la sua più estrema prospettiva organica ... È questa la mia 'Terra Felice': il mondo nuovo, dei rapporti organici, umanistici e naturali" (Rondi, *La terra felice*, viii–ix).
18 "Pochi uomini, come Fellini, ho visto così capaci di mescolarsi, in modo istintivo, gioioso ... alla folla degli 'altri,' alla gente delle strade, nelle occasioni anche più rumorose, violente ... L'umanità con i suoi densi e coloriti grovigli, il suo potente o sottile flusso, piace a Fellini nel suo aspetto, appunto, più beatamente (o angosciosamente) vitalistico ... come oscuro, generoso mistero di presenze ... Sono perfino patetici lo slancio, la violenza quasi, con cui Fellini cerca, si costruisce, aspira alla vita autentica, cioè all'esatto e armonioso svolgimento della persona umana verso la più ricca autenticità, trovata e riconosciuta nell'ambito d'una società armoniosa, rinnovata: direi, nel versante d'una coralità nuova" (Rondi, *Il cinema di Fellini*, 12–13).
19 The letter is included, with no mention of Rondi's input, in Bondanella and Gieri (eds.) *La strada* (211–14). Rondi's possible contribution to this letter has also been suggested by his assistant director, Moraldo Rossi (see Rossi and Sanguineti, *Fellini & Rossi*, 70), and by the critic Alberto Pezzotta in his essay "Brunellone e Federico: La collaborazione con Fellini," 75–6.

20 For a complete account of Angelo Arpa's exchanges with several directors, and with Fellini in particular, as well as for a collection of his fascinating reflections and essays on Fellini, see Arpa, *Io sono la mia invenzione.*

21 Fellini, *The Book of Dreams*, 459, 559.

22 Bondanella, *The Cinema of Federico Fellini*, 154.

23 The information is reported in Parigi and Pezzotta, *Il lungo respiro*, 391.

24 Kezich, *Su La dolce vita*, 124–6.

25 Rondi, *Il cinema di Fellini*, 207.

26 For different reasons, Alberto Arbasino has criticized these characters as "ridicules." See Paolo Conti, "E Arbasino stronca 'La dolce vita,'" in *Corriere della Sera* (21 December 2008), accessed online on 15 March 2009.

27 Minuz, *Viaggio al termine*, 54–5.

28 Both collaborators expressed dissatisfaction with the final result: Scolari, *L'Italia di Fellini*, 272; Rondi, *Il cinema di Fellini*, 28–9.

29 Rondi, *La musica contemporanea*, 133–5.

30 Rondi, *Il ritmo moderno*, 12.

31 Ibid., 32.

32 Rondi, *Il cinema di Fellini*, 207.

33 Fellini, *La dolce vita di Federico Fellini*, 169.

34 Rondi, *Il cammino della musica*, 84.

35 Ibid., 91.

36 Zanzotto, "Motivi di un candore," 83, 92.

37 Kezich, *Su La dolce vita*, 126.

38 Rondi, *Il cinema di Fellini*, 279.

39 Bondanella, *The Cinema of Federico Fellini*, 290–1; Minuz, *Viaggio al termine*, 171–98.

40 Rondi quoted in Faldini and Fofi, *Il cinema italiano d'oggi*, 241.

41 Rondi, *Il ritmo moderno*, 33.

42 Fellini, "Prova d'orchestra," 73. This is the original script archived in the Fondo Norma Giacchero at the Federico Fellini Foundation in Rimini, Italy.

43 What follows is the complete passage: "Un convulso, lacerato montaggio di brani, squarci, momenti, ritagli di episodi estremamente violenti scelti dal repertorio dei cinegiornali di questi ultimi anni. Un sonoro caotico, terrificante di spari, raffiche, grida, slogans urlati con demenziale iterazione attraversati, frantumati da sirene della polizia, dagli ululati delle autoambulanze, dal rimbombo degli altoparlanti, dal fragore e il boato delle molotov, delle bombe. Su questo impasto da incubo che è la dimensione delirante di un 'assurdo universo,' appaiono i titoli del breve filmetto" (Fellini, "Prova d'orchestra," 2).

diminutivi, tutto l'armamentario della pre-grammaticalità pascoliana"
(Pasolini, "Nota su *Le notti*," 700).

79 Siciliano, *Pasolini: A Biography*, 226.

80 Pasolini, "*La dolce vita*," 2277.

81 See my essay "The American *Fanciullino* in Happy Country." For previous impressions regarding Fellini and the *fanciullino* as an explanation of
Fellini's psychological framework, see Renzo Renzi in his introduction to
Il primo Fellini, 13–19. Paolo Pillitteri stresses the difference between the
poetics of Pascoli and Fellini, arguing that a parallel between the two
would lead us to de-emphasize Fellini's modernity (Pillitteri, *Appunti su
Fellini*, 77–8).

82 Pasolini, *La religione del mio tempo*, 86–90. A complete translation of this
section of *La religione del mio tempo* can be found in Pasolini, *Poems*, trans.
by Norman MacAfee and Luciano Martinengo (New York: Noonday Press,
1996), 78–86.

83 "Pier Paolo guarda sfilare alla nostra destra delle antiche mura romane che
affiorano incastonate dentro marmi moderni. 'Come si riuscirà mai a de-
scrivere quelle stupende rovine!' così dice Pier Paolo e sospira, sorridente
e malinconico: 'È la vita anche la morte ...' Ho ancora nell'orecchio quel
canto, quelle note, e il senso misterioso eppure chiarissimo di quel verso.
Era il finale del film?" (ibid., emphasis in the original). Fellini, *The Book of
Dreams*, 336, 534.

84 The note is published (misleadingly) as part of the letter that Fellini wrote
in 1965 to the producer Dino De Laurentis, explaining his idea for the am-
bitious film (Fellini, "Lettera a Dino de Laurentis," 205). This recent edition
is based on the typescript archived at the Swiss publishing house Diogenes
Verlag in Zurich. Even if enclosed within the folder of the original manuscript of the treatment, the note must have been written at a later date,
during or after 1977. Closer examination reveals that the note looks at the
project retrospectively, while the letter to De Laurentis represented the first
presentation of the project.

85 Fellini, "Lettera a Dino De Laurentis," 182.

86 Patriarca, *Totò nel cinema di poesia*, 135.

87 These considerations share common ground with the interpretations that
Maurizio De Benedictis gathered in his essay regarding the centrality of
the theme of death in the work of both Fellini and Pasolini, broadly traced
in the dualism between the dead and the living, and the urban world and
the rural world, as well as in clown-like pairs of characters. The dynamic
of interchangeability between life and death, and between past and
present, found in this dream provides further evidence of the notion of
duplicity that De Benedictis follows in his reflections about the two artists'

poetics. De Benedictis also hints at the common element of the Jungian Great Mother in their poetics, who functions as an intermediary with the beyond, which will be discussed here within the context of their work on the figure of the prostitute, and more broadly in Fellini's work with Zanzotto. De Benedictis, *Linguaggi dell'aldilà*, 45, 63, 81, 100.

88 Fellini, *The Book of Dreams*, 337, 534.

89 A sample of this type of characterization is found in the following excerpt from this early script by Pasolini: "Grigio is not ashamed of being poor ... Resignation is the strength of roaming dogs ... Goodbye, Grigio, the humblest among the humbles, the last of the needy in spirit ... If it is possible – as it will be – to announce one day that a man's life was saved, it will be thanks to you too. You did not have anything, only life. However, everyone knows that you were happy, that what you had was enough for you, and will that it would suffice you forever" (Pasolini, "Grigio," 2077–9).

90 Minuz's *Viaggio al termine*, which is currently the chief source for what concerns the often overlooked dialogue between Fellini's films and a variety of social and political issues in modern Italy, includes a detailed discussion of the director's conflict with Berlusconi (199–222).

91 "La mia strada è segnata – passo a passo – / dalla forza che trovo in me al mattino, / arco del sesso e della fronte ... / amore d'ogni uomo, dei compagni / vivi con me negli anni" (Rondi, "La mia strada è segnata" in *La terra felice*, 7)

92 "Leggeri i polipi / come barbe del mare e come vele/ femminilmente si contraggono e al canto / del pescatore dolce come una bestemmia un orizzonte / di reti spiove fino in fondo all'acqua. // E qui fa preda del mistero mentre al sole / ti componi nel sale delle statue / illuminata e tersa con le cosce / lucide e intatte come il cuoio dei gambali // che quelli impuntano nel mare. / Nella pesca profittevole anche tu sali con l'alga / dal profondo e con questi miei pensieri / che somigliano a quelli del tuo oscuro" (Rondi, "Il mare" in *L'amore fedele*, 34; Light as beards of the sea and like sails / the octopus contracting womanly / to the fisherman's song / sweet, as a curse, a horizon / of nets rains down till the bottom / of the sea. // And here it preys upon mystery while under the sun / you compose yourself in / the salt of statues / lit and terse with your thighs / lucid and whole like the leather of the boots / that they pierce into the sea. / In the profitable fishing you too rise like the algae / from the depth and with these thoughts of mine / that resemble those of feminine / obscurity, which the sea, deep down, mirrored).

93 "La donna è realizzata poeticamente ... nella sua partecipazione unitaria – alla natura e alla Storia. Enorme confine col cuore della terra, con la sua pura maturità (tramite, addirittura, di estrema ambientazione terrestre) la

donna in questi libri è anche espressa come compagna e collaboratrice di
Storia, sorgente a identica unificazione di civiltà attiva." (Rondi, *La terra
felice*, v).

94 Originally, Fellini and Pinelli proposed another story about a tempera-
mental and sentimental prostitute, whom Anna Magnani refused to play;
the story would become the idea for *Le notti di Cabiria* (Rondolino, *Roberto
Rossellini*, 146). The two screenwriters were accused of having plagia-
rized a 1901 novella by Ramón Valle-Inclán entitled *Adega* (José Luis
Guarner, *Roberto Rossellini*, New York, Praeger, 1970, 27–8.). Even though
plagiarism was denied, critics such as Mario Verdone have shown many
similarities between the two (see his *Roberto Rossellini*, Paris, Seghers,
1963, 34–5). Nonetheless, *Il miracolo* remains in any case concerned with
Fellinian themes.

95 For a detailed analysis of the events concerning this important legal battle
see Johnson, *Miracles and Sacrilege: Roberto Rossellini*.

96 For a discussion of the erotic charge of this and other scenes in the film
see Brunette, *Roberto Rossellini*, 100.

97 One of Fellini's accepted roles as screenwriter was inventing comic gags
for Aldo Fabrizi, which is traceable in *Roma, città aperta*, as well as in other
films (Bondanella, *The Cinema of Federico Fellini*, 36, 42).

98 Subini, "Il medioevo di *Francesco, giullare di Dio*," 30–1.

99 For example, when director Giuseppe De Santis cast Silvana Mangano
in *Riso amaro* (1949), it was not only to exploit her commercially as a sex
symbol but to represent how the attractive woman is brainwashed by the
superstructure of the Hollywood star system and objectified by men (see
Antonio Carlo Vitti, "L'affascinante rappresentazione del personaggio
femminile nella cinematografia di Giuseppe de Santis," in *Studi Italiani*
13.1, January–June 2001: 93–114).

100 Rondi quoted in Faldini and Fofi, *L'avventurosa storia*, 5–6.

101 De Martino, *Sud e magia*, 98–103.

102 For further details on this particular anecdote as well as for other intersections between De Martino's work and reputation and Fellini's, see Minuz,
Viaggio al termine (37–41).

103 Rondi, "*La rosa dei venti*," 293–4.

104 For an in-depth analysis of the relationship between the public and
production in these years see Brunetta, *Storia del cinema italiano*, vol. 4,
490–500.

105 For a summary of the process that led to the commercialization of the
sexual revolution and the different positions taken by a number of theo-

rists see David Allyn, *Make Love, Not War*, 228–45. For a history of the Italian erotic and porn genre, and for a closer examination of the commercial phenomenon touched upon in this chapter, see Giovannini and Tentori, *Porn'Italia*.

106 Pezzotta, "La cosa in sé," 50.
107 See Leoni, "Il signore del set," and Martino, "L'entusiasmo della prima volta."
108 Zavattini, "Diario: Roma 17 febbraio 1958," 136.
109 "Brunello Rondi on the branch of a big black tree, fumbling with two steel cables attached to his legs. By pulling on them, he lifts first one leg and then the other. Brunello's actions have the air of an experiment. I chuckled wickedly, and call over Rossellini and the others so that they can come to see what Brunello's doing and make fun of him. Brunello doesn't seem to mind, and keeps doing his strange exercises, as if he wanted to return movement to his legs, teaching them how to walk again" (Fellini, *The Book of Dreams*, 325, 532).
110 Rondi, *Il cinema di Fellini*, 20.
111 Bachmann, "The Cinema Seen as a Woman," 2–9.
112 O'Healy, "Unspeakable Bodies: Fellini's Female Grotesques," 325.
113 Lederman, "Dreams and Vision in Fellini's 'City of Women.'"
114 Fellini quoted in Pellizzari, "Un filo rosso," 93.
115 Here are some of Tonino Guerra's most significant collaborations in cinema: *Un ettaro di cielo* (Casadio, 1957), *La garçonnière* (De Santis, 1960), *Matrimonio all'italiana* (De Sica, 1964), *C'era una volta* (Rosi, 1967), *Lo scatenato* (Indovina, 1967), *I girasoli* (De Sica, 1969), *Un tranquillo posto di campagna* (Petri, 1969), *Tre nel Mille* (Indovina, 1971), *Giochi particolari* (Indovina, 1971), *Cristo si è fermato a Eboli* (Rosi, 1979), *I tre fratelli* (Rosi, 1981), *La notte di San Lorenzo* (Taviani, 1982), *Enrico IV* (Bellocchio, 1983), *Nostàlghia* (Tarkovskij, 1983), *Kaos* (Taviani, 1984), *Taxidi sta Kythira* (Anghelopulos, 1984), *Good Morning, Babylon* (Taviani, 1987), *Topio stin omichli* (Anghelopulos, 1988), *Stanno tutti bene* (Tornatore, 1990), *To meteoro vima tou pelargou* (Anghelopulos, 1991), *To vlemma tou Odyssea* (Anghelopulos, 1995), *La tregua* (Rosi, 1997), and *Mia aioniotita kai mia mera* (Anghelopulos, 1998).
116 Guerra quoted in Faldini and Fofi, *L'avventurosa storia*, 2.
117 "Al so, al so, al so, / Che un om a zinquent'ann / L'ha sempra al mèni puloidi / E me a li lèv do, tre volti e dè, / Ma l'è sultènt s'a ma vaid al mèni sporchi / Che me a m'arcord / Ad quand ch'a s'era burdèll (Fellini and Guerra, *Amarcord*, 7).

118 Ibid., 40–1.
119 Fellini, *The Book of Dreams*, 291, 523.
120 Gaudenzi, "Memory, Dialect, Politics: Linguistic Strategies in Fellini's *Amarcord*."
121 Guerra, *I bu*, 160–1.
122 Guerra, *E' mel*, 66–7.
123 Ginzburg, "Incontrando Tonino Guerra."
124 A similar moment of awe for the simple things of life is found in *Prova d'orchestra*; in a short scene an old man is staring at the ceiling and marvelling at the shape of a spider's web, and he notices that in the midst of the orchestra's chaos the spider is calmly moving up and down. There is no philological evidence, but it is highly probable that the scene originated from Guerra, who contributed thirty pages to the film but had to abandon it for a trip to Russia (Guerra and Martini, "Il cinema di Tonino Guerra," 35).
125 Guerra, *L'equilibrio*, 138.
126 Gramigna, Preface, 5.
127 Guerra, *L'uomo parallelo*, 168–71.
128 Ibid., 103–5.
129 Guerra, *I guardatori della luna*, 7.
130 Guerra, *Tonino Guerra: Poesie nel paesaggio*, 101, 103.
131 The count's peacock is also linked to Guerra's memory of a similarly staggering bird (Pellizzari, "Un filo rosso," 53). The peacock returns in Andrej Krjanovsky's animation film *Il lungo viaggio* (1998) made with Fellini's drawings and written by Tonino Guerra.
132 In his interview with Guerra, Gianfranco Gori hinted at this correspondence between Guerra's poems and *Amarcord* ("Poeta al cinema," 128–9).
133 Fellini, *The Book of Dreams*, 266, 517.
134 See Maurizio Mein's insightful documentary *Diario segreto di Amarcord*, dedicated to the making of *Amarcord*.
135 Guerra, *I bu*, 140–1.
136 Fellini and Guerra, *Ginger e Fred*, 225–6.
137 See my essay "Giuseppe Tornatore in viaggio attraverso il padre" in *Incontri cinematografici e culturali tra due mondi*, ed. Antonio C. Vitti (Pesaro, Italy, Metauro Edizioni, 2012), 205–15.
138 Fellini, *The Book of Dreams*, 386, 546.
139 Ibid., 400, 550.
140 See Guerra's lecture delivered during the event *Fellini Oniricon*: "E la nave va," Padua, 16 October 2008. On various occasions Guerra has alluded to his preference for *E la nave va* over *Amarcord*.

141 Fellini and Guerra, "E la nave va," 49. I am quoting from the unpublished and annotated script archived at the Fondazione Federico Fellini in Rimini.

142 Zanzotto, "E la nave va," 68. For an account of the exchanges related to Zanzotto's work on this film see De Giusti, *Il cinema brucia e illumina*, 18, and the other related documents contained in this anthology.

143 Fellini and Guerra, "E la nave va," 128.

144 Ibid., 129–30.

145 Pasolini, "Nota su *Le notti*," 700.

146 Contini, "Il linguaggio di Pascoli," 219–44.

147 Pasolini, *Passione e ideologia*, 146–9. Pasolini's Friulan poems were first collected in *La meglio gioventù* (1954, The best of youth).

148 Fellini quoted in Chiesi's video, *Pasolini e Fellini: Il poeta e il mago*.

149 Zanzotto, "Stramba crociera," 58.

150 See Zanzotto's "Lo sciamano."

151 Fellini, "Lettera a Andrea Zanzotto," 4–5.

152 "Mi sembra che la sonorità liquida, l'affastellarsi gorgogliante, i suoni, le sillabe che si sciolgono in bocca, quel cantilenare dolce e rotto dei bambini in un miscuglio di latte e materia disciolta, uno sciabordio addormentante, riproponga e rappresenti con suggestive efficacia quella sorta di iconografia subacquea del film, l'immagine placentaria, amniotica, di una Venezia decomposta e fluttuante di alghe, di muscosità, di buio muffito e umido" (Ibid.; English translation by Welle and Feldman in their edition, *Peasants Wake for Fellini's "Casanova,"* 6).

153 Ibid., 5.

154 Zanzotto, "Observations," 88.

155 Ibid., 90

156 Surliuga, "Simulation and Ekphrasis," 226.

157 Gozzano, "Il nastro di celluloide e i serpi di Laooconte," 1093.

158 Ibid., 1098 (see also G. Gozzano, *San Francesco d'Assisi*, Alessandria, Edizioni dell'Orso, 1997). Zanzotto, "Filò," 57.

159 The literature on this subject is vast, but the reader may start with Irene Gambacorti, *Storie di cinema e letteratura: Verga, Gozzano, D'Annunzio* (Florence: Società Editrice Fiorentina, 2003); Nino Genovese and Sebastiano Gesù (eds.), *Verga e il cinema* (Catania: Giuseppe Maimone Editore, 1996); Francesco Callàri, *Pirandello e il cinema, con la raccolta completa degli scritti teorici e creative* (Venice: Marsilio, 1991).

160 Zanzotto, "Filò," 59.

161 Ibid., 63.

Barbanente, Mariangela. "Tullio Pinelli: Ritratto di uno scrittore cinematografico." Diss., Università Degli Studi di Roma La Sapienza, 1994–1995.

Bazin, André. "*Cabiria*: The Voyage to the End of Neorealism." In *Federico Fellini: Essays in Criticism*, ed. Peter Bondanella, 94–102. Oxford: Oxford University Press, 1978.

———. "La strada." In *Federico Fellini: Essays in Criticism*, ed. Peter Bondanella, 54–9. Oxford: Oxford University Press, 1978.

Bernhard, Ernst. "Il complesso della Grande Madre." In *Mitobiografia*, ed. Hélène Erba-Tissot, 168–79. Milan: Adelphi, 1969.

Betti, Liliana. "Alla ricerca di Toby Dammit." In *Tre passi nel delirio*, ed. Liliana Betti, Ornella Volta, and Bernardino Zapponi, 46–9. Bologna: Cappelli, 1968.

Bigini, Antonio. "Prima della dolce vita: Pasolini in viaggio con Anita." *Studi novecenteschi* 35.75 (2008): 273–80.

Bispuri, Ennio. *Federico Fellini: Il sentimento latino della vita.* Rome: Il Ventaglio, 1981.

———. "Il mare e il treno: I segni e i sogni dell'espressionismo di Federico Fellini." *Fellini-Amarcord* 1.2 (June 2008): 47–88. Print.

Boarini, Vittorio. *L'arte di Fellini nella collezione Gèleng e nei costumi di Danilo Donati.* Rimini, Italy: Fondazione Fellini, 2005.

Bondanella, Peter. *The Cinema of Federico Fellini.* Princeton, NJ: Princeton University Press, 1992.

———. ed. *Federico Fellini: Essays in Criticism.* Oxford: Oxford University Press, 1978.

———. *A History of Italian Cinema.* New York: Continuum International Pub. Group, 2009. Previously published as *Italian Cinema: From Neorealism to the Present.* New York: Continuum, 2001.

Bondanella, Peter, and Manuela Gieri, eds. *La strada.* New Brunswick and London: Rutgers University Press, 1987.

Bonnigal, Dorothée. "Il 'Casanova' Di Federico Fellini: Exorcising the Loss of the Baroque Circle." *Veltro:Rrivista della civiltà italiana* 40.1–2 (1996): 58–62.

Borin, Fabrizio. *La filmografia di Nino Rota.* Florence: L.O. Olschki, 1999.

Brunetta, Gian Piero. "Flaiano ed il ritratto linguistico dell'italiano del dopoguerra." In *Flaiano, l'uomo e l'opera: Atti del convegno nazionale nel decennale della morte dello scrittore, Pescara 19–20 Ottobre 1982,* 85–92. Pescara, Italy: Fabiani, 1989.

———. *Storia del cinema italiano: Dal miracolo economico gli anni novanta 1960–1993.* Vol. 4. Rome: Editori Riuniti, 1998.

———. *Storia del cinema italiano: Dal neorealismo al miracolo economico, 1945–1959.* Vol. 3. Rome: Editori Riuniti, 1998.

Brunette, Peter. *Roberto Rossellini*. Berkeley: University of California Press, 1996.

Burke, Frank. *Fellini's Films: From Postwar to Postmodern*. New York: Macmillan/Twayne, 1996.

Buzzati, Dino. *I misteri d'Italia*. Milan: Mondadori, 1978.

———. *Poema a fumetti*. Milan: Mondadori, 1969.

———. "Lo strano viaggio di Domenico Molo." *Omnibus*. (1938 October–November).

———. "Le tentazioni di Sant'Antonio." In *Sessanta racconti*, 305–10. Milan: Mondadori, 1963.

Calabretto, Roberto. "'... Totò e Ninetto: Uno stradivario e uno zufoletto ...' I candidi nel cinema di Pier Paolo Pasolini." In *Storia del candore: Studi in memoria di Nino Rota nel ventesimo della scomparsa*, ed. Giovanni Morelli, 179–99. Florence: Olschki, 2001.

Calvino, Italo. "Autobiography of a Spectator." In *Perspectives on Federico Fellini*, ed. Peter Bondanella and Cristina Degli-Esposti, 25–30. New York: G.K. Hall, 1993.

Camon, Ferdinando. "Cosa c'è sotto le cancellature?" In *Atti del Convegno Federico Fellini: Il libro dei miei sogni. Rimini, 9–10 novembre 2007*, ed. Giuseppe Ricci, trans. Robin Ambrosi, 155–66. Rimini, Italy: Fondazione Fellini, 2008.

Carotenuto, Aldo. *Jung e la cultura del XX secolo*. Rome: Astrolabio, 1977.

Carringer, Robert. "Collaboration and Concepts of Authorship." *PMLA* 116. 2 (Mar. 2001): 370–9.

———. *The Making of Citizen Kane*. Berkeley: University of California Press, 1985.

Casanova, Alessandro. *Scritti e immaginati: I film mai realizzati di Federico Fellini*. Rimini, Italy: Guaraldi, 2005.

Cavazzoni, Ermanno. *Il poema dei lunatici*. Turin: Bollati Boringhieri, 1987.

Cecchi d'Amico, Suso, and Margherita d'Amico. *Storie di cinema (e d'altro)*. Milan: Garzanti, 1996.

Cederna, Camilla. "La bella confusione." In *8½ di Federico Fellini*, ed. Camilla Cederna, 17–85. Modena, Italy: Cappelli, 1963.

Chiamenti, Massimiliano. "Effigi di Dante e di Leopardi in Fellini." *The Italianist*, 24.2 (2004): 224–37.

Chicchi, Francesca. "Fellini–Flaiano: La provincia d'Italia a Cinecittà." *Fellini-Amarcord* 4 (December 2004): 27–46.

Chiesi, Roberto, ed. *Fellini, Pasolini e il progetto dei "ragazzi selvaggi."* Centro Studi-Archivio Pier Paolo Pasolini, Cineteca of Bologna. DVD.

———. ed. *Pasolini e Fellini: Da "Le notti di Cabiria" alla contestazione veneziana*. Centro Studi-Archivio Pier Paolo Pasolini, Cineteca of Bologna. DVD.

————. ed. *Pasolini e Fellini: Il poeta e il mago; Intorno a "Le notti di Cabiria,"* *(1956–1957).* Centro Studi-Archivio Pier Paolo Pasolini, Cineteca of Bologna. DVD.

Contini, Gianfranco. "Il linguaggio di Pascoli." In *Varianti e altra linguistica: Una raccolta di saggi 1938–1968,* 219–44. Turin: Einaudi, 1970.

Corti, Maria. Introduction to *Opere: Scritti postumi; Ennio Flaiano,* eds. Maria Corti and Anna Longoni, v–xiii. Milan: Bompiani, 2001.

Costello, Donald. *Fellini's Road.* Notre Dame, IN: University of Notre Dame Press, 1983.

————. "Layers of Reality: *8½* as Spiritual Autobiography." *Notre Dame English Journal,* 13.2 (1981): 1–12.

Cro, Stelio. "Fellini's Freudian Psyche between Neo-Realism and Neo-Baroque." *Canadian Journal of Italian Studies* 18.51 (1995): 162–83.

Curato, Baldo. *Sessant'anni di teatro in Italia.* Milan: M.A. Denti, 1947.

D'Amico, Silvio. "D'Amico on Pinelli." *Fellini-Amarcord* 3–4 (November 2008): 45–57.

De Benedictis, Maurizio. *Linguaggi dell'aldilà: Fellini e Pasolini.* Rome: Lithos, 2000.

De Giusti, Luciano, ed. *Il cinema brucia e illumina: Intorno a Fellini e altri rari.* Venice: Marsilio, 2011.

Degli-Esposti, Cristina. "Federico Fellini's Intervista or the Neo-Baroque Creativity of the Analyzed on Screen." *Italica* 73.2 (Summer, 1996): 157–72.

Delouche, Dominique. *Les Chemins de Fellini suivi du Journal d'un Bidoniste.* Paris: Les Éditions du Cerf, 1956.

De Martino, Ernesto. *Sud e magia.* Milan: Feltrinelli, 1960.

DeRosa, Steven. *Writing with Hitchcock: The Collaboration of Alfred Hitchcock and John Michael Hayes.* New York: Faber and Faber, 2001.

De Santi, Pier Marco. *La musica di Nino Rota.* Bari, Italy: Laterza, 1983.

Dick, F. Bernard. "Adaptation as Archaeology: *Fellini Satyricon* (1969) from the 'Novel' by Petronius." In *Perspectives on Federico Fellini,* ed. Peter Bondanella and Cristina Degli-Esposti, 130–8. New York: G.K. Hall, 1993.

Faldini, Franca, and Goffredo Fofi, eds. *L'avventurosa storia del cinema italiano: Raccontata dai suoi protagonisti, 1960–1969.* Milan: Feltrinelli, 1981.

————. eds. *Il cinema italiano d'oggi, 1970–1984: Raccontato dai suoi protagonisti.* Milan: A. Mondadori, 1984.

Farassino, Alberto. *Lux Film.* Milan: Il castoro, 2000.

Fellini, Federico. *La dolce vita di Federico Fellini.* Ed. Tullio Kezich. Rocca San Casciano, Italy: Cappelli, 1960.

————. *Fare un film.* Turin: Einaudi, 1993.

————. *Federico Fellini: La voce della luna.* Turin: Einaudi, 1990.

——. *Fellini on Fellini*. Trans. Isabel Quigley. New York: Da Capo, 1996.

——. "A First Draft: A Letter from Federico Fellini to His Friend Brunello Rondi, October 1960." In F. Fellini, *8½: Federico Fellini, Director*, ed. Charles Affron, 227–34. New Brunswick, NJ: Rutgers University Press, 1987.

——. "Io sono aperto voluttuosamente a tutto." *Pianeta* 5 (December–January, 1964–5): 99–106.

——. "Letter to a Marxist Critic." In *La strada*, ed. Peter Bondanella and Manuela Gieri, trans. Isabel Quigly, 211–14. New Brunswick, NJ, and London: Rutgers University Press, 1987.

——. "Lettera a Andrea Zanzotto." In A. Zanzotto, *Filò: Per il Casanova di Fellini*, 3–4. Milan: Arnoldo Mondadori Editore, 1988.

——. "Lettera a Dino De Laurentis." In *Il viaggio di G. Mastorna*, ed. Ermanno Cavazzoni, 169–204. Macerata, Italy: Quodlibet 2008.

——. *Il libro dei sogni*. Milan, Rizzoli, 2007. Translated by Aaron Maines as *The Book of Dreams* (Milan: RCS Libri Spa, 2008).

——. *Le notti di Cabiria*. Ed. Lino Del Fra. Modena, Italy: Cappelli, 1965.

——. Preface to *Fellini's Satyricon*, ed. Dario Zanelli, trans. Eugene Walter and John Matthews, 43–6. New York: Ballantine Books, 1970.

——. *Quattro film*. Turin: Einaudi, 1974.

——. *Il viaggio di G. Mastorna*. Ed. Ermanno Cavazzoni. Macerata, Italy: Quodlibet, 2008.

Fellini, Federico, Ermanno Cavazzoni, and Tullio Pinelli. "La voce della luna." Shooting and continuity script. Fellini MSs. II. Lilly Library of Rare Books, Bloomington, IN.

Fellini, Federico, and Camilla Cederna. *8½ di Federico Fellini*. Ed. Camilla Cederna. Modena, Italy: Cappelli, 1963. English version: *8½: Federico Fellini*, ed. Charles Affron (New Brunswick, NJ: Rutgers University Press, 1987).

Fellini, Federico, and Rita Cirio. *Il mestiere del regista*. Milan: Garzanti, 1994.

Fellini, Federico, and Ennio Flaiano. "Moraldo va in città." In *Scritti e immaginati: I film mai realizzati di Federico Fellini*, ed. Alessandro Casanova, 133–83. Rimini, Italy: Guaraldi, 2005. Edited and translated by John C. Stubbs as *"Moraldo in the City" and "A Journey with Anita."* Urbana and Chicago: University of Illinois Press, 1983.

Fellini, Federico, Ennio Flaiano, and Tullio Pinelli. "Il bidone: Soggetto e sceneggiatura di Federico Fellini, Ennio Flaiano e Tullio Pinelli." Pinelli MS. (Box 3). Lilly Library of Rare Books, Bloomington, IN.

Fellini, Federico, and Giovanni Grazzini. *Intervista sul cinema*. Bari, Italy: Laterza, 1983.

Fellini, Federico, and Tonino Guerra. *Amarcord*. Milan: Rizzoli, 1973.

————. "E la nave va." Fondo Norma Giacchero. Fondazione Federico Fellini. Rimini, Italy. The edited version of this script as been published as F. Fellini, *E la nave va* (Milan: Longanesi, 1983).

Fellini, Federico, and Mino Guerrini. *Ginger e Fred*. Ed. Mino Guerrini. Milan: Longanesi, 1986.

————. "Le strade di Fellini." *Il Mondo*, 19 January 1954: 12.

Fellini, Federico, and Tullio Kezich. "L'intervista lunga." In *Giulietta degli spiriti di Federico Fellini*, ed. Tullio Kezich, 15–72. Rocca San Casciano, Italy: Cappelli editore, 1965.

Fellini, Federico, and Milo Manara. *Due viaggi con Federico Fellini: Viaggio a Tulum; Il Viaggio di G. Mastorna detto Fernet*. Ed. Vincenzo Mollica. Milan: Mondadori, 2001.

Fellini, Federico, and Tullio Pinelli. "'Lo sceicco bianco': Sceneggiatura di Federico Fellini, Tullio Pinelli con la collaborazione di Ennio Flaiano, da un soggetto di: Fellini–Pinelli–Antonioni." Pinelli MSs. Box 1. Lilly Library of Rare Books, Bloomington, IN.

————. "La strada." Pinelli MS. 7 (Box 3 IIA). Lilly Library of Rare Books, Bloomington, IN.

————. *La strada, sceneggiatura*. Rome: Bianco e Nero, 1955. Translated as *"La Strada": Federico Fellini, Director*, ed. Peter Bondanella and Manuela Gieri (Rutgers University Press, NJ, 1987).

————. "Viaggio a Tulun." In F. Fellini, *Block-notes di un regista*, 11–39. Milan: Longanesi, 1988.

Fellini, Federico, Tullio Pinelli, and Ennio Flaiano. "'I Vitelloni' (titolo provvisorio): Soggetto e trattamento di Federico Fellini, Tullio Pinelli, Ennio Flaiano." Pinelli MS. 4 (box 2, ID). Lilly Library of Rare Books, Bloomington, IN.

Fellini, Federico, and Bernardino Zapponi. "Prova d'orchestra." Fondo Norma Giacchero. Fondazione Federico Fellini. Rimini, Italy. The materials contained in this folder have been published with some changes in Fellini, *Prova d'orchestra*, ed. Oreste Del Buono (Milan: Garzanti, 1980).

————. "Roma." Fellini MS. 10 (box 2, ID). Lilly Library of Rare Books, Bloomington, IN.

————. *Roma di Federico Fellini*. Rocca San Casciano, Italy: Cappelli, 1972.

————. "'Toby Dammit' dal racconto di Poe 'Non scommettere la testa col diavolo': Riduzione di Fellini & Zapponi." Fellini MS. 11 (Box 2). Lilly Library of Rare Books, Bloomington, IN.

Fiocco, Achille. *Correnti spiritualistiche nel teatro moderno*. Rome: Editrice Studium, 1955.

Flaiano, Ennio. "Del varietà." *Il Mondo*, 5 May 1951.

——. *Diario notturno*. Milan: Bompiani, 1973.

——. *Il gioco e il massacro*. Milan: Rizzoli, 1970.

——. "Ho parlato male de 'La strada.'" *Cinema* VII. 139, 10 August 1954: 449.

——. "Un marziano a Roma." In E. Flaiano, *Opere*, ed. Maria Corti and Anna Longoni, vol II, 475–88. Milan: Bompiani, 2001. Translated by Philip Balma and Fabio Benincasa as "A Martian in Rome," *Italica* 83.1 (2006): 98–107.

——. *Un marziano a Roma e altre farse*. Milan: Rizzoli, 1975.–. *Media Museum: Le arti e lo spettacolo*. Sanbuceto, Italy: Ediars, 2009.

——. "La notte porta consiglio." In *La notte porta consiglio e altri racconti cinematografici*, ed. Diana Rüesch, 75–106. Milan: Bompiani, 2001.

——. *Ombre fatte a macchina*. Ed. Cristina Bragaglia. Milan: Bompiani, 1997.

——. *Opere: Scritti postumi*. Ed. Maria Corti and Anna Longoni. Milan: Bompiani, 2001.

——. *Soltanto le parole: Lettere di e a Ennio Flaiano (1933–1972)*. Ed. Anna Longoni and Diana Rüesch. Milan: Bompiani, 1995.

——. *Tempo di uccidere*. Milan: Longanesi, 1963. Translated by Stuart Hood as *A Time to Kill* (London: Quartet Books, 1992).

——. *Una e una notte*. Milan: Bompiani 1974.

——. *The Via Veneto Papers*. Trans. John Satriano. Malboro, VT: Malboro Press, 1992.

Flaiano, Ennio, and Giulio Villa Santa. "La satira, la noia e la fede." In *La solitudine del satire*, 215–32. Milan: Rizzoli, 1973.

Fofi, Goffredo. "Flaiano: O dell'ironia come forma intima di sopravvivenza oltre la tragedia." *Script* 3 (1993): 48–52.

Fofi, Goffredo, and Gianni Volpi. *L'arte della visione*. Rome: Donzelli, 2009.

Gaillard, Christian. "Dire et non-dit du reve." In *Atti del Convegno Federico Fellini: Il libro dei miei sogni; Rimini, 9–10 novembre* 2007, ed. Giuseppe Ricci, trans. Robin Ambrosi, 107–29. Rimini, Italy: Fondazione Fellini, 2008.

Gargiulo, Gius. "*Poema a fumetti* trent'anni dopo: Alcune riflessioni sui 'mondi possibili' di Buzzati e Fellini." *Narrativa* 23 (2002): 221–32.

Gatto Trocchi, Cecilia. *Storia esoterica d'Italia*. Casale Monferrato, Italy: Piemme, 2001.

Gaudenzi, Cosetta. "Memory, Dialect, Politics: Linguistic Strategies in Fellini's *Amarcord*." In *Federico Fellini: Contemporary Perspectives*, ed. Frank Burke and Marguerite R. Waller, 155–67. Toronto: University of Toronto Press, 2002.

Gaut, Berys. "Film Authorship and Collaboration." In *Film Theory and Philosophy*, ed. Richard Allen and Murray Smith, 149–72. New York: Oxford University Press, 2003.

Geduld, Carolyn. "*Juliet of the Spirits*: Guido's Anima." In *Federico Fellini: Essays in Criticism*, ed. Peter Bondanella, 137–51. Oxford: Oxford University Press, 1978.

Giammusso, Maurizio. "The Theatre of Tullio Pinelli." *Fellini-Amarcord*, November 2008: 9–19.

Gieri, Manuela. *Contemporary Italian Filmmaking: Strategies of Subversion; Pirandello, Fellini, Scola, and the Directors of the New Generation*. Toronto: University of Toronto Press, 1995.

Ginzburg, Natalia. "Incontrando Tonino Guerra: Un poeta di paesi." *La stampa*, 29 October 1972.

Giordano, Maria Luisa. *Rol e l'altra dimensione*. Milan: Sonzogno, 2000.

Giovannini, Fabio, and Antonio Tentori. *Porn'Italia*. Pavona, Italy: Nuovi Equilibri, 2004.

Gordon, Robert. "Film History Recut." *Times Literary Supplement*, 1 July 2011: 28.

Gori, Gianfranco. "Poeta al cinema." In *Tonino Guerra*, 124–37. Modena, Italy: Regione Emilia-Romagna, 2004.

Gozzano, Guido. "Il nastro di celluloide e i serpi di Laooconte." In *Opere*, ed. C. Calcaterra and A. De Marchi, 1093–101. Milan: Garzanti, 1956.

Gramigna, Giuliano. Preface to *Storie dell'anno Mille* by Tonino Guerra and Luigi Malerba, 5–9. Milan: Bompiani, 1977.

Gramsci, Antonio. *Quaderni dal carcere*. Ed. Valentina Gerratana. Turin: Einaudi, 1975.

Guerra, Tonino. *I bu*. Rimini, Italy: Maggioli Editore, 1972.

———. "*E la nave va*": *Fellini Oniricon*. Lecture given in Padua on 16 October 2008. YouTube Video, accessed on 1 February 2010.

———. *E' mel (Il miele)*. Rimini, Italy: Maggioli Editore, 1982.

———. *L'equilibrio*. Milan: Bompiani, 1967.

———. *I guardatori della luna*. Milan: Bompiani, 1981.

———. *Tonino Guerra: Poesie nel paesaggio*. Rimini, Italy: Ramberti, 2005.

———. *L'uomo parallelo*. Milan: Bompiani, 1969.

Guerra, Tonino, and Luigi Malerba. *Storie dell'anno Mille*. Milan: Bompiani, 1977.

Guerra, Tonino, and Giacomo Martini. "Il cinema di Tonino Guerra." In *Tonino Guerra*, ed. Giacomo Martini, 15–39. Modena, Italy: Regione Emilia-Romagna, 2004.

Hobsbawm, Eric. *The Age of Extremes: A History of the World, 1914–1991*. New York: Pantheon Books, 1994.

Johnson, William B. *Miracles and Sacrilege: Roberto Rossellini, the Church, and Film Censorship in Hollywood*. Toronto: University of Toronto Press, 2008.

Jung, C.G. *Dreams*. Trans. R.F.C. Hull. Princeton: Princeton University Press, 1974.

———. *The Red Book = Liber novus*. Ed. Sonu Shamdasani. New York: W.W. Norton, 2009.

Kezich, Tullio. *Federico, la vita e i film*. Milan: Feltrinelli, 2002. Trans. Minna Proctor, with Viviana Mazza, as *Federico Fellini: His Life and Work*. New York: Faber and Faber, 2006.

———. "Quella sera a Torino con il mago di Fellini." *Corrière della sera*, 24 November 1994: 17.

———. *Su La dolce vita con Federico Fellini*. Venice: Marsilio, 1996.

———. "Tullio Pinelli." In *Enciclopedia dello spettacolo*, vol. 8, ed. Silvio D'Amico, 139–41. Rome: Casa Editrice le Maschere, 1961.

Kipen, David. *The Schreiber Theory*. Hoboken, NJ: Melville House Publishing, 2006.

Klein, M., and G. Parker, eds. *The English Novel and the Movies*. New York: Frederick Ungar Publishing, 1981.

Krjanovsky, Andrej, dir. *Il lungo viaggio*. 1998. YouTube video, accessed on 15 March 2010.

Lederman, Marie Jean. "Dreams and Vision in Fellini's 'City of Women.'" *Journal of Popular Film & TV* 9.3 (1981): 114–22.

Leoni, Roberto. "Il signore del set." In *Il lungo respiro di Brunello Rondi*, ed. Parigi, Stefania and Alberto Pezzotta, 248–53. Rieti, Italy: Edizioni Sabinae, 2010.

Luciani, Sebastiano Arturo. *L'antiteatro*. Rome: La voce, 1928.

———. *Verso una nuova arte: Il cinematografo*. Ed. Francesco Bolzoni. Rome: Edizioni della cometa, 2000.

Lugli, Remo. *Gustavo Rol: Una vita di prodigi*. Rome: Mediterranee, 1995.

Luzzi, Joseph. "Verbal Montage and Visual Apostrophe: Zanzotto's 'Filò' and Fellini's *Voce della luna*." *MLN* 126.1 (January 2011): 179–99.

Mammì, Alessandra. "Fellini segreto." *L'Espresso*, 10 March 2011: 102–7.

Marcus, Millicent. *After Fellini: National Cinema in the Postmodern Age*. Baltimore: Johns Hopkins University Press, 2002.

———. "Fellini's *La strada*: Transcending Neorealism." In *Perspectives on Federico Fellini*, ed. Peter Bondanella and Cristina Degli-Esposti, 87–99. New York: G.K. Hall, 1993.

———. "Fellini's *La voce della luna*: Resisting Postmodernism." In *Filmmaking by the Book: Italian Cinema and Literary Adaptation*, 225–48. Baltimore: Johns Hopkins University Press, 1993.

———. *Filmmaking by the Book: Italian Cinema and Literary Adaptation*. Baltimore: Johns Hopkins University Press, 1993.

Maroni, Oriana, and Giuseppe Ricci, eds. *I libri di casa mia: La biblioteca di Federico Fellini*. Rimini, Italy: Fondazione Federico Fellini, 2008.

Martino, Luciano. "L'entusiasmo della prima volta." In *Il lungo respiro di Brunello Rondi*, ed. Stefania Parigi and Alberto Pezzotta, 254–7. Rieti, Italy: Edizioni Sabinae, 2010.

McBride, Joseph. "The Director as Superstar." In *Federico Fellini: Essays in Criticism*, ed. Peter Bondanella, 152–60. New York: Oxford University Press, 1978.

McDonald, Ian. "Disentangling the Screen Idea." *Journal of Media Practice* 5:2 (2004): 89–99.

———. "The Silent Screenwriter: The Re-discovered Scripts of Eliot Stannard." *Comparative Critical Studies* 6.4 (2009): 385–400.

Mein, Maurizio, dir. *Diario segreto di Amarcord*. 1974. DVD.

Melanco, Mirco. "Il motivo del viaggio nel cinema italiano (1945–1965)." In *Identità italiana e europea nel cinema italiano dal 1945 al miracolo economico*, ed. Gian Piero Brunetta, 217–308. Turin: Edizioni della Fondazione Agnelli, 1996.

Merola, Nicola. "Flaiano sceneggiatore." In *La critica e Flaiano*, ed. Lucilla Sergiacomo, 208–9. Pescara, Italy: Ediars, 1992.

Micciché, Lino. "Un cinema senza sceneggiatori?" *Fellini-Amarcord* 1–2 (October 2001): 31–4.

Minuz. Andrea. *Viaggio al termine dell'Italia: Fellini politico*. Soveria Mannelli, Italy: Rubbettino, 2012.

Moravia, Alberto. "Dreaming Up Petronius." In *Federico Fellini: Essays in Criticism*, ed. Peter Bondanella, 161–7. Oxford: Oxford University Press, 1978.

Morelli, Giovanni, ed. *Storia del candore*. Florence: Olschki, 2001.

Moretti, Vito, ed. *Flaiano e 'oggi e domani.'* Pescara, Italy: Ediars, 1993.

Muscio, Giuliana. *Scrivere il film*. Milan: Savelli Editori, 1981.

Naldini, Nico. *Pasolini: Una vita*. Turin: Einaudi, 1989.

Natalini, Fabrizio. *Ennio Flaiano: Una vita nel cinema*. Rome: Artemide Edizioni, 2005.

———. "Flaiano sceneggiatore di scrittori." *Studi novecenteschi* 31.67–68 (2004): 251–65.

Neumann, Erich. *The Great Mother*. Trans. Ralph Manheim. Princeton: Princeton University Press, 1991.

O'Healy, Aine. "Unspeakable Bodies: Fellini's Female Grotesques." *Romance Languages Annual* 4 (1992): 325–9.

O'Leary, Alan. "After Brunetta: Italian Cinema Studies in Italy, 2000 to 2007." *Italian Studies* 63.2 (Autumn 2008): 279–307.

O'Leary, Alan, and Catherine O'Rawe. "A 'Certain Tendency' in Italian Film Criticism." *Journal of Modern Italian Studies* 16.1 (2011): 107–8.

O'Rawe, Catherine. "The Condition of Italian Cinema Studies: Gender, Genres, Auteurs, and Absences." *Italian Studies* 61.2 (Autumn 2006): 271–7.

Pacchioni, Federico. "The American Fanciullino in 'Happy Country.'" *Fellini-Amarcord: Rivista di studi felliniani / Fellinian Studies Magazine* 1–2 (October 2006): 15–25.

———. "Il retro di 'Happy Country': Il processo Tarnowska e altri frammenti." *Fellini-Amarcord: Rivista di studi felliniani / Fellinian Studies Magazine* 1–2 (August 2007): 61–70.

Parigi, Stefania, and Alberto Pezzotta, eds. *Il lungo respiro di Brunello Rondi.* Rieti, Italy: Edizioni Sabinae, 2010.

Pascoli, Giovanni. *Canti di Castelvecchio.* Milan: Rizzoli, 1998.

Pasolini, Pier Paolo. "Alla passeggiata archeological." In *Pasolini per il cinema,* ed. Walter Siti and Franco Zabagli, vol. 2, 2145–8. Milan: Mondadori, 2001.

———. "Amarcord." In *Saggi sulla letteratura e sull'arte,* ed. Walter Siti and Silvia De Laude, vol. 2, 2631–7. Milan: Mondadori, 1999.

———. "*La dolce vita*: Per me si tratta di un film cattolico." In *Saggi sulla letteratura e sull'arte,* ed. Walter Siti and Silvia De Laude, vol. 2, 2269–79. Milan: Mondadori, 1999.

———. *Empirismo eretico.* Milan: Garzanti, 2000. Translated by Ben Lawton and Louise K. Barnett as *Heretical Empiricism* (Washington, DC: New Academia Publishing, 2005).

———. "Federico Fellini e Tonino Guerra, *Amarcord.*" In *Saggi sulla letteratura e sull'arte,* ed. Walter Siti and Silvia De Laude, vol. 2, 1894–9. Milan: Mondadori, 1999.

———. "Grigio." In *Pasolini per il cinema,* ed. Walter Siti and Franco Zabagli, vol. 2, 2077–9. Milan: Mondadori, 2001.

———. "L'irrazionalismo cattolico di Fellini." *Filmcritica,* XI. 94 (February 1960): 80–4.

———. *Lettere, 1955–1975: Con una cronologia della vita e delle opera.* Ed. Nico Naldini. Turin: Einaudi, 1988.

———. "Marcello, Maddalena e la prostituta" In *Pasolini per il cinema,* ed. Walter Siti and Franco Zabagli, vol. 2, 2299–307. Milan: Mondadori, 2001.

———. "Nota su *Le notti.*" In *Saggi sulla letteratura e sull'arte,* ed. Walter Siti and Silvia De Laude, vol. 1, 699–707. Milan: Mondadori, 1999.

———. *Passione e ideologia.* Milan: Garzanti, 1994.

———. *Ragazzi di vita.* Milan: Garzanti, 2009.

———. *La religione del mio tempo.* Milan: Garzanti, 1961.

214   Bibliography

———. "La sceneggiatura come 'struttura che vuole essere altra struttura.'" In *Empirismo eretico*, 188–97. Milan: Garzanti, 2000.

———. "Sette punti per una polemica: Un elenco per Marotta." In *Saggi sulla letteratura e sull'arte*, ed. Walter Siti and Silvia De Laude, vol. 2, 2285–9. Milan: Mondadori, 1999.

———. "L'umile Italia." In *Le ceneri di Gramsci*, 39–49. Milan: Garzanti, 1976.

Patriarca, Emanuela. *Totò nel cinema di poesia di Pier Paolo Pasolini*. Florence: Firenze Atheneum, 2006.

Pellizzari, Lorenzo. "Un filo rosso per il cinema italiano." In *Tonino Guerra*, ed. G. Martini, 42–109. Modena, Italy: Regione Emilia-Romagna, 2004.

Pelo, Riikka. "Tonino Guerra: The Screenwriter as a Narrative Technician or as a Poet of Images? Authorship and Method in the Writer–Director Relationship." *Journal of Screenwriting* 1.1 (2010): 113–29.

Pezzotta, Alberto. "Brunellone e Federico: La collaborazione con Fellini." In *Il lungo respiro di Brunello Rondi*, ed. Stefania Parigi and Alberto Pezzotta, 75–86. Rieti, Italy: Edizioni Sabinae, 2010.

———. "La cosa in sé: Un percorso nei primi e negli ultimi film." In *Il lungo respiro di Brunello Rondi*, ed. Stefania Parigi and Alberto Pezzotta, 41–55. Rieti, Italy: Edizioni Sabinae, 2010.

Pillitteri, Paolo. *Appunti su Fellini*. Milan: Fraco Angeli, 1990.

Pinelli, Tullio. "Il ciarlatano meraviglioso." In *Tullio Pinelli*, 141–202. Rome: Editori & Associati, 1996.

———. "Una diversità complementare." *Cinema* 139 (August 1954): 449.

———. "Il giardino delle sfingi." In *Il giardino delle sfingi e altre commedie*, 97–160. Turin: Giulio Einaudi Editore, 1975.

———. *Il giardino delle sfingi e altre commedie*. Turin: Giulio Einaudi Editore, 1975.

———. "Gorgonio." In *Il giardino delle sfingi e altre commedie*, 19–96. Turin: Giulio Einaudi Editore, 1975.

———. *Innamorarsi: Racconti*. Nardò, Italy: Controluce, 2008.

———. "La lotta con l'angelo." In *Tullio Pinelli*, 93–139. Rome: Editori & Associati, 1996.

———. *Le notti di Cabiria*. Nardò, Italy: BESA Editrice, 2004.

———. "I padri etruschi." In *Tullio Pinelli*, 43–91. Rome: Editori & Associati, 1996.

———. "La pulce d'oro." In *Tullio Pinelli*, 9–42. Rome: Editori & Associati, 1996.

———. "La sacra rappresentazione di Santa Marina." In *Tullio Pinelli*, 203–37. Rome: Editori & Associati, 1996.

———. "Sono in tre a remare sulla barca di Fellini." *L'Espresso* 31 (May 1964): 2.

———. "Lo stilita." In *Il giardino delle sfingi e altre commedie*, 3–18. Turin: Giulio Einaudi Editore, 1975.

———. *Tullio Pinelli*. Rome: Editori & Associati, 1996.

Pinelli, Tullio, and Maricla Boggio. "Tullio Pinelli intervistato da Maricla Boggio." In *La strada: Dramma in due atti*, 11–26 . Nardò, Italy: BESA Editrice.

Pinelli, Tullio, and Federico Fellini. "La strada: Soggetto e sceneggiatura – Tullio Pinelli / Federico Fellini." Pinelli MS. 5 (Box 2, IE). Lilly Library of Rare Books, Bloomington, IN. Now published in *Fellini-Amarcord* 2.3 (October 2004): 19–48.

Pinelli, Tullio, and T. Kezich. "Il teatro del mondo." Trans. Robin Ambrosi. *Fellini-Amarcord* 3–4 (November 2008): 21–43.

Pinelli, Tullio, and Federico Pacchioni. "Intervista a Tullio Pinelli." *Italica* 85. 2–3 (Summer/Autumn 2009): 311–18.

Pinelli, Tullio, and Demetrio Salvi. "Tullio Pinelli fra teatro e cinema." *Cineforum* 331 (January–February 1994): 33–40.

Pinelli, Tullio, and Bernadino Zapponi. *La strada: Dramma in due atti*. Nardò, Italy: BESA Editrice, 2000.

Pirandello, Luigi. *On Humor*. Trans. Antonio Illiano and Daniel Testa. Chapel Hill: University of North Carolina Press, 1960.

Placido, Beniamino, dir. *La Roma di Flaiano*. Video archived at the Media Museum of Pescara, Italy. Rai. VHS.

Poe, Edgar Allan. "Never Bet the Devil Your Head." In *The Complete Tales and Poems of Edgar Allan Poe*, 482–9. New York: Random House, 1975.

Renga, Dana. "Irony and the Aesthetics of Nostalgia: Fellini, Zanzotto, and Casanova's Redemption." *Quaderni d'italianistica* 20.1–2 (1999): 159–90.

Renzi, Renzo, ed. *Il primo Fellini*. Rocca San Casciano, Italy: Cappelli, 1969.

Risset, Jacqueline. *L'incantatore: Scritti su Fellini*. Milan: Scheiwiller, 1994.

Rol, Gustavo Adolfo."*Io sono la grondaia ...*": *Diari, lettere, riflessioni di Gustavo Adolfo Rol*. Florence: Giunti, 2000.

Rondi, Brunello. *Amore fedele*. Padua: Rebellato, 1958.

———. *Il cammino della musica d'oggi e l'esperienza elettronica*. Padua: Rebellato, 1959.

———. *Il cinema di Fellini*. Rome: Bianco e Nero, 1965.

———. *Cinema e realtà*. Rome: Cinque Lune Editore, 1957.

———. *Esistenza e relazione*. Padua: Rebellato, 1958.

———. *La musica contemporanea*. Rome: Edizioni dell'Ateneo, 1952.

———. *Il neorealismo italiano*. Parma: Guanda Editore, 1956.

———. *Il nuovo teatro*. Rome: Bulzoni, 1979.

———. *Il ritmo moderno*. Rome: Petrignani, 1949.

———. "*Rosa dei venti.*" *Filmcritica* 96 (1960): 293–338.

———. *La terra felice*. Padua: Rebellato, 1961.

Rondolino, G. *Roberto Rossellini*. Turin: UTET libreria, 2006.

Rossi, Moraldo, and Tatti Sanguineti. *Fellini & Rossi: Il sesto vitellone*. Bologna: Le Mani, 2001.

Russel, Lawrence. "Fellini Satyricon." *Film Court*, 1999. Accessed online on 15 September 2009.

Russo, Giovanni. *Con Flaiano e Fellini a via Veneto*. Catanzaro, Italy; Rubbettino, 2005.

Ryan-Scheutz, Colleen. *Sex, the Self, and the Sacred: Women in the Cinema of Pier Paolo Pasolini*. Toronto: University of Toronto Press, 2007.

Sainati, Augusto. *Ciò che abbiamo detto è tutto vero*. Venice: Marsilio, 2008.

Schwartz, Barth David. *Pasolini Requiem*, New York: Pantheon Books, 1992.

Scolari, Giovanni. *L'Italia di Fellini*. Rieti, Italy: Edizioni Sabinae, 2008.

Sepa, Maria. "Flaiano scrittore per il cinema." Diss. Brown University, 1990.

Sergiacomo, Lucilla, ed. *La critica e Flaiano*. Pescara, Italy: Ediars, 1992.

Sesti, Mario, and Andrea Crozzoli, eds. *Il viaggio di Fellini: Fotografie di Gideon Bachmann*. Pordenone, Italy: Cinemazero, 2003.

Sharrett, Christopher. "'Toby Dammit,' Intertext, and the End of Humanism." In *Federico Fellini: Contemporary Perspectives*, ed. Frank Burke and Marguerite R. Waller, 121–36. Toronto: University of Toronto Press, 2002.

Siciliano, Enzo. *Pasolini: A Biography*. Trans. John Shepley. New York: Random House, 1982.

Siti, Walter, and Franco Zabagli. *Pasolini per il cinema*. Ed. Walter Siti and Franco Zabagli. Milan: Mondadori, 2001.

Spicer, Andrew. "The Author as Author: Restoring the Screenwriter to British Film History." In *The New Film History: Sources, Methods, Approaches*, ed. James Chapman, Mark Glancy, and Sue Harper, 89–103. New York: Palgrave McMillan, 2007.

Stillinger, Jack. *Multiple Authorship and the Myth of Solitary Genius*. Oxford: Oxford University Press, 1991.

Stoja, Stefano. "Ennio Flaiano e la fontana di Trevi: Lo scrosciare ticchettante delle idee." *Cartevive* XXI.45 (November 2010): 129–39.

Stubbs, C. John. *Federico Fellini as Auteur: Seven Aspects of His Films*. Carbondale: Southern Illinois University Press, 2006.

Subini, Tomaso. "Il medioevo di *Francesco, giullare di Dio*." *Doctor Virtualis*, 6 (2007): 23–50.

Surliuga, Victoria. "Simulation and Ekphrasis: Zanzotto's Poetry in Fellini's *Casanova*." *Literature Film Quarterly* 37.3 (2009): 224–33.

Tassone, Aldo. "From Romagna to Rome: The Voyage of a Visionary Chronicler (*Roma* and *Amarcord*)." In *Federico Fellini: Essays in Criticism*, ed. Peter Bondanella, 261–88. New York: Oxford University Press, 1978.

Tatò, Anna Maria, dir. *Marcello Mastroianni: Mi ricordo, sì, io mi ricordo*. 1997. DVD.

Testa, Carlo. "Cinecittà and America: Fellini Interviews Kafka." In *Federico Fellini: Contemporary Perspectives*, ed. Frank Burke and Marguerite R. Waller, 188–208. Toronto: University of Toronto Press, 2002.

Tillson, Victoria G. "Making the Implicit Explicit: Finding Pasolini in Fellini's Le notti di Cabiria." *Studi pasoliniani* 6 (2012): 67–81.

Tornabuoni, Lietta, ed. *Federico Fellini*. New York: Rizzoli, 1995.

———. "Fellini oniricon." *Dolce vita* 1.3 (1987): 2–9.

Tripodi, Antonio, and Marco Dalla Gassa. *Approdo a Tulum: Le Neverland a fumetti di Fellini e Manara*. Venice: Studio LT2, 2010.

Trubiano, Marisa. "Flaiano and Fellini, Fellow Travelers on Parallel Tracks." *NEMLA Italian Studies* 27–8 (2003): 75–91.

Van Order, Thomas. *Listening to Fellini: Music and Meaning in Black and White*. Madison. NJ: Fairleigh Dickinson University Press, 2009.

Wagner, G. *The Novel and the Cinema*. Rutherford, NJ: Faireleigh Dickinson University Press, 1975.

Welle, John. "Fellini's Use of Dante in *La dolce vita*." *Studies in Medievalism* 2.3 (1983): 49–65.

Welle, John, and Ruth Feldman, eds. *Peasants Wake for Fellini's "Casanova" and Other Poems*. Urbana and Chicago: University of Illinois Press, 1997.

West, Rebecca. "Tonino Guerra and the Space of the Screenwriter." *Annali d'italianistica* 6 (1988): 162–78.

Wood, Mary. *Italian Cinema*. Oxford: Berg, 2005.

Zabagli, Franco. "Pasolini per 'Le notti di Cabiria.'" *Quaderni dell'Antologia Vieusseux* 1–2 (May–August 1995): 119–78.

Zambelli, Massimo, and Giuseppe Acone, eds. *Campane nel pozzo: La voce della luna; Il testamento spirituale di Federico Fellini*. Rimini, Italy: Il cerchio, 1997.

Zanelli, Dario. *L'inferno immaginario di Federico Fellini: Cose dette da F.F. a proposito di "Il viaggio di G. Mastorna."* Rimini, Italy: Guaraldi, 1995.

Zanzotto, Andrea. "Cantilena londinese." In *Peasants Wake for Fellini's "Casanova" and Other Poems*, ed. and trans. John P. Welle and Ruth Feldman, 42–9. Urbana and Chicago: University of Illinois Press, 1997.

———. "E la nave va." *Positif* 507 (2003): 104–9.

———. "E la nave va." In *Il cinema brucia e illumina: Intorno a Fellini e altri rari*, ed. Luciano De Giusti, 67–9. Venice: Marsilio, 2011.

———. "Filò." In *Peasants Wake for Fellini's "Casanova" and Other Poems*, ed. and trans. John P. Welle and Ruth Feldman, 54–85. Urbana and Chicago: University of Illinois Press, 1997.

———. *Filò: Per il "Casanova" di Fellini*. Milan: Mondadori, 1988.

———. "In margine al copione de 'La città delle donne."·In *Il cinema brucia e illumina: Intorno a Fellini e altri rari*, ed. Luciano De Giusti, 103–7. Venice: Marsilio, 2011.

———. "Ipotesi intorno alla 'Città delle donne.'" In *La città delle donne*, ed. Liliana Betti, 19–31. Milan: Garzanti, 1980.

———. "Motivi di un candore." In *Il cinema brucia e illumina: Intorno a Fellini e altri rari*, ed. Luciano De Giusti, 83–92. Venice: Marsilio, 2011.

———. "Observations on the Meaning of the Situation in the Dialects in Italy in the Late Twentieth Century." In *Peasants Wake for Fellini's "Casanova" and Other Poems*, ed. and trans. John P. Welle and Ruth Feldman, 87–91. Urbana and Chicago: University of Illinois Press, 1997.

———. "Recitativo veneziano." In *Peasants Wake for Fellini's "Casanova" and Other Poems*, ed. and trans. John P. Welle and Ruth Feldman, 10–39. Urbana and Chicago: University of Illinois Press, 1997.

———. "Lo sciamano." In *Il cinema brucia e illumina: Intorno a Fellini e altri rari*, ed. Luciano De Giusti, 119–22. Venice: Marsilio, 2011.

———. "Stramba crociera." In *Il cinema brucia e illumina: Intorno a Fellini e altri rari*, ed. Luciano De Giusti, 57–61. Venice: Marsilio, 2011.

———. "Versi in onore di Federico." In *Il cinema brucia e illumina: Intorno a Fellini e altri rari*, ed. Luciano De Giusti, 65. Venice: Marsilio, 2011.

Zapponi, Bernardino. *Casanova: In un romanzo la storia del film di Fellini*. Milan: Mondadori 1977.

———. ed. *Il Delatore*. Rome: Arte della stampa, 1958–65.

———. "Edgar Poe e il cinema." In *Tre passi nel delirio*, ed. Liliana Betti, Ornella Volta, and Bernardino Zapponi, 15–19. Bologna: Cappelli, 1968.

———. *Gobal*. Milan: Longanesi, 1967.

———. *Il mio Fellini*. Venice, Marsilio, 1995.

———. *Nostra signora dello spasimo*. Milan: Sugar Editore, 1963.

———. *Passione*. Milan: Milano libri, 1974.

———. "Roma & Fellini." In *Roma di Federico Fellini*, ed. Bernadino Zapponi, 11–73. Rocca San Casciano, Italy: Cappelli, 1972.

———. "The Strange Journey." In *Fellini's Satyricon*, ed. Dario Zanelli, trans. Eugene Walter and John Matthews, 33–9. New York: Ballantine Books, 1970.

———. *Trasformazioni*. Genoa: Il melangolo, 1990.

Zapponi, Bernardino, and Maricla Boggio. "Bernardino Zapponi intervistato da Maricla Boggio." In *La strada: Dramma in due atti*, 27–33. Nardò, Italy: BESA Editrice, 2000.

Zapponi, Bernardino., and Olivier Curchod. "Entretien avec Bernardino Zapponi." *Positif* 413/414 (1995): 69.

Zapponi, Bernardino, and Tullio Pinelli. "Fellini au travail." *Cahiers du Cinéma* XLII, 474 (December 1993): 60–1.

Zavattini, Cesare. "Diario: Roma 17 febbraio 1958." *Cinema nuovo* 126 (March 1958): 136–7.

Index

The abbreviation "FF" is used to refer to Federico Fellini. Page numbers followed by "f" refer to pages containing figures.